Merchant Ships of the World
1910–1929
in color

Merchant Ships of the World
1910–1929
in color

Written and illustrated
by
Laurence Dunn

Macmillan Publishing Co., Inc.
New York

Macmillan Publishing Co., Inc.
866 Third Avenue, New York, N.Y. 10022

Library of Congress Cataloging in Publication Data
Dunn, Laurence
Merchant ships of the world in color, 1910–1929

Macmillan color series

1. Merchant Ships.   2. Ocean liners   I. Title.
   VM378.D8 1975   623.82'4'09041   74-23925

First American Edition 1975

Printed in Great Britain

Contents

Introduction

As regards the design and appearance of ships, the period covered by this book was one of particular interest and variety. For the first half at least, the sailing ship was still a common sight; and various borrowings from the era of sail still showed in many of the older steamers—in such things as height of mast, rake and sheer. A suit of canvas was often carried, mainly for steadying purposes, while clipper stemmed steamers were still quite often seen.

For passenger ships, in particular, the pre-war years up to 1914 were ones of outward elegance. Air travel was decades away; the passenger liner represented the height of sophistication and was the accepted means of travel between the world's far-flung ports. Few vessels could beat the high speeds of today's great container ships, but what matter? Unless they could reach their destination overland, travellers had no alternative to what now seems a leisurely voyage.

Nowadays, undue emphasis is apt to be placed on the liners of the North Atlantic, this at the expense of those engaged on other, longer routes. While the transatlantic giants had their appeal, so too did these others which, as regards size and speed, were more comparable to the intermediate Atlantic ships. Of various categories, they ranged from quite fast mail ships with high-class passenger accommodation to those which in the main catered for emigrants. As a type the cargo liner was less clearly defined than now, since despite their much smaller superstructure they too often carried large numbers of emigrants or steerage passengers. Those too were the days when as a type, the tramp steamer was approaching its zenith. Generally conforming to one of only three or four basic layouts, they differed rather in detail, yet each seemed to have a rugged personality of its own. Small wonder, for they were designed to carry almost anything anywhere and their worldwide voyagings could well keep them from their home port for a year or more.

Prior to 1914 only a minute proportion of the world's merchant ships burned anything but coal in their boilers, but during the 'twenties the switchover to oil gradually gained momentum. Growing oil consumption demanded more oil tankers. Apart from a few giants of around 17,000 tons d.w., the tanker seldom exceeded 8,000–10,000 tons and was often very much smaller. While the earlier generation of tankers built just before or around the turn of the century showed many interesting variations, their successors conformed much more to one main layout—the three island—and were frequently built in series. So, excepting the light-painted Scandinavians, the overall image presented by this type was generally somewhat drab.

On the shorter routes there were almost countless old-established fleets of

miniature liners—many of them mail ships—which also carried varying proportions of passengers and cargo. In more recent years and with the advent of air
travel it seemed that such ships and services were past history, but to meet the
needs of the motorist, this type has been reborn—as the ubiquitous car ferry.
Another traditional type which did become a casualty was the British coastwise
passenger-cum-cargo liner. The development of the long distance motor coach
in the 'twenties (far cheaper than train) killed the passenger aspect of this trade,
while later, the next generation of purely cargo carriers had their *raison d'être*
stolen by the heavy lorry.

The advent of the First World War cut right across the hitherto steady line of
evolution and this did not really become apparent again until some years after
the war had ended. By then, the whole pattern of world shipping, both passenger
and cargo, had changed. During the actual war years Britain's whole output as a
shipbuilding nation had to be concentrated on her own urgent needs—the
construction and repair of war vessels and the building of standard-type cargo
ships to replace her appallingly heavy war losses. She was thus unable to build
for much of the world as of old, and this led inevitably to the creation of many
new shipyards overseas which, once established, remained as future competitors.
Prior to the First World War American shipyards were geared to meet that
nation's own requirements, but no more. Soon, however, the world saw American creative genius at its best with the build-up of a vast shipbuilding organisation which, apart from Naval tonnage, turned out an enormous armada of
standard-type merchant ships. However, once the wartime emergency had passed
so did the need for most of these hurriedly produced American cargo ships.
Soon these were laid up in their hundreds, while most of the shipyards which
built them passed into oblivion.

As for Japan, so as to aid the war effort America supplied large quantities of
steel to that nation, who from having a very minor shipbuilding industry was
able to rapidly expand this and build very considerable numbers of ships for
America, some for Britain and others for herself.

The end of the war was characterised by a state of disarray with whole fleets
of passenger ships needing conversion from trooping and other wartime duties.
Shipyards in Britain were choked with orders for new purpose-designed ships,
among them many cargo liners and bigger passenger ships. Then, too, there was
the great dispersal of the ex-German merchant fleet between the Allies. Many
units were elderly and had been long laid up and merely served as stopgaps
until new tonnage was ready. Other new or almost completed ships proved far
more valuable and served their new owners well. It was largely through the
intake of interned ex-German vessels that some Latin American merchant fleets
really came into being. In like fashion, Portugal was another country to acquire
a number of useful additions.

Born of the war were many new ideas, the best of which were incorporated
in the next generation of ships. These embraced actual hull design, the grouping
of deckhouses and superstructure, new cargo handling gear and alternative
forms of propulsion. The turbine in its original form had a direct drive and was

therefore only suitable for very fast ships. The introduction and subsequent perfection of reduction gearing greatly widened its scope and made it well suited for other categories. Then there was the diesel engine. While the Danish-built *Selandia* (plate 3) of 1912 was the world's first ocean-going motor liner, it should be remembered that in the years prior to the war several motorships of comparable size were built in Britain. Thereafter, preoccupied with the war, it was some time before Britain could give very much attention to the development and application of the diesel engine. Meanwhile the flow from Scandinavia continued, most of these vessels being distinguished by having their machinery and superstructure in a new position—aft of amidships. Another break with tradition was the elimination of the usual funnel, its place being taken by a very small one resembling a stove pipe, or else tall, but even slimmer exhausts led up one of the masts. But within a few years, and despite the forecasts of some diesel enthusiasts, the funnel returned to favour—even on motorships. Instead of being merely an uptake for smoke as of old, the motorship funnel, generally more squat and much wider, housed not only the exhausts and silencers but often a variety of other equipment as well.

In early steamers there was a widespread reluctance to make any great use of kingposts (known alternatively as sampson- or king-posts), probably on aesthetic grounds. Such niceties died with the First World War and twin stump masts or kingposts were a prominent feature of many of the larger American ships built then (*see* plates 61–63). The liner *Minnewaska* of 1923 (plate 32) was another to have a great array of these. One of the greatest cargo carriers of her day, she needed six pairs to work her derricks. Yet even at that date her owners were somewhat coy about them, for in their publicity literature she was often shown without them!

As to the ships which feature in this book, each has been chosen either for her own particular interest or as representative of a particular type or hull layout. While many famous vessels have been included, I have—for the sake of interest —generally turned towards those which, for one reason or another, have tended to be overlooked. My aim has been to portray the general pattern of development during this period. To see this most clearly one needs to bear in mind not only the dates of construction but also purpose and trade, owners' individual approach, national characteristics, variations on a particular theme and the inter-borrowings between nations. Also, that always fascinating theme—wartime improvisation. This, for instance, led to the construction of both concrete- and wooden-hulled steamships, the conversion of sailing ships into full-powered motorships and, too, the building of a bizarre-looking series of French schooners which, besides their suit of sails, had twin funnels and, below, two sets of steam triple expansion engines.

Mention has been made of the lack of the usual funnel on early Scandinavian motorships. One such ship was the Norwegian *Brabant* (plate 89). Designed for service between Oslo and Antwerp, she was for some years unique among North Sea passenger ships in having no funnel. However, in due course, her owners found it worth while to improve her looks by removing one mast and in its place fitting a funnel of reasonable proportions. In somewhat similar fashion, certain German-built cargo liners carried what was in effect a national 'hallmark', this being the very short, forward well deck—to be seen in plates 51 and 54. Other pointers to German origin lay in the details and layout of the two elements of their superstructure and the casing at the funnel-base. In conjunction with all these features, the two thin, closely spaced funnels of the *Brant County* (plate 51) revealed to the knowledgeable that she had been built for the German–Australian Line.

The conversion of ships is no new thing. Early in her career, the cargo ship *Glenapp* was rebuilt to become the mail and passenger-carrying liner *Aba* (plate 27). An even greater transformation was achieved with the American motor cargo ship *Missourian* (plate 95). In this she is shown as built and below, as an end-piece, as she appeared in the 'sixties when, after several reconstructions, she was trading as the emigrant ship *Flaminia*. In that guise she carried no cargo whatsoever, the forward hold being used only for passengers' baggage.

The Color Plates

CANADA

S.S. EMPRESS OF RUSSIA, 1913
Canadian Pacific Railway Co.
16,810 tons gross

PLATE I

s.s. LADY RODNEY, 1929
Canadian National Steamships
8,194 tons

PLATE 2

DENMARK

m.v. SELANDIA, 1912
East Asiatic Co.
4,964 tons

PLATE 3

FRANCE

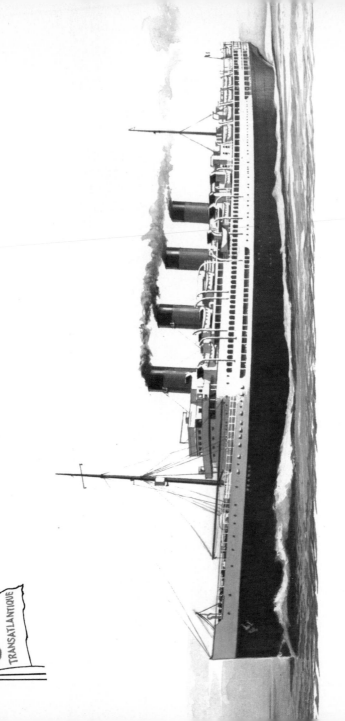

s.s. FRANCE, 1911
Cie. Générale Transatlantique
23,666 tons

PLATE 4

FRANCE

S.S. PROVIDENCE, 1914

Fabre Line
11,996 tons

PLATE 5

m.v. ERIDAN, 1929
Cie. des Messageries Maritimes
9,928 tons

PLATE 6

GERMANY

PLATE 7

s.s. IMPERATOR, 1913
Hamburg-American Line
52,117 tons

GERMANY

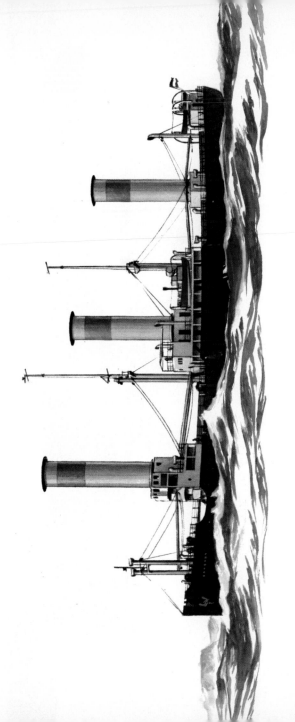

m.v. BARBARA, 1926
Managers: Rob. M. Sloman, Jr.
2,077 tons

PLATE 8

GERMANY

PLATE 9

m.v. ORINOCO, 1928
Hamburg–American Line
9,660 tons

GREAT BRITAIN

PLATE 10

S.S. BALMORAL CASTLE, 1910
Union-Castle Mail S.S.Co. Ltd.
13,361 tons

s.s. HOWICK HALL, 1910

Chas. G. Dunn & Co. Ltd.

4,923 tons

PLATE II

GREAT BRITAIN

S.S. LACONIA, 1911
Cunard Line
18,000 tons

PLATE 12

S.S. OLYMPIC, 1911
White Star Line
46,359 tons

PLATE 13

GREAT BRITAIN

s.s. ROTORUA (ex-SHROPSHIRE), 1911

New Zealand Shipping Co. Ltd.

12,112 tons

PLATE 14

S.S. ERINPURA, 1911
British India S. Nav. Co. Ltd.
5,128 tons

PLATE 15

GREAT BRITAIN

S.S. VAUBAN, 1912
Lamport & Holt Line
10,680 tons

PLATE 16

s.s. BRITISH MARSHAL, 1912

British Tanker Co. (BP)

4,158 tons

PLATE 17

GREAT BRITAIN

s.s. SAN JERONIMO, 1914
Eagle Oil Transport Co. Ltd.
12,028 tons

PLATE 18

GREAT BRITAIN

S.S. AQUITANIA, 1914

Cunard Line

45,657 tons

PLATE 19

GREAT BRITAIN

PLATE 20

s.s. MELROSE ABBEY, 1929
Associated Humber Lines
1,908 tons

s.s. MACCLESFIELD, 1914
Associated Humber Lines
1,018 tons

S.S. BENRINNES, 1914
Ben Line Steamers Ltd.
4,798 tons

PLATE 2I

GREAT BRITAIN

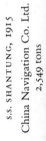

s.s. SHANTUNG, 1915
China Navigation Co. Ltd.
2,549 tons

PLATE 22

GREAT BRITAIN

s.s. BELGIC, 1917

Managers: White Star Line

24,547 tons

PLATE 23

PLATE 24

CONCRETE SHIPS

aux. m.v. MOLLIETTE, 1919

B. Oppenheimer
293 tons

s. tug CRETECABLE, 1919

Stelp & Leighton Ltd.
267 tons

GREAT BRITAIN

s.s. YORKSHIRE, 1920

Bibby Line
10,184 tons

PLATE 25

GREAT BRITAIN

s.s. HUNTSMAN, 1921
T. & J. Harrison
8,196 tons

PLATE 26

m.v. ABA after 1921 conversion
Elder Dempster & Co. Ltd.
7,937 tons
(above – as built 1918 as GLENAPP)

PLATE 27

GREAT BRITAIN

LONDON COLLIERS

PLATE 28

S.S. CHARTERED, 1921
Gas Light & Coke Co.
2,021 tons

S.S. CORCHESTER, 1927
Cory Colliers Ltd.
2,374 tons

s.s. AUTOMEDON, 1922

Alfred Holt & Co.

7,628 tons

PLATE 29

PLATE 30

s.s. JERVIS BAY, 1922

Aberdeen & Commonwealth Line

14,164 tons

GREAT BRITAIN

PLATE 31

s.s. DORIC, 1923
White Star Line
16,484 tons

GREAT BRITAIN

PLATE 32

s.s. MINNEWASKA, 1923
Atlantic Transport Co. Ltd.
21,716 tons

PLATE 33

WELSH CONTRASTS

m.v. MARGRETIAN, 1923
O. & W. Williams & Co.
2,578 tons

s.s. USKHAVEN, 1923
Richard W. Jones & Co. Ltd.
2,464 tons

GREAT BRITAIN

FORMER SAILING SHIPS

PLATE 34   m.v. CANIS, rebuilt c. 1918   m.v. CAPABLE, converted 1924

Det Bergenske D/S A/S.   F.T. Everard & Sons Ltd.

934 tons   216 tons

GREAT BRITAIN

S.S. AVILA (later AVILA STAR), 1927

Blue Star Line Ltd.

12,872 tons

PLATE 35

GREAT BRITAIN

m.v. PACIFIC RELIANCE, 1927
Furness Withy & Co. Ltd.
6,717 tons

PLATE 36

PLATE 37

s.s. KEDAH, 1927
Straits S.S.Co. Ltd.
2,499 tons

GREAT BRITAIN

s.s. BEAVERFORD, 1928
Canadian Pacific Railway Co.
10,042 tons

PLATE 38

s.s. PARRACOMBE, 1928

Pyman Bros. Ltd.
4,698 tons

PLATE 39

S.S. SOUTHERN EMPRESS
(ex SAN JERONIMO), 1914
Southern Whaling & Sealing Co. Ltd.
12,398 tons

PLATE 40

m.v. HIGHLAND CHIEFTAIN, 1929
Nelson Steam Navigation Co. Ltd.
14,131 tons

PLATE 41

GREECE

s.s. VASILEFS CONSTANTINOS, 1914

National S. Nav. Co. of Greece, Ltd.

9,272 tons

PLATE 42

s.s. PATRIS II, 1926
National S. Nav. Co. of Greece, Ltd.
3,854 tons

PLATE 43

HOLLAND

PLATE 44

s.s. KARIMOEN, 1911
Stoomvaart Mij. 'Nederland'
6,940 tons

N.A.S.M.

PLATE 45

s.s. SPAARNDAM, 1922
Holland–America Line
8,857 tons

HOLLAND

s.s. KLIPFONTEIN, 1922
Holland-South Africa Line
7,063 tons

PLATE 46

m.v. BALOERAN, 1929

Rotterdam Lloyd

16,981 tons

PLATE 47

ITALY

s.s. SAN GUGLIELMO, 1911
"Sicula Americana" Soc. di Nav.
8,341 tons

PLATE 48

s.s. SUWA MARU, 1914

Nippon Yusen Kaisha
10,927 tons

PLATE 49

JAPAN

ARABIA MARU, 1918

Osaka Shosen Kaisha

9,500 tons

PLATE 50

s.s. BRANT COUNTY, 1915

Det Bergenske D/S A/S (County Line)

5,001 tons

PLATE 51

NORWAY

s.s. STAVANGERFJORD, 1918
Den Norske Amerikalinje A/S

PLATE 52

m.v. SARDINIA, 1920

Fred. Olsen & Co.

2,060 tons

PLATE 53

PORTUGAL

s.s. CUNENE, 1911

Soc. Geral de Commercio, Industria e
Transportes, Ltd.

6,876 tons

PLATE 54

SPAIN

PLATE 55

S.S. INFANTA ISABEL, 1912
Pinillos Izquierdo & Co.
8,170 tons

SPAIN

PLATE 56

S.S. REINA VICTORIA-EUGENIA, 1913
Compania Trasatlantica
10,136 tons

m.v. INFANTA BEATRIZ, 1928
Compania Trasmediterranea
6,279 tons

PLATE 57

SWEDEN

s.s. ATLAND, 1910
Axel Brostrom & Son
5,029 tons

PLATE 58

U.S.A.

s.s. TIVIVES, 1911
United Fruit Corporation
5,017 tons

PLATE 59

s.s. MATSONIA, 1913
Matson Navigation Co.
9,402 tons

PLATE 60

S.S. AMERICAN MERCHANT, 1920

United States Lines

7,430 tons

PLATE 61

U.S.A.

S.S. PRESIDENT VAN BUREN, 1920
United States Lines
10,533 tons

PLATE 62

U.S.A.

S.S. PRESIDENT HARDING, 1921

United States Lines

14,187 tons

PLATE 63

s.s. MOUNT CLINTON, 1921

United American Lines

7 510 tons

PLATE 64

AUSTRALIA

PLATE 65

S.S. INDARRA, 1912

Australasian United S.Nav.Co.Ltd.
9,735 tons

BELGIUM

PLATE 66

S.S. STAD ANTWERPEN, 1913

Belgian Government
1,384 tons

CANADA

PLATE 67

S.S. PRINCESS MARGUERITE, 1925

Canadian Pacific Rly. Co.
5,875 tons

FINLAND

PLATE 68

S.S. CARELIA, 1921

Finland S.S.Co. Ltd.
1,123 tons

FRANCE

PLATE 69   steam schooner COMMANDANT DE ROSE, 1918

French Government
2,114 tons

GERMANY

PLATE 70   S.S. ISAR, 1929

Norddeutscher Lloyd
9,026 tons

GREAT BRITAIN

PLATE 71

s.s. ROYAL SCOT, 1910

London & Edinburgh S.Shpg. Co. Ltd.
1,726 tons

GREAT BRITAIN

PLATE 72

s.s. LONDON QUEEN, 1910

London & Channel Islands S.S.Co. Ltd.
599 tons

PLATE 73

S.S. NORMANNIA, 1911

London & S.Western Rly. Co.

1,567 tons

PLATE 74

S.S. LADY CLOE, 1916

British & Irish Packet Co. Ltd.

1,581 tons

GREAT BRITAIN

PLATE 75   s.s. DARINO, 1917

Ellerman Lines Ltd.

1,349 tons

GREAT BRITAIN

PLATE 76   s.s. WAR VIPER, 1918

The Shipping Controller

5,160 tons

PLATE 77

wooden s.s. WAR MINGAN, 1918

The Shipping Controller
2,217 tons

PLATE 78

s.s. JOLLY BRUCE, 1920

Walford Lines Ltd.
553 tons

GREAT BRITAIN

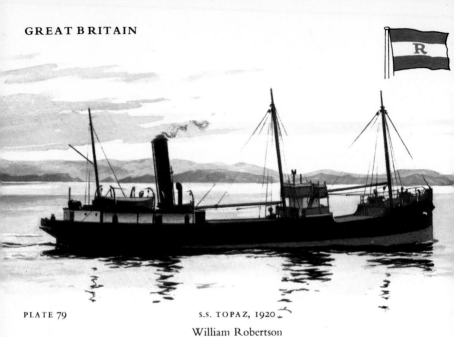

PLATE 79   S.S. TOPAZ, 1920

William Robertson
577 tons

GREAT BRITAIN

PLATE 80   S.S. GANNET, 1921

General S. Nav. Co. Ltd.
1,443 tons

PLATE 81

S.S. MALINES, 1922

London & N. Eastern Rly. Co.
2,969 tons

PLATE 82

S.S. BERNICIA, 1923

Tyne-Tees S. Shipping Co. Ltd.
1,839 tons

PLATE 83

S.S. AVOCETA, 1923

Yeoward Line Ltd.

3,442 tons

PLATE 84

S.S. INVERLAGO, 1925

Lago Shipping Co. Ltd.

2,372 tons

GREAT BRITAIN

PLATE 85   S.S. NERISSA, 1926

C.T. Bowring & Co. Ltd.
5,583 tons

GREAT BRITAIN

PLATE 86   M.V. ULSTER MONARCH, 1929

Belfast S.S. Co. Ltd.
3,735 tons

HOLLAND

PLATE 87
S.S. BATAVIER II, 1920
Wm. H. Muller & Co.
1,575 tons

MALTA

PLATE 88
S.S. KNIGHT OF MALTA, 1929
Cassar Co. Ltd.
1,553 tons

PLATE 89   m.v. BRABANT, 1926

Fred. Olsen & Co
2,335 tons

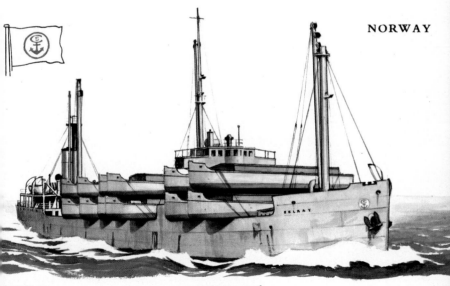

PLATE 90   m.v. BELRAY, 1926

Christen Smith
2,888 tons

RUSSIA

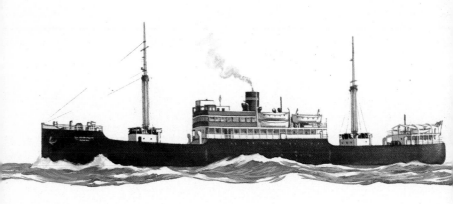

PLATE 91

m.v. SMOLNI, 1929

Sovtorgflot
3,767 tons

SWEDEN

PLATE 92

m.v. SUECIA, 1912

Axel Axelson Johnson
3,730 tons

PLATE 93

S.S. BRITANNIA, 1929

Swedish Lloyd
4,216 tons

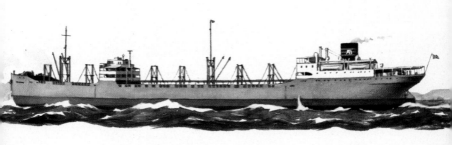

PLATE 94

M.V. SVEALAND 1925

Tirfing S.S. Co. Ltd.
15,598 tons

PLATE 95   m.v. MISSOURIAN, 1922

American-Hawaiian S.S. Co. Ltd.
7,899 tons

PLATE 96   -and rebuilt 1955 as FLAMINIA

Cogedar Line
8,776 tons

1 s.s. EMPRESS OF RUSSIA, 1913, Canada

The *Empress of Russia* and her sister *Empress of Asia* represented the third generation of ships used by the Canadian Pacific Rly. Co. on their service between Western Canada and the Orient. This was opened by the C.P.R. in 1887 with three chartered vessels, the *Abyssinia*, *Batavia* and *Parthia*, all one-time Cunarders built in 1870 and of between 2,500 and 3,600 tons gross. They were replaced in 1891 by a trio specially designed for the trade—on which they immediately took premier position. These were the yachtlike *Empress of India*, *Empress of Japan* and *Empress of China*, 16-knot ships of just under 6,000 tons gross. They in turn eventually became out-classed by others, notably the very much larger ships of the Toyo Yusen Kaisha.   But in 1913 such competition was more than met by the introduction into the trans-Pacific trade of the two new, three-funnelled *Empress* liners. Nearly three times the size of those they replaced, they were, incidentally, the world's first large liners to have cruiser sterns. Among Pacific ships, however, they were not quite the first, this feature having previously been incorporated in two Canadian National coastal ships, the 3,300-ton *Prince George* and *Prince Rupert* of 1910.

Both the *Empress of Russia* and her sister were built by the Fairfield Shipbuilding & Engineering Co. Ltd., Glasgow. The former was launched on 28 August, 1912, the other following three months later. Of 16,810 tons gross and 8,789 tons net, the *Russia* measured 590 ft in length overall (570·2 ft b.p.) × 68 ft breadth mld × 46 ft mld to the shelter deck. The load draught was 29 ft and the hull was topped by a long, combined bridge and forecastle which extended for 394 ft. She had quadruple screws, each driven by a set of Parsons turbines. These took steam from six D.E. and four S.E. boilers which had a working pressure of 190 p.s.i. On trials, with a draught of 26 ft 8in., the *Empress of Russia* did 21·4 knots, just one knot above the speed stipulated. However, her nominal service speed was 19 knots, about 3 knots better than that of the Japanese ships. In the trans-Pacific trade, speed was of particular importance owing to the very high freights earned from the carriage of silk, the insurance rates for this being so high that every day saved had a considerable effect on the shipper' costs.

The passenger accommodation was reputedly equalled only by the finest Atlantic liners. It catered for about 200 first, 100 second and 800 steerage. The officers and crew numbered some 475. The main, first-class public rooms were on the promenade deck, the dome of the forward lounge rising between the forward and second funnels and that of the smoke room aft of the third stack. Also on that deck, but facing aft, was the first-class veranda café. Apart from these and the writing room, the promenade deck and the one below were devoted to first-class cabins, mainly two-berth. The shelter deck had a domed, 200-seat first-class dining saloon, the café and reception room forward, the second-class dining saloon and the open decks for the second-class and steerage aft. The rest of the passenger cabins, both first- and second-class, were on the upper deck, the after part of which was devoted to steerage. Lessons having been learned from the *Titanic* disaster, the ship was exceptionally well sub-divided and it was claimed that she would remain afloat with any four compartments flooded.

On 1 April, 1913, the *Empress of Russia* left Liverpool on her long maiden voyage to the Orient via the Suez route. On her first trans-Pacific run made that May, she crossed from Yokohama to Vancouver in 8 days, 18½ hours, a record which stood for nine years. As a reminder of conditions at that time it is worth recording that en route she called at Nagasaki where, in the space of 6 hours, local labour carried on board 3,200 tons of coal. With the commencement of the First World War the ship was requisitioned to spend about 18 months in the Indian Ocean, operating as an A.M.C. A brief return to commercial service was followed by a spell of trans-Atlantic trooping. By 1919 she was back on her old run and on this she continued until the winter of 1940–41. Then, after she had made 310 trans-Pacific crossings, she was once again requisitioned as a troopship and sent to the U.K. In September 1945, while undergoing a post-war refit at Barrow-in-Furness, she was gutted by fire and was subsequently broken up there by T. W. Ward Ltd. Her sister *Empress of Asia* was equally successful in service. In January 1941 she arrived at Vancouver on the conclusion of her 307th scheduled Pacific crossing and was requisitioned a month later for service as a troopship. In this capacity she was sunk off Singapore in February 1942 by Japanese aircraft.

2   s.s. LADY RODNEY, 1929, Canada

The *Lady Rodney* and her sister *Lady Somers* formed part of a five-ship group built 1928–29 for Canadian National Steamships of Montreal. They resulted from a trade agreement of 1925 which called for improved passenger and cargo services between Canada and the British Colonies in the Caribbean. Although very much alike in hull and appearance, these two groups were designed to work on two quite distinct services and as a result their passenger accommodation and cargo facilities differed appreciably.

The *Lady Rodney* and *Lady Somers* were intended for the shorter of these two routes, which terminated at Jamaica and in this the emphasis was on through traffic—passengers travelling to and from the mainland—and on the northward carriage of bananas. The other three ships, the *Lady Drake*, *Lady Hawkins* and *Lady Nelson*, operated on the much longer Eastern Caribbean service which extended as far South as Georgetown. On this there was a considerable amount of inter-island passenger traffic, which called for extra, cheaper grades of accommodation.

All five ships were built and engined by Cammell Laird & Co. Ltd., Birkenhead. The *Lady Rodney* and *Lady Somers* were constructed to Lloyd's Register classification and the other three to that of the British Corporation. Each of the two former ships had a gross tonnage of 8,194 and carried a deadweight of 4,620 tons on a draught of 23 ft. Their main dimensions were length o.a. 438 ft (420 ft b.p.), breadth mld 60 ft and depth mld to upper deck 32 ft 9 in. Their hulls had four decks and four holds. Besides 24,000 cu. ft of space for general, and 15,500 cu. ft for refrigerated cargo, these two ships had 204,000 cu. ft of ventilated space, enough for 1 million stems of bananas. Amidships the two 'Ladies' had very attractive accommodation for 107 (later 125) passengers. This was first-class only—in contrast to that on the other three ships which, in addition, carried up to 32 second-class passengers and 102 steerage. Twin screws were driven by two sets of Parsons S.R. geared turbines. These were of impulse-reaction type and developed 7,500 s.h.p, giving a service speed of 14 knots. Superheated steam at 220 p.s.i. was supplied by four S.E. boilers which were oil-fired and worked under forced draught.

The *Lady Rodney*, the last of the quintette, was launched on 30 November, 1928, and completed in April 1929. From then until the war she and the *Lady Somers* maintained the fortnightly Western Caribbean service between Montreal (Halifax and St. John, N.B., in winter) and Jamaica, calling en route at Bermuda and Nassau. The *Lady Rodney* came through the war unscathed. Government service as a troopship lasted from June 1942 to November 1945. In the following year she was used to repatriate Canadian soldiers and their dependants and she also made five Channel voyages, bringing 'war brides' from Rotterdam and Antwerp to England, thence to Canada. After having travelling 165,000 miles on Government service she arrived at St. John, N.B., in December 1946 to undergo a major overhaul.

Of the other *Lady* ships three were sunk, among them the *Lady Somers*—in mid-Atlantic in July 1941—while serving as an Armed Boarding Vessel. This left only the *Lady Rodney* and *Lady Nelson*, and in July and August 1947 these two re-entered commercial service, this time on the Eastern Caribbean service. This took them via Boston to Bermuda, St. Kitts, Antigua, Montserrat, Dominica, St. Lucia, Barbados, St. Vincent, Grenada, Trinidad and Georgetown, the round voyage lasting about a month. Air competition made their operation increasingly uneconomic and in October 1952 both were withdrawn from service.

Sold to Egypt, they were refitted at Alexandria in 1953, the *Lady Nelson* becoming the *Gumhuryat Misr* (later *Alwadi*) and the *Lady Rodney* the *Mecca*. The former was intended for east–west Mediterranean service and the latter for the trade between North Africa, Egypt and Jeddah, in which there was a considerable flow of native labour as well as pilgrims. Her cabin accommodation was accordingly modified somewhat and her 'tween decks fitted out to take nearly 1,300 steerage. Her career in this capacity ended somewhat ignominiously in the Summer of 1967 when, during the brief war between Egypt and Israel, she was scuttled in the Suez Canal. As to the *Alwadi*, there have been no movement reports for a quite considerable time, but at the time of writing her name still features in Lloyd's Register. To those who may wonder at the system of naming adoped for the *Lady* ships, these commemorated the wives of Admirals intimately associated with the British West Indies, through exploration, colonisation or conquest. The Admirals themselves shared the honour with their wives, and a life-size portrait of each was hung in the liner bearing his consort's name.

3 m.v. SELANDIA, 1912, Denmark

The Danish-owned *Selandia* of the East Asiatic Company has a special place in maritime history as being the world's first ocean-going motorship. She was built and engined by Burmeister & Wain, Copenhagen, whose executives had from a very early stage shown great interest in a new form of engine invented by a young German engineer named Rudolf Diesel. In 1895 B. & W. secured the Danish patent rights for the engine, which they set about improving, having determined not to market it until absolute reliability had been attained. In December 1910, even before it had been tried out afloat, Mr. H. N. Andersen, founder of the East Asiatic Co., was so convinced of its superiority over steam that he placed the order for this pioneer motorship—which by current standards was large.

The name chosen for her was the latinised version of Sjaelland, the island on which Copenhagen stands. The ship was launched on 4 November, 1911, and all went so smoothly that she was ready for delivery by mid-February. Five days later, on 22 February, 1912, she left for London and her long maiden voyage to Bangkok. Interest in her was such that the Crown Prince and other members of the Danish Royal Family travelled in her as far as Elsinore. Each day while in London she was visited by hundreds, including Winston Churchill, then First Lord of the Admiralty, at whose request various Admiralty officials joined the ship for the run to Antwerp.

The *Selandia*'s main dimensions were: length (b.p.) 370·4 ft, (overall) 386 ft, breadth 53·2 ft and depth mld to upper deck 30 ft. Her twin screws were driven by two 8-cylinder engines of 4-stroke single-acting type, the power being kept low at 1,250 i.h.p. apiece at about 140 r.p.m. The cylinders were of 530 mm diameter and 730 mm stroke and gave the ship a sea speed of 11–12 knots. Her gross tonnage was 4,964, the deadweight 7,400 tons, and displacement 9,800 tons. Oil fuel to a maximum of 1,056 tons was carried in the double bottom and in tanks abreast the shaft tunnel.

Outwardly, the ship broke from tradition in having no funnel, merely exhausts. Her hull layout was also unusual in having four islands, giving one long and two short well decks. She had two continuous decks and below the 'tween deck spaces she had five holds, three forward and two aft of the machinery space. These were served by 11 derricks and—another novelty—electric winches. The crew was berthed in the poop and the engineers and officers abreast the engine casing; while the accommodation for the 26 first-class passengers was arranged under the bridge. There, on the centreline, she also had the main saloon (forward), dining saloon and galley. Above these, on the bridge deck, was the Captain's cabin, one or two passenger cabins and a smoking room for passengers.

The route for which the *Selandia* was intended was exceptionally long and it was 26 June, 1912, before she returned to Copenhagen after her triumphant 22,000-mile maiden voyage. In the course of her first 12 years she travelled over 600,000 miles and in that time the engines caused only 10 days delay in port. She remained in the Company's service until 1936. Then sold to Norway, she traded first as the *Norseman*, next—from 1940—as the *Tornator*, owned by the Finland Amerika Linjen O/Y of Helsingfors. Service as such was brief, for late in January 1942 she was wrecked off the Japanese Coast, in Omaisaki Bay.

The *Selandia* was the first of three similar ships. Her builders were also responsible for the *Fionia*, while on the Clyde Barclay, Curle & Co. built the *Jutlandia*, whose launching followed only a week after that of the *Selandia*. The new diesel engines so justified themselves that thereafter the East Asiatic Co. only ordered motorships.

4   s.s. FRANCE, 1911, France

The *France* joined the ranks of the North Atlantic élite in the same year as the White Star *Olympic* and four years after the Cunard *Lusitania* and *Mauretania*; and she preceded the giant *Imperator* of the Hamburg–American Line by one year. Viewed against these, the *France* appears a relative lightweight but, save only the two Cunarders, she was the fastest merchantman afloat. Her owners, the Cie. Générale Transatlantique (the French Line) operated from Le Havre, a port which at that time could not handle unduly large vessels, nor did the amount of traffic to and from France warrant a ship of exceptional size. But what she lacked in this direction was offset by the rich, lavish elegance of her appointments—to say nothing of the service traditional to 'Transat' ships.

For the Company, however, she represented a very great advance, for her immediate forbears, with which she operated for some years, were the 11,000-ton, 20-knot sisters *La Lorraine* and *La Savoie* of 1900–1 and the 21-knot *La Provence* of 13,700 tons, which had been built in 1906. Curiously, since these were all two-funnelled, two-masted ships, there was, in their appearance, a strong family resemblance, common features being the degree of rake and the relative height and proportions of the funnels—plus something else which was undefinable. The *France* was the largest and fastest merchant ship yet built in that country, also the first of any size there to be turbine driven. Of all French liners, she was the only one to have four funnels.

She had a gross tonnage of 23,666 and displaced 26,760 tons. Her length b.p. was 685 ft (approx. 712 ft o.a.), breadth mld 75 ft 5 in., depth mld to D deck 52 ft 10 in. (to B deck 70 ft 6 in.), and load draught 29 ft 10 in. Quadruple screws were driven by French-built, Parsons-type, three-stage turbines of 45,000 s.h.p. Steam at 200 p.s.i. was provided by 11 double-ended and 8 single-ended boilers. These were arranged in four boiler rooms which extended for 279 ft of the ship's length, the engine room occupying another 147 ft. The coal capacity was 5,000 tons and the daily consumption around 575 tons. Three classes of passengers were carried, 535 first, approximately 440 second and 950 third, the precise numbers varying over the years.

The ship was built and engined by the Chantiers de l'Atlantique, St. Nazaire. The keel-laying ceremony took place on 20 April, 1909, and she was launched—on the top of an exceptionally high tide—on 20 September, 1910. On 3 April, 1911, she left for trials and on a 24-hour run she averaged about 25 knots at 47,000 s.h.p. and attained a maximum of 25·9 knots. Since she always operated with slower ships, there was seldom need for full power, her great reserves in this direction being used instead to ensure the utmost regularity in time-keeping. Thus on her maiden voyage to New York—which commenced on 20 April, 1911–she only averaged 22·2 knots outwards and 22·4 knots homewards.

In her early years the ship sailed direct between Le Havre and New York and although a particular favourite with Americans, she was not well known in England. Even after a call at Plymouth had been instituted (in 1922) she remained a ship remote, and passengers were taken off or landed there by tender. During the early days of the war the *France* remained laid up at Brest. Then requisitioned for Government service, she became the *France IV* and in the role of transport she was present at the Dardanelles. After that she spent about three years as a hospital ship. The final period of the war she spent trooping on the Atlantic. Her return to commercial service in 1919 was followed by a bonanza period of easy money and her popularity was such that those wishing to travel in her had to bid for their cabins.

In June 1921, premier position in the French Line fleet passed to the 34,569-ton *Paris*, which was joined in 1927 by the 43,153-ton *Île de France*. Meanwhile, the *France* had been converted to burn oil and had had her accommodation modernised so as to cater for the very travel-conscious, but nevertheless less affluent, section of the American market. After making some economy cruises the *France* made a final trans-Atlantic crossing in August 1932. Early the following year, while laid up at Le Havre, she incurred some fire damage and in December 1934 she was sold for demolition at Dunkirk.

5   s.s. PROVIDENCE, 1914, France

Among the international range of passenger lines which competed on the North Atlantic for the main flow of traffic between the U.S.A., England and Northern Europe there was one and only one French representative, the Cie. Générale Transatlantique. There was, however, one other French concern which operated between Marseilles and New York, the Fabre Line which, although of much smaller stature, had been involved in this trade since the 'eighties. The fact that they used a more southerly and therefore warmer route was a strong selling point to Americans and Frenchmen alike. Another aspect, much stressed in the States, was the ease with which a Fabre Line crossing could be coupled with a holiday tour embracing North Africa, the Levant, Greece and the Italian and French Rivieras. The Company was founded in 1881 as the Compagnie Francaise de Navigation à Vapeur Cyprien Fabre. Latterly it became the Cie. de Navigation Cyprien Fabre but, over the years, it was familiarly known as the Fabre Line or else Cyprien Fabre. The quality of its fleet was considerably improved by the construction of four vessels in 1902–7, the *Roma*, *Germania*, *Madonna* and *Venezia*, two-funnelled ships of 14–15 knots speed and some 5,000 to 6,000 tons gross. These were joined in 1911 and 1912 by the *Sant Anna* and *Canada*, both of over 9,000 tons. Not long afterwards two much more ambitious liners, the *Patria* and *Providence*, each of nearly 12,000 tons, were ordered but the completion of these was delayed by the war. Both were built at La

Seyne, the Forges et Chantiers de la Méditerranée being responsible for both their hulls and machinery.

The Fabre Line had never ordered exact sisterships, each vessel showing slight variation in size. This applied to the *Patria* and the *Providence*, the latter being the longer by 25 ft. Even so, the difference in gross tonnage was very small. The *Providence*, of 11,996 tons gross and 6,693 tons net, had a cargo capacity of 5,665 tons and displaced 14,800 tons. Her registered dimensions were length 511·8 ft, breadth 59·7 ft and depth 43·5 ft. A twin-screw ship, she was propelled by two sets of triple-expansion engines with cylinders of approximately 30½, 49½ and 79½ in. diameter and 51¼ in. stroke. These had an i.h.p. of 9,500, took steam from nine Prudhon Capus coal-fired boilers and gave a service speed of about 17 knots. Accommodation was provided for about 200 first-class, 300 second- and 1,800 third-class passengers. The ship had seven decks in all. Four holds were served by 8 steam winches and 10 derricks of 3 to 5 tons capacity.

Even after the Armistice , a considerable time elapsed before the *Providence* was finished. However, by May 1920 she was ready for trials and on these, carried out off the Îles d'Hyeres, she attained 18·23 knots. Less than a fortnight later, on 3 June, she left Marseilles on her maiden voyage to New York, calling en route at Lisbon, the Azores and Providence (Rhode Island). For a number of years she and the *Patria* plied between New York and a range of Mediterranean ports, together with other Fabre ships, the most important of these being the pre-war *Canada* and the 8,567-ton *Sinaia*, which entered service in 1924. The service was then at its peak of prosperity and in 1929 the Company carried 70,000 passengers. Then came the great depression which hit the Company with particular severity. In 1931 the two big ships were withdrawn from the New York trade and in January of the following year they were both chartered to the Messageries Maritimes for their service between Marseilles, Egypt and the Levant. Hitherto the hulls of the *Providence* and her sister had been all white, but during this charter period they were painted as shown, black, but with the red, white and blue Fabre funnel colours. Soon afterwards the *Providence* stranded off the Island of Imbroz, but was refloated with the aid of a Turkish salvage vessel, an episode which served as the subject for a Turkish stamp issued in 1951.

In January 1940 the two ships were sold outright to the M. M. and from then on they had all black funnels. But in November the long partnership was brought to an end by saboteurs, an internal explosion causing the *Patria* to sink in Haifa harbour where, years later, her wreck was broken up. Back in the years of war and Vichy control, the *Providence* had been laid up at Berre where, during a gale, she had dragged her anchors and run ashore, her condition being such that she was ignored by the occupying German forces. There she remained until December 1944, when she was refloated and reconditioned. Her passenger capacity now became 222 first-, 294 second- and 284 third-class. A further period on the Marseilles–Levant service followed and this, starting in 1949, became coupled with the seasonal carriage of Mohammedan pilgrims from Dakar and Casablanca to Jeddah, the port for the Muslim holy city. In October 1951, after the season's flow had ended, the ship was sold and subsequently broken up at La Spezia.

6   m.v. ERIDAN, 1929, France

The first motor liner to be built for the Messageries Maritimes was the 8,194-ton *Theophile Gautier* of 1926. In terms of appearance she followed the lead set by some early post-war French liners in having two funnels so under-sized and ill-designed as to make her not merely ugly but, worse still for a passenger ship, devoid of personality. The

Eridan was the M.M.'s second motorship and with her the Company introduced a different funnel style; this was repeated for their next five motor liners, the last of which entered service in 1931. In fact, the idea of a square funnel with overhanging top was not original, although new to the passenger trade. It was inspired by that fitted on a small German cargo vessel, the m.v. *Vulcan,* which was built in 1924 to try out a new form of gearing.

The style scandalised the purists, but seen in retrospect, it served several useful purposes. It was eye-catching, gave the Company's new generation of ships a definite corporate image and certainly made the world more M.M. conscious. This was badly needed, for seen against the latest P. & O. liners on the Eastern and Australian trades (most of which were faster), the older M.M. ships lacked presence. Viewed from a wider aspect, the adoption of this new style served as a much needed antidote to the ultraconservative attitude which then applied to the externals of ships. Soon the *Eridan* with her square funnels was followed by such novelties as single-masted liners, raked stems and the first touch of streamlining. A new impulse was asserting itself.

For most of her career the *Eridan* was owned by the Soc. des Services Contractuels des Messageries Maritimes, a State-aided offshoot of the Cie. des Messageries Maritimes. After the war she become the property of the parent Company. She was built by a firm long associated with the M.M., the Soc. Provençale de Cons. Navales, of La Ciotat. A twin-screw ship, she was designed for the Company's passenger, mail and cargo service to Australia. This was emphasized by the decor of many of her public rooms, which centred around the Australian landscape, fauna and flora. Despite this, she was used on a variety of routes.

Her tonnage was 9,928 and she had a load displacement of 14,135 tons, corresponding to a draught of 27 ft 1 in. The overall length was 468 ft 7 in. (442 ft 11 in. b.p.), breadth mld 61 ft and depth mld (to upper deck) 46 f t 3 in. The five holds had a capacity of 10,680 cu. metres and were served by 14 derricks and electric winches. The main propelling machinery comprised two 2-stroke, S.A., 8-cylinder, French-built Sulzer diesels. The contract speed was 15 knots, but on trials she attained 16·1. As for passengers, the *Eridan* was fitted to accommodate 56 first-, 86 second- and 436 third-class (emigrants). Of the first-class public rooms on t he promenade deck, the smoking room was furnished in a French provincial style, but for the others in that class a modern idiom was chosen. The first-class cabins were nearly all for one or two persons, the second-class for two or four.

When launched on 3 June, 1928, the *Eridan* had the distinction of being the largest and highest-powered motorship yet built in France. On 19 November, 1929, she sailed from Marseilles on a short maiden voyage to Alexandria, Jaffa (Haifa) and Beirut. Early in the new year, on 10 January, she started on her designed service to Australia, via Suez. Her voyages took her as far as Sydney and Brisbane in one direction and Dunkirk (her port of registry) and Antwerp in the other. Later her itinerary, still via Suez, was extended to Nouméa. However, at the end of 1935, she started sailing in the opposite direction, from Marseilles to Papeete and Nouméa, by way of the French Antilles and the Panama Canal. This continued until 1940, at least.

The *Eridan* was one of those which came under Vichy control. This ended on 8 November, 1942, when, as one of a four-ship convoy, she was intercepted off the North African Coast by the Allied invasion ('Torch') covering forces, and sent first to Arzew and then Oran. Subsequently she was used by the Allies, her managers at that time being the British India Line. While at Saigon late in December 1945 she had an engine-room fire, but this caused no great delay. In March 1946, after the dissolution of the Inter-

Allied pool, the ship was returned to her owners. After a brief spell of Mediterranean trooping she underwent a refit at Toulon which lasted far into 1947. From this she emerged with her passenger capacity raised to 95 first- and 112 second-class, plus space for 900 troops. The *Eridan* then spent several years on the Company's Indian Ocean Line. This started from Marseilles and took her along the East African Coast to Madagascar, Reunion and Mauritius.

In 1951 the ship returned to her builders and was given another refit and improved accommodation, also a 'new look' with one large oval funnel. That over, the *Eridan* returned to the Madagascar run. This phase ended in 1953, when she made one or two voyages to Haiphong, possibly with troops. Thereafter she operated from Marseilles across the Atlantic and through the Panama Canal to Papeete and Nouméa. Her last scheduled voyage ended at Marseilles on 28 January, 1956, and by March she had been sold for breaking up at La Seyne.

7   s.s. IMPERATOR, 1913, Germany

Even now, over half a century later, the years which preceded the First World War stand out—more than any others—as those of grandiose schemes and giant passenger ships such as the world had never seen before. Between the summers of 1911 and 1914 seven great liners, each of 45,000 tons or over, were either commissioned or launched, three each for the White Star and Hamburg-American lines and one for the Cunard. Yet of these only two were destined to serve their owners as planned.

It was the White Star which took the lead in this direction by ordering the *Olympic* and *Titanic* and subsequently the *Britannic*. Inspired from an early stage by the scale of the White Star project, Albert Ballin, head of the Hamburg-American Line, decided on a trio which would outstrip all others, as regards both size and luxury. The *Imperator* was the first of the resultant ships which were launched at yearly intervals, she by the Vulcan-Werke, Hamburg, the *Vaterland* and the *Bismarck* by Blohm & Voss. There had been ideas that the three should be built at Belfast, as had many other big German liners. However, the terms of a government subsidy stipulated construction within Germany. However good this was for national pride, it posed a somewhat daunting challenge to those made responsible, since in general German builders lacked the long experience of their British counterparts.

At the time of writing there is an excess of container tonnage on the North Atlantic. In the 'thirties the same applied to passenger ships. It is perhaps worth considering the position of this type had there been no *Titanic* loss, no war and all these giants had served their owners as planned. That the Cunard Line should order the *Aquitania* to run with their express ships *Lusitania* and *Mauretania* was logical enough, since the elderly *Campania* made poor showing against the other two. The White Star pattern was for the 17,000-ton *Oceanic* of 1899 to be joined by three *Olympic* class ships, the former acting as a stand-in as required. Before the advent of the *Imperator* the Hamburg-American express service to New York (one of six North Atlantic lines then operated by the Company) was maintained by the 22,000-ton *Amerika* of 1905, the 24,000-ton *Kaiserin Auguste Victoria* of 1906 and the 16,000 to 17,000-ton *Cincinatti* and *Cleveland* of 1909. Of these, the first two were 18-knot ships and the latter pair 16-knot. As seen by other major companies, such as the Norddeutscher Lloyd (with four existing fliers built 1897–1907 and a 34,000-tonner launched in 1913) and the Cie. Générale Transatlantique (with the 24,000-ton *France* newly completed and the 34,000-ton *Paris* on the stocks), the future must have seemed somewhat perilous.

The *Imperator* had a gross tonnage of 51,969 and a displacement of 56,000 tons, the latter corresponding to a draught of 35 ft 6 in. Her length overall was 919 ft (882·9 ft b.p.), breadth extreme 98·3 ft, depth of hold 57·1 ft and depth mld 63 ft. She had quadruple screws and these were driven by German-built, Parsons-type turbines of 62,000 s.h.p. which were designed to give a speed of 23 knots (about 24 knots maximum). The astern power was 35,000 s.h.p. Steam at 235 p.s.i. was supplied by no less than 46 single-ended boilers which were arranged in four compartments.

In the hull there were five continuous decks, E to J, the lowest of these being at about water level. Yet lower there were two partial decks forward and one aft. Above, D deck was continuous but open beneath at the stern. Even though the construction of the *Imperator* was well advanced it was inevitable that the *Titanic* disaster should lead to some changes to her design and equipment. One new precaution was the addition of an extra skin 5 ft inside the outer hull. This was carried the length of the three forward holds and to well above the waterline. More embarrassing was the universal demand that there should be lifeboats for all, 83 boats (two of them motor-driven) having to be fitted. Problems of space and stability necessitated the grouping of many of these in a new position, in the lower part of the superstructure.

In terms of appearance the ship was impressive but stiff, the amount of sheer and flare being limited, far less than on her British contemporaries. Aft, round the stern, she had gold scroll work, while the stem was briefly dominated by a great eagle—as shown—but after heavy weather damage this unloved fitting was removed. Just as in size the *Imperator* was intended to outstrip all others, so was her accommodation designed to surpass all by its magnificence. It is remarkable how those responsible for the outfitting and decor of her passenger spaces—cabins included—should so ignore the aspects of weight and stability. Even so, very great credit must be given to Charles Mewès for the elegance and charm which he achieved in most of the public rooms.

The number of passengers carried was vast, 908 first-class, 972 second-class, 942 third-class and 1,772 steerage, a total of 4,594. The crew numbered 1,180. Comparable passenger capacities for the *Olympic* and *Aquitania* were 3,300 and 4,200 respectively. The first-class passengers had the use of six decks amidships, their promenade spaces being on A, B and C decks. Among the most outstanding features were the two Imperial suites, the loftiness of the public rooms and the provision of a magnificent swimming pool. This was situated on G deck—its base near the waterline—at a point midway between the first and second funnels.

The *Imperator* was launched by the Kaiser in person on 23 May, 1912 and after various minor troubles she left Cuxhaven on 10 June, 1913, on her maiden voyage to New York. Lack of stability soon asserted itself and that winter the ship was withdrawn for drastic alterations. Her appearance was altered from that shown by the removal of 9 ft from the tops of her funnels. Internally she was stripped of much of her heavy marble and panelling, while she was given 2,000 tons of cement ballast. Even so she remained a tender ship. The *Imperator* spent the war laid up at Hamburg, her sister the *Vaterland* (later *Leviathan*) at New York. The former put to sea in May 1919 after being assigned to the U.S.A. to carry home American troops from France. Allocation to Britain was followed by Cunard management and a refit. Early in 1922 she and the unfinished *Bismarck* (later *Majestic*) were bought jointly by the Cunard and White Star lines, and the risk of over-bidding was thus avoided. Although each firm was responsible for its own vessel, joint ownership continued until 1932.

Her career as the *Berengaria* started in 1921, but the ship still did not come up to Cunard standards, so that in October she was sent to the Tyne for an overhaul which included conversion to oil burning, the stripping of her steerage accommodation and

general improvement of the rest of the passenger spaces. She then started a very successful period of service, running alongside the *Aquitania* and *Mauretania* between Southampton, Cherbourg and New York. In the late 'twenties much of her old third-class
accommodation was converted into tourist, her passenger capacity subsequently stand-
ing at 811 first-, 661 second-, 525 tourist and 606 third-class. By the late 'thirties the
state of the North Atlantic trade was such that after a fire in her main lounge—at New
York in the Spring of 1938—she returned home empty and late that year she was sold
for breaking up on the Tyne. This work was not finished until after the war, when the
lower hull, in two pieces, was towed to Rosyth for final demolition.

8 m.v. BARBARA, 1926, Germany

The Flettner rotor ship was a German invention of the 'twenties. Only a few decades
earlier steamships had carried sails and used them when the wind was fair, to gain
additional speed; so it was with the rotor ship, the tall towers being the scientist's
equivalent of auxiliary sail power. Wind blowing on them, so it was claimed, created
far more power than on well-trimmed sails, the thrust developed being dependent on
direction and speed of rotation.

Only two ships were given these rotors. The first was the *Buckau*, 497 tons gross, a
converted schooner which was fitted with two towers but retained her original propeller
and the small diesel which drove it. The results gained prompted the German Admiralty
to carry out further tests on the larger and specially built *Barbara*. She was chartered to
a Hamburg firm, Rob. M. Sloman, Jr., whose fleet included some similarly sized, but
conventionally powered steamships against which the performance of the *Barbara*
could be judged.

She had a gross tonnage of 2,077 and a cargo capacity of about 2,800 tons. Her overall
length was 294 ft, breadth mld 43 ft 4 in. and depth mld 19 ft 3 in. The draught was
approximately 18 ft 5 in. She had four hatches served by electric winches and ten
derricks of 3- to 30-tons capacity. Her main propelling machinery, light and compact,
consisted of two high-speed, 6-cylinder M.A.N.-type diesels (360 mm × 520 mm)
which together developed 1,060 b.h.p. Their normal speed was 300 r.p.m. and they were
connected to Vulcan hydro-mechanical gear which reduced the speed of the single
propeller to 80 r.p.m. A Vulcan clutch enabled the propeller to be disengaged when
required. The ship was also fitted with the then new Flettner type of rudder.

As to the three rotors, these were approximately 55 ft tall and 13 ft in diameter. They
were made of an aluminium alloy, were carried on steel pivots and ran on ball bearings
in oil baths. Their weight was 1·4 tons apiece. The rotors were both started and controlled from the bridge. The power needed for them was very small, the maximum
figure mentioned being 75 h.p.

The *Barbara* was launched on 28 April, 1926, and started her trials that July. Such
details as were released covered an occasion when the wind speed was 3 to 5 on the
Beaufort scale. With the wind at 105° from the vessel's course, the propeller disengaged
and the rotors revolving at 140 r.p.m., the ship attained a speed of 5·5 knots. The power
needed was 75 h.p. With the wind 40° from aft 5·5 knots was achieved at only 45 h.p.
With one main engine running (500 h.p.) and no rotor movement, the ship's speed was
7 knots. With rotors running—at an additional 45 h.p.—and the wind on the beam, the
speed was raised to 9·5 knots. Again, with the two main engines giving a speed of 9
knots and the wind still on the beam, a 45 h.p. to the rotors raised the speed to 10·5
knots.

Eventually the idea was dropped as not being worth while. The stripping of the first ship, the *Buckau* was therefore soon followed by that of the *Barbara*. In 1933 she became the *Birkenau*, owned by another Hamburg firm, the Bugsier Reed. -und Bergungs A.G. Her appearance was now completely different, since the forward bridgehouse as well as the rotors had gone. Amidships she had a new wheelhouse, but no funnel and only short stumps for topmasts. In 1947 she was bought by Ove Skou, of Copenhagen, who renamed her *Else Skou* and later gave her new, higher-powered diesels, also a new profile with two tall, conventionally placed masts (where the end rotors had been), a larger bridge and a very wide, but squat, funnel. The ship kept that name until 1963, when she became the *Fotis P.*, the larger of a two-ship fleet owned by the Greek Libyan Lines, of Piraeus. The latest change of ownership came about 1966, when she was bought by a Saudi Arabian firm, Orri Navigation Lines, of Jeddah, who renamed her *Star of Riyadh*.

9 m.v. ORINOCO, 1928, Germany

By the mid-'twenties, after a major building programme and the purchase of other companies and individual ships, the Hamburg-American Line had once again acquired a massive fleet. The urgent early need was for numbers, so a degree of austerity had to be accepted. However, by 1928 the results of a second building programme were really apparent, for in that year the Company took delivery of eight new ships. If the early ones were of the bread and butter category, these were of more sophisticated design and, unlike most of their forbears, were all diesel-driven. Of the three which were designed for passenger service the *Orinoco* and *Magdalena* were the most interesting, being by far the most luxurious the Company had ever put on the Central American trade.

The *Orinoco*, of 9,880 tons gross and 6,500 tons d.w., was built by the Bremer Vulkan, Vegesack, her sister coming from the Schichau yard at Danzig. Both had twin screws and were propelled by Schichau-Sulzer type engines. These were of single-acting, two-cycle type and had eight cylinders apiece. At 95 r.p.m. they had an output of 6,800 b.h.p. corresponding to a speed of about 15 knots. The *Orinoco* had an overall length of 480 ft, her breadth and depth being 61 ft and 38 ft respectively. The load draught was 29 ft.

As regards external appearance these two ships (also the rather larger *General Osorio* of 1929) were unique, for relative lack of freeboard was offset by an unusually massive superstructure, the base of which extended forward to the foremast. Another unusual feature, but one very popular in the tropics, was the placing of two of the main dining rooms high up in the superstructure. The *Orinoco* could accommodate 140 first-class, 100 intermediate and 100 third-class passengers. For the first-class, A deck (one below the bridge) was devoted to public rooms, the aftermost one—its arched windows visible below the second funnel—being the gallery over the first-class dining room. The third-class was arranged forward and the intermediate-class from amidships aft. The ship had a large open-air pool which formed the core of what appeared to be the poop deckhouse. The *Orinoco* was launched in February 1928, yet on April 25 she called at Southampton on her maiden voyage. Thereafter the two ships operated together, alternating with some freighters. However, in 1934 the *Magdalena* grounded near Curacao and remained fast for over three months. While being repaired she was also given higher-powered machinery and lengthened forward, returning to service in 1935 as the one-funnelled *Iberia*.

In April 1941, while at Vera Cruz the *Orinoco* was seized by the Mexican Government and renamed *Puebla*. Proving too large for the Mexican–U.S. trade, she was leased to the U.S. Maritime Commission. Several years' service as a U.S. troopship—still named

Puebla—ended with her return to Mexico in 1946. Promptly sold to Southern Steamships (Pty.) Ltd. of Cape Town, she became the *Olympia*, but only for a very brief spell, for early in 1947 she was resold to become the *Juan de Garay*, owned at Buenos Aires by the Transoceanica Line (Cia. Transoceanica Argentina S.R.L.). During this final phase she had a white hull and funnels painted in national colours (light blue with white band) and operated as a one-class ship with accommodation for 850. Her owners' only vessel, she traded between the River Plate and ports in Spain and Italy in conjunction with Spanish ships of the Ybarra Line. In April 1961 she left Montevideo on her final transatlantic voyage. Laid up at Barcelona, she remained there until November 1962 when she left for the breakers' yard at Castellon. Meanwhile, her one-time sister has continued in service as the Russian *Pobeda*. Based on the Black Sea and used mainly for cruises in and around that area, she has also made some much longer voyages.

10 s.s. BALMORAL CASTLE, 1910, Great Britain

On the South African mail service, the *Balmoral Castle* and her sister the *Edinburgh Castle* represented the end of an era, that of the slim, elegant liner with her counter stern and two tall, rim-topped funnels. They were the last Union-Castle mail ships to be built during the regime of Sir Donald Currie, that dominant personality who had founded the Castle Line and had continued as head after the merger of the Union and Castle Lines in 1900. His place as Chairman was taken by Lord Pirrie, whose period as such was marked by the introduction of very different, more built-up styles.

In their shaping and hull dimensions, the *Balmoral Castle* and the *Edinburgh Castle* conformed to two earlier pairs, the *Kenilworth Castle* and the *Armadale Castle* of 1904/1903 and the *Walmer Castle* and *Saxon* of 1902/1900. The design, however, had originated in a much earlier ship, the 7,537-ton *Norman* of 1894. The *Balmoral Castle* was built and engined by the Fairfield S. B. & E. Co. Ltd. Launched into the Clyde on 13 November, 1909, she entered service the following Spring. Of 13,361 tons gross, she had a d.w. tonnage of 11,800 and a load draught of 31 ft 5 in. Her overall length was 590 ft 9 in. (570 ft b.p.), breadth 64 ft 6 in. and depth mld 42 ft 6 in. She had four continuous decks and above these a 116-ft long forecastle and a 74-ft poop, the latter being linked to the long 'open' promenade deck. Incidentally, it was by this joining of the main superstructure with the poop, also the use of the more modern Welin davits, that the new ships could be distinguished from the previous pair. Like the four which preceded them they were propelled by twin screws and two sets of quadruple expansion engines of 12,500 i.h.p. The cylinder diameters were 32, 46, 66½ and 96 in. and the stroke 60 in. For steam-raising there were 6 double-ended and 4 single-ended boilers which had a working pressure of 220 p.s.i. The *Balmoral Castle*'s coal bunker capacity was approximately 3,760 tons. In the Union-Castle the subject of speed was generally played down, sufficient that their vessels could fulfil the terms of the Mail contract and have plenty of power in reserve. Lloyd's Register quotes 17½ knots, but this was probably near her maximum, the service speed being about one knot less.

As built, the ship had accommodation for 317 first-class, 220 second- and 268 third-class passengers. The first-class cabins were on the upper and main decks and were fitted with chests of drawers, wardrobes 'and all the usual fittings, including an electric fan'. Above, on the promenade deck, there was a group of larger staterooms which could be divided as required into suites of two, three or four rooms. The *Balmoral Castle* had the distinction of being the first Cape liner to be fitted with wireless telegraphy.

After making two round voyages she was commissioned as a man-of-war—with buff

funnels—to carry various members of the Royal Family to Cape Town for the inaugura-
tion of the Union of South Africa in 1910. Her functions as a Royal Yacht over, she had
a brief but very successful reign as the crack ship on the Cape route. In South Africa
when war was declared, she was one of the first to bring South African troops to England.
After that brief phase as a trooper she returned to her designed Mail service, but later
in the war was taken up under the Liner Requisition Scheme, put under Cunard management and used to ferry American troops across the Atlantic. Then came a final spell of
war work, helping to take home Australian troops. She was home in time to carry
members of the House of Lords, as guests of the Admiralty, to the Victory Naval Review
off Southend. After that she returned to her old run between Southampton and South
African ports, retaining her popularity even after the advent of newer and larger ships.

As with most liners, her accommodation underwent modification during the years,
and early in 1939, when she was offered for sale, her passenger capacity was given as
307 first-class and 206 tourist, her crew, incidentally, numbering 284. In May 1939, while
laid up off the Isle of Wight, she was sold to John Cashmore, the shipbreaking firm at
Newport, Mon., for about £37,000.

11   s.s. HOWICK HALL, 1910, Great Britain

Not only was the *Howick Hall* a fine example of the pre-war cargo liner but her owners,
Chas. G. Dunn & Co. Ltd., of Liverpool, were determined that she should appear so.
Their most ambitious ship yet, she was designed for the U.S.—Latin American trade, on
which she had to compete with ships of companies both larger and longer-established.
As built, the *Howick Hall* had a gross tonnage of 4,923 (later increased to 5,096) and a
d.w. capacity of 8,079 tons. Her overall length was 413 ft (400 ft b.p.), breadth mld
51·5 ft, depth mld 29·7 ft and load draught just under 26 ft. Her hull had two continuous
decks and, above these, a long combined bridge and forecastle and a short poop, which
resulted in the rather unusual small well deck aft. Thoroughly up-to-date in design, she
was one of the first cargo liners to have longitudinal framing and her derricks included
one capable of 35-ton lifts.

A ship without sisters, she was launched by Wm. Hamilton & Co. Ltd., Port Glasgow,
on 1 October, 1910, and given a single set of triple-expansion engines supplied by David
Rowan & Co., Glasgow. She had four S.E. boilers with a working pressure of 180 lb
and bunker capacity for 800 tons of coal. Her speed was about 10 knots. On completion
she sailed direct for the States, to enter service on the New York and South America
Line, of which Dunn's were the managers. This phase was a brief one, for by 1915 she
and three other *Hall*s, together with five other British ships—those of the Isthmian
S.S. Co. Ltd.—had been bought by the newly formed United States Steel Products Co.
Inc., of New York. This firm, an offshoot of the United States Steel Corporation, later
adoped the title Isthmian Line in favour of its own more cumbrous one. Today, decades
later, the Isthmian Line is still a major concern, one now associated with the States
Marine Corporation.

Under the Stars and Stripes the *Howick Hall* retained her grey hull but was given plain
buff funnels. This ended in October 1929 when she was sold to a London firm who
renamed her *Dovenden*. Active service as such was minimal, for she spent most of 1930
laid up at New York, a collision there hardly helping matters. By October she had
crossed the Atlantic to Rotterdam, where she became a near-permanent feature. Sale to
another London concern late in 1932 was followed by continued idleness. In January
1935 she was sold for £7,500, reputedly to be broken up. However, as with various
other Italian purchases made then, demolition did not follow. Instead, her new owners,

Ditta Luigi Pittaluga Vapori, Genoa, put her back into service as the *Ircania*. In 1937 she changed hands yet again, this time locally. The Pittaluga funnel mark—a white band on black—then gave way to the green, white and red bands of the S.A. Co-operativa di Nav. 'Garibaldi'. This was at the time of the Abyssinian war and the *Ircania* was one of the many ships used to carry Italian military supplies to Massowah. In 1941 she was lying at Jacksonville when she and other Axis ships then in American ports were taken over by the U.S. Government. Recommissioned as the Panamanian flag *Raceland*, she was bombed and sunk south of Bear Island in March 1942.

12 s.s. LACONIA, 1911, Great Britain

The *Laconia* of 1911 and her sister *Franconia* of 1910 were intended to spend most of the year on the Cunard Line's service between Liverpool and Boston, but to be used during the winter months on the Mediterranean–New York trade. On both routes their sophisticated layout and fine appointments showed those previously employed— four masters like the *Ivernia*—for what they were, worthy but unenlightened examples of nineteenth-century design.

In their external shaping the *Laconia* and *Franconia* represented the first of several variations on the theme introduced into the Cunard fleet by the 19,000-ton *Carmania* and *Caronia*. The new pair were scaled down versions of these, smaller by some 1,400 tons and shorter by 15 ft, but more apparent to the eye was the fact that they had one less promenade deck. The last applications of the *Carmania* style—but with a single funnel—appeared in two different series built in the 'twenties. These were the 14,000-ton, A-class ships built for the Canadian trade and a 20,000-ton quintet—in which the names *Franconia* and *Laconia* featured once again.

Possibly because of their brevity of service, relatively little has been written about the *Laconia* of 1911 and her sister, yet they were built and finished to the highest Cunard standards. In that fleet they were the first to have a gymnasium and also movable—not swivel—chairs in the main dining rooms. The *Laconia* also had the distinction of being the first British passenger liner to be fitted with Frahm anti-rolling tanks. The subject of much interest, these were placed in the lower part of the forward cross-bunker. There were two tanks each side, their combined length being 39 ft. Each was about 15 ft wide and nearly three decks high. Three 20-in. valves controlled the flow of water from one side to the other. The *Laconia*'s main dimensions were length overall 625 ft, length b.p. 600 ft, breadth mld 71 ft and depth mld to B deck 60 ft 3 in. The load draught was 29 ft 6 in. corresponding to a displacement of 24,290 tons. The gross tonnage was 18,099. Both she and her sister were built by Swan, Hunter & Wigham Richardson, Ltd., but their propelling machinery, which drove twin screws, came from the Wallsend Slipway & Engineering Co. Ltd. This comprised two sets of 4-crank, quadruple-expansion engines with cylinders of 33, 47, 67 and 95 in. diameter and 60 in. stroke. To keep vibration to the minimum they were balanced on the Yarrow, Schlick and Tweedy system. Steam at 210 p.s.i. was supplied by six D.E. boilers which relied on natural draught and were grouped in two separate compartments. The coal bunker capacity was 2,500 tons and the service speed 17 knots.

The *Laconia* had accommodation for approximately 250 first-, 450 second- and 2,000 third-class passengers, while her officers and crew numbered about 450. The first-class public rooms were arranged on the boat deck and were furnished in Colonial style. They included a writing room, lounge, smoking room and veranda café, also gymnasium. The main dining saloon, with its balcony, was two decks down on C deck. The first-class cabins, which had the innovation of fixed washbasins—and running water—

instead of the old tip-up type, were arranged on B, C and D decks. Because of labour troubles the *Laconia* spent a year on the stocks. Eventually launched on 27 July, 1911, she left the Tyne on 10 December for Liverpool where, two days later, she was delivered to the Cunard Line. Her first sailing from the Mersey, on 20 January, 1912, was to New York. From there she proceeded to the Mediterranean, her entry into the Boston service following two months later. For a brief period Cunard ships served Boston as never before, but with the outbreak of the First World War various units were called up, thus neccessitating the suspension of the service.

For the first two years of the war the *Laconia* was used as a liner-cruiser and flew the White Ensign. During part of this period she acted as base ship for the expedition mounted against the German cruiser *Koenigsberg* which had retreated up the Rufidji River (Tanganyika). Returned to the Cunard, the *Laconia* then resumed trans-Atlantic service, but only for a brief final phase. On 25 February, 1917, she was torpedoed and sunk, with the loss of 12 lives, when 160 miles N.W. by W. from the Fastnet. Her sister had previously been sunk, while serving as a troopship near Malta on 4 October, 1916. As for the second *Laconia* and *Franconia* of 1922 and 1923, the former was likewise torpedoed—in 1942—but the latter continued in service until sold for scrap in 1956.

13   s.s. OLYMPIC, 1911, Great Britain

The idea of building the *Olympic* and her two sisters was conceived in its earliest form in 1907, when the Cunard Line's *Lusitania* was showing her paces and the *Mauretania* still fitting out. The White Star were firmly set on their policy of putting supreme comfort and great size before excessive speed. Quite apart from the *Lusitania*'s abilities as a record breaker, she and her sister had a gross tonnage of over 30,000, making them the largest in the world. Against them the White Star ships made poor showing. True, they were headed by the 21,000 to 24,000-ton 'big four', the *Celtic, Cedric, Baltic* and *Adriatic* in the 16½-knot range (the *Adriatic* was good for about 17). But in the faster category the Company had only the 17,000-ton *Oceanic* of 1899 and the 10,000-ton *Majestic* and *Teutonic*, which dated back to 1889–90.

The plan envisaged was that the *Oceanic* would work with the first two ships of the new trio, and that when the third one was ready the *Oceanic* would be relegated to reserve, being brought out when overhaul of the others made this neccessary. Compared with the two Cunarders, the projected White Star vessels represented a 50 per cent increase in size. At that time the relationship between the White Star Line and Harland & Wolff was such that the construction of ships elsewhere was not considered. In any case, where giant ships were involved Harland & Wolff were in an unassailable position.

The *Olympic* was launched at Belfast on 20 October, 1910, and she left for sea on 31 May, 1911, taking with her the guests who, a few hours earlier, had witnessed the launch of the *Titanic*. The gross tonnage of the *Olympic* was 45,324 (later 46,329). Her registered length was 852 ft 6 in., overall length 882 ft 9 in., breadth extreme 92 ft 6 in. and depth mld (to bridge deck) 73 ft 3 in. The height from keel to navigating bridge was 104 ft and the load draught 34 ft 6 in. She and the two which followed were the last great liners to have hulls of three-island type. Thus, although there was no superstructure aft, the stern was exceptionally tall, likewise the rudder, which was of non-balanced type.

In the *Laurentic* of 1909, the builders had introduced a new and very satisfactory machinery arrangement and this was adopted for the *Olympic* class. It comprised two sets of 4-cylinder, triple-expansion engines (with cylinders of 54, 84 and (two) 97 in. diameter and 75 in. stroke), which together totalled 30,000 i.h.p. and drove the wing shafts. Steam was exhausted into an L.P. turbine which contributed a further 16,000 s.h.p. through the centre shaft. Steam at 215 p.s.i. was provided by 24 D.E. and 5 S.E. boilers. Her service speed was 21 knots.

The *Olympic*, which had accommodation for 1,054 first-, 510 second- and 1,030 third-class passengers, sailed from Southampton on 14 June, 1911, on her maiden voyage, and on it averaged 21·7 knots. Three months later she was in collision with H.M. cruiser *Hawke* and, as a result of the damage incurred aft, she had to return to Belfast for repairs. On 10 April, 1912 the second of the new series, the *Titanic*, left Southampton on her first and final voyage; her loss a few days later brought disaster of the first magnitude. As a result of this catastrophe extensive alterations were made to the *Olympic*: the construction of an inner skin, the insertion of extra bulkheads and the heightening of others. She was also given additional lifeboats, while the numbers carried in the first class were considerably reduced.

The 1914–18 war was in its early stages when the *Olympic* distinguished herself by taking H.M.S. *Audacious* in tow. However, the mined battleship was too heavily damaged and sank. As a troopship the *Olympic* proved invaluable and while serving in this capacity in 1918 she had the satisfaction of ramming—and sinking—a submarine which had attacked her. In August 1919 the *Olympic* returned to Belfast to refit after five years of hard war service and while there she was converted to oil burning. The third of the series, the *Britannic*, which was never delivered to the Company, had been sunk in the Aegean in November 1916, while acting as a hospital ship. Instead of working with her as planned the *Olympic* started a long and successful period on the North Atlantic, operating between Southampton and New York with two purchased ex-German prizes, the 34,000-ton *Homeric* (formerly the N.D.L *Columbus*) and the 56,000-ton *Majestic* (launched as the Hamburg-American Line's *Bismarck*). The Cunard–White Star merger took place in 1934 and in the following Spring the *Olympic* was finally withdrawn and laid up. She remained at Southampton until the Autumn of 1935 when she was sold to be broken up at Jarrow. Two years later what remained of this most successful ship was towed north to Inverkeithing for final demolition. In the following year her two opposite numbers, the *Homeric* and *Majestic* were also sold, but before the latter left Southampton for Rosyth, the new generation, in the form of the *Queen Mary*, arrived from her builders to carry on the premier North Atlantic service.

14   s.s. ROTORUA, 1911, Great Britain

Originally known as the *Shropshire*, this impressive looking ship was one of three five-masted passenger and cargo liners built for a joint service to Australia via the Cape. She and the *Wiltshire* were owned by the Federal Steam Navigation Co. Ltd. and the *Argyllshire* by the Scottish Shire Line (Turnbull, Martin & Co. Ltd.), also of London. The three were alike as to size and design and all were built and engined by John Brown & Co. Ltd., Clydebank.

The *Shropshire* was 11,911 tons gross and carried a dead weight of 12,100 tons—large for her time—on a draught of 29 ft 9 in. Her length b.p. was 526·4 ft, breadth mld 61 ft and depth mld to shelter deck 45 ft. The ship had twin screws and quadruple-expansion machinery of 5,500 i.h.p. This received steam at 215 p.s.i. from two D.E. and two S.E. boilers and gave a speed of 14 knots. As a coal burner she had bunker space for 2,700 tons and consumed about 100 tons per day. The hull had three continuous decks and beneath these there were six holds. Of these, four and their 'tween deck spaces were insulated. Early descriptions reveal little about the original accommodation, save that she could carry 120 first-class passengers.

The *Shropshire*, the second of the trio, was launched two months after the *Argyllshire* and ten months before the *Wiltshire*. The actual launch date was 27 April, 1911, and on 28 October she left Liverpool on her maiden voyage to Australia. Service as a group was brief, virtually ending with the war. Of the other two, the *Wiltshire* was wrecked in 1922, while the *Argyllshire* continued trading as such until 1932 when she became the *Clan Urquhart*. Five years later she was broken up.

As to the *Shropshire*, she became a troopship in 1914, but returned to commercial service three years later. Since 1912 her owners, the Federal S.N. Co. Ltd., had been controlled by the New Zealand Shipping Co. Ltd. and, at the end of the war, the latter found itself left with only four passenger ships, one fewer than was needed to maintain a monthly service to New Zealand. In 1922 it was therefore decided that the *Shropshire* should be transferred to the N.Z.S. service, and take the place—and name—of the previous *Rotorua*, which had been torpedoed in 1917. The *Shropshire*, then at Falmouth where, late in 1921, she had caught fire while refitting, was accordingly brought to London. There she spent the rest of 1922 and more while she received a very thorough overhaul, was converted to oil burning and given much improved accommodation for approximately 130 first-class passengers and 270 in the second- and third-classes. In her new guise as the *Rotorua* (*II*) she sailed from London and Southampton late in March 1923 bound for New Zealand by way of the Panama Canal and soon she became a very popular unit of the N.Z.S. passenger fleet. In 1929 the very much larger *Rangitiki* and her two sisters were commissioned, but even so six years elapsed before the *Rotorua*—by then getting elderly—was made into a one- (tourist) class ship, the actual capacity remaining about the same.

The *Rotorua*'s career ended on 11 December, 1940, when she was torpedoed and sunk 110 miles west of St. Kilda. At the time she was bound from Lyttelton, Panama and Halifax (where she joined a convoy) for Avonmouth, carrying a full cargo of meat, dairy produce, etc., but no passengers. She sank in 20 minutes taking with her 19 of her complement, but the remaining 106 were rescued by Naval craft.

As seen, both at the time and in retrospect, the *Rotorua* stood rather as a ship apart, lacking the glamour of many, but immensely impressive to the eye. Over the years her profile was subject to slight variation, mainly in the number of topmasts carried. As for the N.Z.S. houseflags shown, the use of the pennant was later discontinued, a few years before the Company and its fleet was absorbed into the P. & O.

15 s.s. ERINPURA, 1911, Great Britain

The British India Steam Navigation Co.—more familiarly known as the B.I.—was the greatest of all shipping firms to be based East of Suez, and at the time of the *Erinpura*'s construction owned well over 100 steamers. Although some ships and services were operated from Bombay, Calcutta was the real centre, and from there a complex of services covered the Bay of Bengal, to Burma, the Straits and far beyond. Westwards they extended round the coast of India to Bombay, the Persian Gulf and East Africa. Then, too, other ships maintained regular sailings to and from Britain. Of all its services, that between Calcutta and Rangoon was the oldest, having been opened by a forbear of the Company in 1856.

The *Erinpura* of 1911 was one of a class of seven fast passenger and cargo steamers which were built mainly for use on the Calcutta–Rangoon–Straits route, also on that between Madras and Rangoon. Although not the Company's largest, the group nevertheless represented a very important addition to the B.I. fleet. As was then customary, most of the E class came from Clydeside yards. The *Erinpura* was built by Wm. Denny & Bros, of Dumbarton, the *Edavana* and *Elephanta* by Barclay Curle, *Ellenga* and *Ellora* by Alexander Stephen and the remaining pair, *Egra* and *Ekma* by Workman Clark of Belfast. Eleven years later Denny's were to build the eighth and final ship of this series, the *Ethiopia*. Besides incorporating various improvements, she differed machinery-wise in being turbine-driven. Of the original seven, the Barclay Curle pair were slightly shorter than the rest, being only 400 ft long b.p. The dimensions of the others varied only fractionally from each other, but the ships from each yard could be distinguished by slight variations as to detail.

The *Erinpura*'s length b.p. was 411 ft, her breadth being 52·5 ft and depth of hold 24·7 ft. Her gross tonnage, originally 5,128, was later raised to 5,142. Her d.w. on a draught of 23 ft 5 in. was 4,750 tons. She had twin screws driven by two sets of triple-expansion engines with cylinders of 24½, 41 and 69 in., and a stroke of 48 in. In her stoke-hold she had two double-ended and two single-ended boilers, all coal-fired and with a working pressure of 200 p.s.i. The bunker capacity was almost 1,300 tons. The hull had three continuous decks with side openings on the upper deck, while above, on the shade deck, there was a bridge structure 177 ft long.

Company records show that as built she could carry 51 first-class and 39 second-class passengers. On long voyages she was certified to carry up to 659 native deck passengers but on short ones the permitted maximum was 2,359, although this figure was reduced somewhat during the monsoon season.

The *Erinpura* was completed in December 1911 and on trials averaged 16·7 knots; her deadweight was then 2,881 tons. When she arrived at Calcutta she had the distinction of being the first Indian Coastal ship to be fitted with wireless. Commercial service was interrupted by the First World War, during which she was used as a hospital ship.

Her career nearly ended in June 1919 when she was serving as an ambulance carrier. It was during a sandstorm on the 15th, when the ship was out on a voyage from Aden to Port Said, that she stranded on the Mushejera Reef off the Great Hanish Islands. There she remained for over a year. Salvage of the whole ship proved impracticable, but in September 1920, after being cut in two, the stern portion was towed back to Aden. On 16 February, 1921, this half ship left port in tow for Bombay, where she arrived on 5 March. There she was rebuilt with an entirely new forward half, the work being finally completed in 1923.

At the time of her stranding, total loss seemed probable, and it would seem likely that the *Ethiopia* was ordered as a replacement. In fact, the *Erinpura* lasted many more years. In 1941, when she was still maintaining her regular mail services between Madras and Rangoon/Singapore, she sailed from the last named just as its fall became imminent and took with her a load of refugees to Colombo. May 1943 saw her in the Mediterranean, the Commodore ship of a heavily protected convoy of 23, all bound westwards for Malta. Against the convoy came a wave of enemy torpedo-carrying aircraft and, above them, high-level bombers. One of the latter scored a direct hit on the *Erinpura*, causing her to sink in 4 minutes. Loss of life, at 66, was high because most of her personnel had been ordered to seek shelter below decks. As she went down, bow first, her gunners aft were still firing their 12-pdr. at the enemy.

16   s.s. VAUBAN, 1912, Great Britain

In its trading activities, the Lamport & Holt Line—one of Liverpool's oldest—has been primarily associated with the Americas, South America in particular. Except for one series, its ships have been essentially cargo liners and all have borne the names of artists, writers, scientists, etc. As the Company's interests broadened, so names commencing with the letter V became reserved for their larger, passenger-carrying ships.

Of these the first of note were the 8,000-ton *Voltaire* and *Vasari* of 1907 and 1909. From these a more ambitious 15-knot, 12,000-ton design was evolved. But in the year when the first of the resultant ships was built, Lamport & Holt was made into a public company and control passed to the then rapidly expanding Royal Mail Steam Packet Co. and this had considerable effect on the future employment of the three new ships.

The *Vauban* was the second of the series, being preceded by the *Vandyck* and followed by the *Vestris*. The intention was to use them on a fast service between Liverpool, Brazil and the River Plate, carrying three classes of passengers plus a considerable amount of cargo. Workman Clark & Co. Ltd., Belfast, were responsible for all three ships and their machinery. Outwardly there were some small differences in the superstructure, but their hull dimensions were alike. The overall length was 511 ft (495·5 ft b.p.), breadth 60·8 ft and depth of hold 28·7 ft. Twin screws were driven by two sets of quad-ruple-expansion engines which, to keep vibration to the minimum, were balanced on the Yarrow, Schlick & Tweedy system. The boilers, five in number, were double-ended and coal-fired. For cargo there were five holds, with some compartments insulated for the carriage of chilled meat, fruit, etc.

The *Vauban* was of 10,680 tons gross and 7,200 tons d.w. She had accommodation for about 280 first-class passengers and 130 second-, also 200 emigrants, the last named being embarked during calls at Vigo, Leixoes and Lisbon. The new service from Liverpool to Buenos Aires was opened by the *Vandyck* in 1911. The *Vauban* was launched on 20 January, 1912, ran trials in April and took up station soon afterwards. The last of the trio, the *Vestris*, followed in the Autumn of 1912. The venture was destined to be short lived and regularity of service—closely allied with popularity—was made impossible by the action of the R.M.S.P. That company was then commencing a new and accelera-ted service between Southampton and the Plate and for this they chartered the *Vauban*, repainted her in their colours and used her as the *Alcala*. However, by the end of 1913 she had resumed her original name and was back on her designed trade. After this Lamport & Holt were virtually forced out by the R.M.S.P., who intended that the service should be handled by their new D-class ships. The *Vauban* and her two sisters were therefore soon transferred from Liverpool to reinforce an existing Lamport & Holt service between New York and Buenos Aires. There, by their size and luxury, they eclipsed all others. However, the war claimed early toll, for on 18 October, 1914, the *Vandyck* was captured and sunk by the German raider *Karlsruhe*. Soon after the war the *Vauban*, *Vestris* and the older *Vasari* resumed sailings between New York and the Plate but made a triangular voyage. From the Plate they returned to Britain and then made a Cunard charter passage to New York before going South again. By the end of 1923 the service had been re-established on a proper fortnightly basis, but by then new and subsidised competition had become intense. The final blow came in November 1929 when the *Vestris*, then on a South-bound voyage, foundered in heavy weather with the loss of over 100 lives. This disaster, coupled with adverse publicity and de-clining profits, led to the abandonment of this once proud passenger service. The V-ships returned to Britain and in January 1932, after a long period of idleness, the *Vauban* was sold for scrap, realising a mere £8,500. Even so, at the time of writing in 1973 the Lamport & Holt Line Ltd. still owns a fleet of quite considerable size, while those of its former rivals on both trades are but memories.

17 s.s. BRITISH MARSHAL, 1912, Great Britain

The great fleet of oil tankers now owned by the B.P. Petroleum Co. Ltd. had its beginnings in the First World War. The formation of what was then known as the

Anglo-Persian Oil Co. Ltd. was followed in 1915 by that of a subsidiary, the British Tanker Co. Ltd., whose functions were to own and manage the tanker fleet about to be established. During the initial period of the war it became necessary to make do with second-hand tonnage; some years elapsed before the Company could build ships to its own specifications.

The *British Marshal* has her place in tanker history as being one of the best of these early purchases made by the British Tanker Co. Although in no way outstanding in terms of design she was nevertheless very representative of the good quality, popular size tanker of her time. She came from a well-known firm and although she was soon eclipsed by larger and more sophisticated ships, she served the B.T.C. for over a decade, by which time their fleet—owned and managed—had reached the 100 mark.

The ship was one of a pair bought in 1918 from the Prince Line Ltd., of Newcastle. Previously the *Russian Prince*, she had been delivered by the Tyne Iron Shipbuilding Co. Ltd. in September 1912. A year later that shipyard had completed the other ship bought, the *Roumanian Prince*—which duly became the *British Major*. The fact that the Prince Line, well known for its great fleet of dry cargo ships, also owned tankers then is something often overlooked. Their first tanker, also a *Russian Prince*, but of 2,716 tons gross, was built in 1888. Her namesake of 1912 was their sixth and after the *Roumanian Prince* of 1913 they built no more until a pair in 1960–61.

The *British Marshal* was a ship of 4,158 tons gross and carried a deadweight of 6,031 tons on a draught of 23 ft 3 in. Her main dimensions were length b.p. 357·2 ft, breadth 48·2 ft and depth 28·2 ft. The propelling machinery comprised a set of triple-expansion engines with cylinders of 25, 42 and 68 in. diameter and 48 in. stroke. The two S.E. boilers had a working pressure of 180 p.s.i. and had been oil-fired from the very start— this being somewhat rare for a ship of 1912. The speed was about 10½ knots. Longitudinal framing was used in the hull and the cargo space was subdivided by a single fore-and-aft (centreline) bulkhead and a series of transverse ones. Along the sides of the cargo tanks there were the then customary 'summer' tanks, which were about one deck deep and about 10 ft or so wide. Inboard of these the main tanks were full height. Externally, the ship was of the usual three-island type, with a raised forecastle, bridge deck and poop, these measuring 39, 25 and 85 ft respectively. Only two derricks were fitted, one on each mast and these were worked by steam winches.

Just prior to her purchase by the B.T.C. the ship had only narrowly escaped destruction, for on 8 July, 1917, when off the S.W. coast of Ireland, she had been attacked by a U-Boat and incurred quite considerable damage. Otherwise her career under the Red Ensign appears to have been without great incident. In the early 'twenties the British Tanker fleet started to expand rapidly. Soon various of the older purchased ships, some of them dating back to the previous century, were disposed of. As to those which replaced them, the size soon adopted as standard was a deadweight tonnage of 10,000 on dimensions 440 ft × 57 ft. However, the *British Marshal* was kept until late in 1929, when she was sold to become the Genoese-registered *Tritone*. Under the ownership of the Societa Italiana Transporti Petroliferi she continued trading until 1933. In March that year she grounded in the Mediterranean, but was refloated and towed to La Spezia, where she arrived on 12 May. Examination showed that she was not worth repairing, so she was accordingly sold for scrap. By chance, her sister *British Major* met her end about the same time. Previously sold to another Italian concern, who renamed her *Riva Sicula*, she reached the safety of Dakar on 20 April, 1933, after being ashore, only to sink in port on 24 May.

The *British Marshal* is shown bearing the British Tanker Co.'s original funnel marking. The central white disc had the Company's initials painted black, the middle letter being taller than the others and curved at the top. The next of the several styles used had three plain bands, white–red–white, between the red base and the black top.

18 s.s. SAN JERONIMO, 1914, Great Britain

Probably the most remarkable shipping development of recent years has been the tremendous growth in the size of tankers. In pre-1914 years the construction of only one tanker as large as the *San Jeronimo* would have made news, but she was but one of a series of ten, each ranking among the world's largest. This combination of individual size and numbers was outward evidence of a remarkable British success in a trade which was then virtually dominated by America.

The story started in 1901 when a civil engineer of international repute, Weetman Pearson, later Lord Cowdray and one of the figureheads in the Mexican oil industry, bought his first land there. The company which he formed—Mexican Eagle (Cia. Mexicana de Petroleo 'El Aguila' Soc. Anon.)—soon extended its activities to include refining and then to the distribution by ship of its products around the Gulf of Mexico. The growth of production was so rapid that a large, ocean-going fleet soon became a vital necessity and, to this end, Lord Cowdray formed the Eagle Oil Transport Co. In 1912 this initiated the largest tanker-building programme the world had yet seen. It comprised nine ships, each of 9,000 tons d.w. and ten like the *San Jeronimo*, of 15,000 to 16,000 tons d.w., their combined tonnage representing 10 per cent of the world's tanker fleet.

Of the larger ones, four were launched in 1913, five in 1914 and the remaining one in 1915. All conformed to the first company's practice of using Mexican Saint names. Two of them, the *San Jeronimo* and *San Nazario*, were built by Wm. Doxford & Sons, Ltd. of Sunderland, three each by Swan, Hunter & Wigham Richardson and Armstrong Whitworth and two by Palmers, of Hebburn. The *San Jeronimo*, which was typical of the series, had a d.w. tonnage of 15,578, the gross measurement being 12,028. Her length o.a. was 540 ft (525 ft b.p.), breadth 66·5 ft and depth mld 42 ft. Her load draught was 28 ft, this later being increased to 29 ft 6 in.

She had a single screw and a set of quadruple-expansion engines of about 4,100 i.h.p. Of considerable size, its cylinders were of 28½, 41, 58 and 84 in. diameter, the stroke being 54 in. Steam at 220 p.s.i. was provided by four S.E. boilers. The speed loaded was about 10–11 knots. The use of oil fuel at sea was then still somewhat novel, but these boilers were fitted to burn oil or coal. Thus they could use cheap Mexican oil for the Eastward loaded voyage and then, in Britain, load coal sufficient for the return ballast trip. But as time went on, only oil was used. The navigational equipment and accommodation was of an unusually high standard. Special novelties were wireless, the library and the freezer store, the last named banishing for ever the need for the traditional hard tack and salted meat.

Instead of the single deck now customary in tankers, the *San Jeronimo* and her sisters had three, these reading downwards, being the shelter, upper and main. The upper of the two spaces thus provided a long crews' recreation area, one which could be used irrespective of weather. Seen in cross-section, the main cargo tanks, which reached to main deck level, were divided by a single longitudinal bulkhead. Above that level, the space between the main and upper decks was divided equally, to form long fore-and-aft compartments. Of these, the outboard ones served as extra permanent cargo tanks, the inner ones as oil expansion tanks. Above all this, the upper deck area was broken by a series of narrow expansion tanks which reached from the many side tanks upwards to the shelter (top) deck. Close to the centreline were the hatches from the main tanks. Small and grouped in fours, they came just under the top (shelter deck) hatches, which were as large as those of any dry-cargo ship.

As regards the fore and aft layout of this area, there were 12 pairs of main tanks, which were divided into three groups by the two pump rooms. At each side of the ship there were four long upper cargo tanks and these, like all the rest, had heating coils. For the discharge of cargo there were four Duplex pumps which could together handle 1,200 tons per hour. Right forward, and separated from the oil tanks by a cofferdam, there was a large hold for dry cargo. This was served by derricks on the foremast. As was then customary, the officers were housed in the bridge, the engineers and crew having their cabins aft, on the upper deck and either side of the engine casing.

The *San Jeronimo* was launched at Sunderland on 13 December, 1913, and delivered on 10 February, 1914, after attaining 11·4 knots on trials. Initially the experts criticised the use of 15,000-ton ships as being uneconomical, but in practice it was found that on an average voyage they carried oil 10 per cent more cheaply than the 9,000-tonners. The ship's great size, and that of her sisters, was especially valued by the Royal Navy, by whom they were used, in a static role, as fleet oilers. During the First World War the first to be requisitioned for this duty were the *San Jeronimo*, which was stationed at Portland, and the *San Lorenzo*. Later they were joined by two more of this class.

War over, the *San Jeronimo* resumed commercial service, remaining in the Eagle fleet until May 1928. She was then sold to the Southern Whaling & Sealing Co. Ltd., of Liverpool and reconstructed to start a new career as the whale factory ship *Southern Empress* (plate 40).

19 s.s. AQUITANIA, 1914, Great Britain

The *Aquitania* was designed for the North Atlantic mail and passenger service and to operate with the *Lusitania* and *Mauretania* of 1907. Their high speed earned them an annual subsidy; in the planning which lay behind the *Aquitania* the aim was to create a ship which would earn as much without a subsidy as the others did with one. The service speed aimed at was 23–23½ knots, which was sufficient to sail from either terminal at three-weekly intervals. In the event, she proved able, in later years, to maintain a fortnightly schedule. In terms of speed she was thus superior to the White Star *Olympic* and broadly comparable to the Hamburg-American Line's *Imperator*. The White Star *Olympic* class ships were the last of the giant liners to have triple screws and combination machinery while the *Aquitania* was the last British-built one to have direct-drive turbines. She was also the last four-funnelled liner to enter the North Atlantic trade; with her withdrawal in 1949 four funnels disappeared from the North Atlantic scene.

Seen in relation to her length, and the lengths of the *Olympic* and *Imperator*, her gross tonnage—45,647—was somewhat low. Her displacement was approximately 53,000 tons and load draught 36 ft 2 in. Her hull weighed approximately 29,150 tons and her machinery 9,000 tons. The overall length was 901 ft (865 ft b.p.), breadth mld 97 ft, and depth mld 64 ft 6 in. The *Aquitania* had quadruple screws and these were driven by Parsons direct-drive turbines, there being one H.P., one intermediate and two L.P. units, also an astern turbine on each shaft. The L.P. ahead turbines actuated the two inner shafts, while the H.P. and intermediate-pressure ahead turbines operated the outer ones. The designed i.h.p. was 60,000. Steam at 195 p.s.i. was provided by 21 double-ended (Scotch) boilers. Judged by present standards the length of hull occupied by the boiler rooms and bunker space was tremendous. It extended from a point midway between the foremast and the bridge to the after side of the fourth funnel. Yet the turbines compartment, the next astern, ended before the after edge of the main superstructure. The top of the boiler rooms approximated to the waterline. Above, there were five decks in the hull and three in the superstructure. Forward, there were two holds, with C to H decks above. Other special features were a large internal swimming pool, Frahm anti-rolling tanks and a rudder/stern shape which resembled those of the *Lusitania* and *Mauretania* but was quite different from that of the *Olympic*. Unlike hers, the rudder was of balanced type and completely submerged.

As built, the *Aquitania* was fitted to carry 618 first-, 614 second- and 1,998 third-class passengers. The crew numbered about 970. Officers' accommodation excepted, the whole of the main superstructure was devoted to the first-class. Down one deck, at a point beneath the two forward funnels, there was also the first-class entrance foyer. Just forward of this, there was the lowest block of first-class cabins and, aft of it, the great first-class dining saloon. The second-class occupied the after superstructure. Most of the third-class was also aft, but at a lower level, with some forward.

The *Aquitania* was built and engined by John Brown & Co. Ltd. and launched at Clydebank on 21 April, 1913. At the end of May 1914 she left Liverpool on her maiden voyage to New York and made three round trips before the declaration of war. On 8 August, armed with some 6 in. guns, she left the Mersey on her first patrol as an auxiliary cruiser. Later she was more sensibly used as a troopship and hospital ship and served in the Dardanelles campaign. In 1919 she made some commercial voyages to the States, but in November she commenced a 7-month refit on the Tyne. During this she was converted to oil-burning and given a bunker capacity of 7,000 tons, sufficient for a round voyage and more.

She then commenced the main period of her North Atlantic career, operating between Southampton, Cherbourg and New York with the *Mauretania* and *Berengaria*. During the Second World War she again became a troopship. Mainly used to carry U.S. servicemen across the Atlantic, she also travelled as far afield as Australia and Pearl Harbour. In 1948 she was returned to the Cunard and, after making 25 voyages to Halifax with settlers, she was sold to the British Iron and Steel Corporation and in 1950 was scrapped at Faslane on the Firth of Clyde.

20 (right)   s.s. MACCLESFIELD, 1914, Great Britain

For their service between Grimsby and Rotterdam the Great Central Railway had built—by Swan, Hunter & Wigham Richardson, Ltd.—two 13-knot cargo ships, each with accommodation for 12 passengers. The first of these sisterships was the *Chesterfield* of 1913 and the other the *Macclesfield* which, in the event, proved to be the final ship built for the G.C.R.

The *Macclesfield* had a gross tonnage of 1,018 (finally 1,049) and a cargo capacity of 1,054 tons. Her main dimensions were length b.p. 250 ft, breadth mld 34 ft and depth mld 16 ft, while the load draught was 14 ft 11 in. She appeared to be of well-deck type, but in fact had three islands, a 31 ft forecastle, a 92 ft bridge deck and a 30 ft poop, the existence of the after well being hidden by full-height bulwarks. She had one continuous deck and 'tween deck spaces in each of her three holds. Besides general cargo, she was designed to carry horses and considerable quantities of vegetables and dairy produce. For propulsion she had a single screw and triple-expansion machinery of 1,600 i.h.p., its cylinders being of 21½, 35 and 58 in. diameter and 39 in. stroke. Her two S.E. boilers had a working pressure of 180 p.s.i. and for them she had bunker space for 160 tons of coal.

She was launched at Walker-on-Tyne on 22 May, 1914, and delivered the following month. In common with all Great Central ships, she then had a white, black-topped funnel. Commercial service was soon disrupted by the First World War, in the course of which—on 18 May, 1918—the *Chesterfield* was torpedoed near Malta. The *Macclesfield* subsequently returned to her old route, but on New Year's day 1923 she and all other railway-owned ships came under new ownership, she and other G.C.R. ships becoming part of the London & North Eastern Rly. For some years this continued to be one of several fleets operating independently out of Grimsby, Goole and Hull to the Continent, but in 1935 Associated Humber Lines was formed to provide unified management for the L.N.E.R. (ex-G.C.R.) Grimsby ships, and the L.M.S. Goole-based fleet, together with those of the Wilson's & N.E. Rly. Shipping Co. and Hull & Netherlands Line. All these vessels were given a common funnel mark, black initials AHL on a red band set between a black top and buff base.

The new arrangement made it possible to switch ships—the *Macclesfield* included—from one route to another. In her new livery the ship operated at different times out of both Grimsby and Hull and, after the Second World War, from the Humber ports on the services to Antwerp, Rotterdam and, more particularly, Hamburg. In 1958 the completion of new tonnage made the *Macclesfield* redundant, and at the close of the year she was sold to Dutch breakers.

In her general shaping, with three hatches and sharply raked funnel and masts, she was representative of many pre-1914, railway-owned ships operating on North Sea routes. The next generation, built in the 'twenties, lacked their grace of line, had no rake and were sometimes, like the *Melrose Abbey*, given an extra hatch and cruiser stern. In turn, this style gave way to motorships, generally with machinery aft.

20 (left)   s.s. MELROSE ABBEY, 1929, Great Britain

The introduction of this ship brought a somewhat overdue degree of rejuvenation to the Hull & Netherlands S.S. Co.'s fleet, since this had previously comprised an elderly pair of steamships, the 1,188-ton *Jervaulx Abbey* and *Whitby Abbey*, both of which dated back to 1908. Like them, she was designed for regular North Sea service, carrying passengers and cargo, much of the latter consisting of dairy produce, vegetables and so on.

The new vessel and her machinery were built locally at Hull, by the Earle's Shipbuilding & Engineering Co. Ltd. Considerably larger than her forbears, the *Melrose Abbey* had a gross tonnage of 1,908 (later raised to 1,941) and a cargo capacity of 1,091 tons. Her length b.p. was 281·3 ft, breadth mld 38 ft, depth mld 18 ft 3 in. and load draught 15 ft 3 in. She had single-screw, triple-expansion machinery with cylinders of 21½, 37 and 64 in. diameter and 42 in. stroke. The three coal-fired boilers worked under forced draught and supplied steam at 221 p.s.i. The service speed was 14 knots. Although at first glance her hull appeared to be flush-decked, there were in fact, two well decks, their existence being hidden by deck-high bulwarks. At the after end of the bridge 'tween decks there were stalls for some 20 horses. Amidships, besides the public rooms and two de-luxe cabins, she had 2- and 3-berth cabins for 84 first-class passengers. Aft, in the poop 'tween deck, there was further accommodation for 38 steerage.

The *Melrose Abbey* was launched on 28 February, 1929, and entered service late in April. Initially, like the others, she had a plain buff funnel with black top. In 1935 this was changed, following the creation of a new company, Associated Humber Lines, whose function was to provide unified management for the Hull & Netherlands and several other fleets which operated out of Goole, Hull and Grimsby. The funnels of all the ships involved were then repainted as shown, with buff base, black top and, in between, a red band bearing the black-painted initials AHL.

At the outset the *Melrose Abbey* had operated with the *Jervaulx Abbey*, but after the latter's sale and that of her sister, she appears to have mostly alternated with the *Dewsbury*, an ex-L.N.E.R. ship built in 1908. After proving her worth as a wartime Convoy Rescue Ship, the *Melrose Abbey* was refitted and returned to service with somewhat modified passenger accommodation. After further changes had been made this provided for 92 first-class and 24 second-class. Early in 1958 she became the *Melrose Abbey II*, her old name being allocated to one of two new passenger and cargo ships then under construction. She continued trading to Rotterdam until January 1959, but a few months later she was sold to the Typaldos Lines, of Piraeus. There she was converted into the 2,069-ton *Kriti*. With cabins built into her former holds, and a much enlarged and altered superstructure, she was able to accommodate some 180 first-class and 130 tourist, in addition to dormitory-class passengers. In this form she was used on a variety of routes in and around the Aegean. Typaldos activities virtually ended as a result of the *Heraklion* disaster in December 1966 and the *Kriti*, like the rest of the fleet, was laid up at Piraeus, and there, at the time of writing, she still remains.

21 s.s. BENRINNES, 1914, Great Britain

In the development of the ocean-going cargo liner, the *Benrinnes* can claim a special distinction, since she was in all probability the last of her type to be built with a clipper stem. By 1914, when she was built for Ben Line Steamers Ltd. (William Thomson & Co.), Edinburgh, this feature, despite its elegance, had become an anachronism in which only a famous and long established company could afford to indulge. Lesser companies aimed instead at stressing modernity. Among passenger ships there were a few later isolated examples, such as the *Stella Polaris* of 1927 and the small Scottish steamer *St. Sunniva* of 1931. Otherwise the true clipper stem has become a feature associated with large yachts and sail training ships.

Since the latter part of the nineteenth century, the steamships built for the Ben Line's Far Eastern trade had conformed to a three-island type profile which was coupled with a rare elegance of line. Most, but not all, of these early ships had clipper stems, but up to 1930 all built for the Company (as distinct from those bought) conformed to this layout. In her design the *Benrinnes* very closely resembled two earlier ships which, like her, had been built by Bartram & Sons, Sunderland. These near-sisters of hers were the *Benlomond* of 1911 and the *Benmohr* which was completed in 1912.

The *Benrinnes* had a registered length of 405 ft, her breadth being 51·5 ft and depth of hold 26 ft 9 in. The gross tonnage was 4,798 and deadweight capacity 7,500 tons, this on a load draught of 23 ft 10 in. She had two continuous decks, four holds and five hatches, the last named being served by 11 steam winches and 12 derricks. Her machinery, supplied by the North Eastern Marine Engineering Co. Ltd., was conventional for its time and comprised a set of triple-expansion engines of 2,150 i.h.p. with cylinders of 25, 43 and 72 in. diameter and 48 in. stroke. Steam at 190 p.s.i. was supplied by three S.E. boilers. Early records are scanty, but by 1928 she was quoted as burning 36 tons of coal per day, this for a speed of 12 knots.

The *Benrinnes* was delivered in July 1914, only a month before the outbreak of war. Almost at the end of this, on 21 October, 1918, she was in the Atlantic when she twice missed being hit by torpedoes fired at her by a U-boat. The *Benmohr* had been less lucky, for early on, in October 1914, she had been sunk by the German raider *Emden* when off the Malabar Coast. The other of this class, the *Benlomond*, survived the war and continued trading until 1932 when she was broken up in Hong Kong. The *Benrinnes*, however, lasted longer and had served the Company for a quarter of a century by the time she was sold in 1937.

As the *Thorpeness*, owned by the Westcliff Shipping Co. Ltd., of London, the tenor of her changed, for she and three other new purchases in that fleet were used as blockade runners, carrying supplies to the government forces in Spain, which was then in a state of Civil War. If profitable, this work was also dangerous, for in January 1938 the *Thorpeness* was anchored off Tarragona when she and the city were attacked by Franco's Nationalist planes. As a result, seven of her crew were killed and seven injured. Five months later, on 22 June, 1938, the ship was again lying at anchor, but off Valencia, when she was bombed and sunk by Franco seaplanes. Hit amidships below the waterline, she sank in ten minutes, but this time all her crew escaped. The *Benrinnes* of 1912 was the first of her name, but since then there have been three others. The fourth *Benrinnes*, which was the 100th ship to join the Ben Line fleet, is of 8,088 tons gross and is still in service in 1972.

22   s.s. SHANTUNG, 1915, Great Britain

On 1 January, 1867, John Swire and Sons, who had been established as merchants at Liverpool since 1812, opened their first Branch in China—at Shanghai—under the trade name of Butterfield & Swire. This business later spread to Hong Kong and all the major ports in China and Japan. In 1872 the China Navigation Co. Ltd. was formed under the management of John Swire & Sons, and since that date has operated services on the Yangtsze as far as Chungking and Suifu, along the China Coast from Canton to Manchuria and overseas to Java, Japan, the Philippines, Australia and New Zealand.

For long the China Navigation Co.'s ships were mainly employed on the Yangtsze, but meanwhile a series of other coastal and longer services were being developed. The *Shantung* was one of a class of six steamers built for the Company during and just after the First World War. The leadship in the series was the *Sinkiang* and, like so many in the fleet, she came from Scotts' of Greenock. However, the *Shantung* and the four which followed were built by a member of the Swire Group, the Taikoo Dockyard & Engineering Co. Ltd., of Hong Kong. Of these the *Sunning* was completed in 1916, the *Suiyang* a year later and the *Szechuen* and *Soochow* both in 1920.

The gross tonnage of the *Shantung* was 2,549 and her deadweight 2,970 tons. Her length b.p. was 310·2 ft, breadth 41·1 ft, depth of hold 22·1 ft and load draught approximately 18 ft. She had steam triple-expansion machinery of 1,400 i.h.p., with cylinders of 22, 35 and 56 in. diameter amd 39 in. stroke. She had coal-fired boilers and a service speed of 11·5 knots, but on trials attained 12·48 knots. Besides a cargo capacity of 164,728 cu. ft bale, she had accommodation for six first-class passengers, 32 second-class, 64 third and 100 deck.

From the time of their construction right up to the Second World War the *Shantung* and her sisters formed the backbone of the China Navigation Co.'s coastal services South of Shanghai, sailing from that port every Tuesday and Friday for Swatow, Hong Kong and Canton. Piracy was then much to the fore and despite the very elaborate precautions carried out on each ship and voyage, pirates over the years contrived to loot a number of the Company's vessels. The most outstanding instance was that of the *Sunning* in 1926, for having been surprised and overcome by pirates, the first and second officers reversed the situation—likewise by surprise—and regained the vessel. In the affray both parties suffered casualties and the *Sunning* herself incurred damage by fire.

Of the six the *Sunning* was declared a Constructive Total Loss after a Hong Kong typhoon in 1936. The *Soochow* was scuttled at Hong Kong in December 1941. In 1942 the *Sinkiang* and *Szechuen* both became war losses, while in 1946 the *Suiyang* was mined in the Bangkok River. So the *Shantung* outlived the rest, continuing in service until 1948 when she was sold for scrap.

23 s.s. BELGIC, 1917, Great Britain

Because of the desperate need for tonnage during the First World War several large passenger ships then under construction were hurriedly completed in austerity fashion. Some were sent to sea devoid of their intended furnishings, but in certain cases they were not even given their planned superstructure. Among the latter were the 15,120-ton *Orca* of the Pacific Steam Navigation Co., the Dominion Line's *Regina* and the *Minnekahda* of the Atlantic Transport Co. The largest of all was the *Belgic* which in her austerity state had a gross tonnage of 24,547, nearly 3,000 tons less than that originally intended.

She had been ordered by the International Navigation Co. Ltd. for the Red Star Line's service between Antwerp and New York. Her chosen name, *Belgenland*, was appropriate since, had the original plans gone through, she would have been the largest liner ever to fly the Belgian ensign. Her launch took place at Belfast on the last day of 1914. The war was then some four months old and the ship was laid aside for a while, top priority being given to the yard's programme of Naval construction. However, in June 1917 the ship was delivered as the *Belgic*, a cargo carrier pure and simple. Her profile was then as shown; bridge excepted, she was minus her intended superstructure. She had two abbreviated funnels not three, as planned, but instead an extra, third, mast to give some effect of balance. Later, as the great Eastward flow of American troops developed it was decided to fit her out as a troop transport. This work was done in the States, the accommodation installed being enough for three battalions.

Her main dimensions were length overall 696·5 ft (670·4 ft b.p.) breadth mld 78 ft and depth mld 49 ft. The load draught was 36 ft 3 in. Her d.w. capacity in that state was 22,025 tons and her gross tonnage 24,547. Wartime figures are scanty, but she was credited with having accommodation for 1,796 'third-class passengers'. She was a triple-screw ship and her machinery was of combination type, with two 4-cylinder triple-expansion engines (each with cylinders of 35½, 56 and (two) 64 in. diameter and 60 in. stroke). These developed 12,000 i.h.p. and were connected to the wing shafts. The centre shaft was driven by a L.P. turbine which added a further 6,500 s.h.p. Steam at 215 p.s.i. was supplied by 10 double-ended boilers and in her days of wartime grey paint the fact that she was a coal-burner was made obvious by the long row of dirt-streaked coaling ports which stretched along her topsides. Her service speed was about 17 knots.

Although registered in the name of the International Nav. Co., the *Belgic* was managed by the White Star Line. Initially she operated between Liverpool and New York but after the war she made some passages from Hamburg. In April 1921 she was laid up at Liverpool to await her turn for overhaul. In March 1922 she was sent to Belfast, where her builders, Harland & Wolff, completed her according to the original specifications. She emerged as the British-flag, 27,132-ton *Belgenland*, looking completely different with two extra promenade decks, three taller funnels and two, not three, masts. In her new glory she had accommodation for some 2,700 passengers in three classes, first, second and third. But by April 1923 when she made her first voyage on her intended Red Star Line service between Antwerp and New York, she was nearly ten years old. The flow of emigrants had fallen away, as had the amount of cargo available, so from an early date she was used in a dual capacity, working part-time on the Atlantic and also as a long-distance cruise ship, a role in which she proved very popular.

She made her last Antwerp–New York crossing in January 1932. Further cruises which alternated with periods of idleness were followed by transfer to the American flag. During a refit at Tilbury she was renamed *Columbia* and early in 1935 she arrived at New York, her new home port. By now she was owned by an associated firm, the Atlantic Transport Co. of West Virginia. After a short spell on the Panama Pacific Line service and some further cruises she was laid up. Her final voyage ended on 4 May, 1936, with her arrival at Bo'ness on the Firth of Forth, where she was beached at P. & W. MacLellan's breaking-up berth.

24 (left) Concrete schooner MOLLIETTE, 1919, Great Britain

Although a few small ferro-concrete ships had been built many years prior to 1914, the large-scale construction of sea-going concrete ships in Britain was basically the result of wartime shortages. Not only were the established shipyards working to capacity, but steel and also skilled labour were in short supply. Concrete ships could be built in new and open sites largely by unskilled labour, factors which more than offset the greater weight of hull. In the United Kingdom the Admiralty-sponsored building programme was centred on the large-scale construction of 1,000-ton d.w. sea-going barges and a lesser number of powerful tugs. However, by the time the Armistice was signed, only one barge had been completed. Meanwhile, outside the official programme, there was a number of interesting 'one-off' concrete vessels, one of the oddest being the little auxiliary schooner *Molliette*. She was built at Faversham, Kent, by James Pollock & Sons, Ltd., a firm long known as specialists in the construction of small craft.

The *Molliette*, which had the distinction of being Britain's first sea-going concrete ship, was launched broadside (a necessity at Faversham) in 1918 and was completed either in January or February 1919. Her overall length was 131 ft (125·6 ft b.p.), breadth mld 25 ft and depth mld 9 ft 9 in. She had a d.w. capacity of 320 tons and a draught of 9 ft 9 in. Her gross tonnage was 293, net tonnage 160. Her hull had a single deck and was completely devoid of curves. Forward it was capped by a 23-ft long forecastle, while aft the level was raised slightly to end in a 30-ft long quarter deck. Between these two she had one long hold served by two hatches. For cargo handling there was one winch near the entrance to the forecastle. In the latter, slightly lower than the deck outside, the crew and 2nd engineer had their quarters, the officers being accommodated aft. For propulsion, other than by sail, the *Molliette* was given a single-cylinder Bolinder, crude-oil engine of 120 b.h.p. and in calm weather this gave a speed of about 7 knots.

According to contemporary descriptions she was built on the monolithic system, the re-inforcing consisting of round rods; no sections of steel were used. Classed by Lloyds as experimental and subject to annual survey, her sphere of operations was limited to English Channel and coasting service between the Thames and Milford Haven. This included the Channel Islands, where her visits are still recalled. Late in 1919 she had two adventures, one when she grounded near Calais. However, by running her engine full astern she was eventually able to get off. Soon afterwards she stranded on the Goodwins, but fortunately on a rising tide. Some time later she inflicted some damage to herself by hitting London's Tower Bridge.

Initially the *Molliette* was managed by Straughan & Green, London, on behalf of her owner, Mr. B. Oppenheimer. However, her appearance in Lloyd's Register under their names and as an auxiliary was brief. Her engine was apparently removed after about a couple of years, and the *Molliette* was thereafter shown as a sailing ship. She and a conventional steam coaster were owned by Mr. R. A. Gray, of London and Steeple, Essex. In all, she was officially listed for about ten years. Quite probably she was withdrawn before then, but as a hulk she may well have lasted many years longer.

24 (right)   concrete tug CRETECABLE, 1919, Great Britain

Of all the sea-going concrete ships to be built in Britain during or just after the First World War, the most important comprised a group of 12 powerful, ocean-going tugs for the Admiralty. Products of four new and specially established shipyards, all 12 were launched in 1919, their completions being more or less evenly divided between that year and 1920. Parallel with their construction was that of a large number of non-propelled lighters, each of 1,000 tons d.w. It has been said that the original concept was the creation of a fleet able to bring urgently needed supplies of iron ore from Spain to Britain. However, with the signing of the Armistice, any such need passed and the contracts for most—those not already laid down—were cancelled. Even so, about 50 lighters were built, most of them being launched in 1919.

All these vessels, tugs and lighters alike, had names commencing with *Crete*. Of the former the *Cretecable* was one of three built at Southwick-on-Wear, near Sunderland, by the Wear Concrete Building Co. Ltd., the others being the *Cretehawser* and *Creterope*. A vessel of 262 tons gross, she was launched in July 1919 and ran trials four months later, these proving very successful despite bad weather. Her main dimensions were length b.p. 125 ft, breadth 27 ft 6 in. and depth 14 ft 9 in., the draught being 13 ft 4 in. A triple-expansion engine of 750 i.h.p. and two boilers using forced draught gave a speed of 10 knots. Her coal bunker capacity was 80 tons and her daily consumption 10 tons. Like many trawlers she had a short turtle-back style forecastle. Amidships, just forward of the funnel, was the galley and by it the entrance to the officers' quarters. These comprised cabins for the Captain, Chief Engineer and four petty officers, a dining saloon and a pantry. The crew, which numbered 12, was berthed aft.

The *Cretecable*'s career was brief, for while some of the dozen tugs lasted until the mid-'thirties, she was wrecked in October 1920 off the north-east coast. As to the subsequent operation of these tugs and lighters, it is worth recalling the initiative shown by the London firm of Stelp & Leighton Ltd. Appreciating their commercial potentials, the Company formed the Crete Shipping Co. Ltd. and bought ten of the tugs, the *Creteblock, -boom, -gaff, -hawser, -mast, -stem* etc., and 39 of the lighters. The result was the largest commercially-owned fleet of concrete ships in the world and this was mainly used for the carriage of coal from Newcastle to the Continent. Laden barges were discharged at their destination, while the tug, instead of waiting, returned home towing two or more empty barges. This proved very profitable until the port authorities decided to levy port dues on each separate unit. This meant that a tug and two barges paid the equivalent in dues of three ships. A thriving trade was thus made uneconomic, so the barges were sold and the tugs laid up. As a next step, Stelp & Leighton ordered a series of small freighters from Swan Hunters', each of which was given the engine and boilers taken from one of the concrete tugs. These vessels, of some 1,750 tons d.w. apiece, were delivered in 1923–25 and gave good service, notably one (sold to Australia in 1934) which was only scrapped in 1968.

25   s.s. YORKSHIRE, 1920, Great Britain

One of the best known and most obvious examples of Company tradition, as applied to externals, was the Bibby Line's adherance to a four-masted profile. With the exception of two cargo ships (built 1920–21) this held good for every Bibby -*shire* liner built between 1889 and 1935. Even though the *Yorkshire* adhered to this style, she was the first, and only, Bibby liner to have a completely flush weather deck, this adding materially to her good looks. She was the Company's first turbine ship and also their last for many years, the series which followed being diesel-driven. The latter came from the Clyde, whereas the *Yorkshire* and all the Bibby liners before her had been built at Belfast by Harland & Wolff, Ltd. Another thing distinguished the *Yorkshire* from those that preceded and followed her: in both world wars Bibby ships played an important part as hospital ships, troop transports and armed merchant cruisers, etc. The *Yorkshire*, ordered just after one war, had a career which spanned the years of peace. But her service under war conditions was minimal, for the Second World War was only about six weeks old when she was sunk.

The *Yorkshire*, of 10,184 tons gross, was the first in the Company's fleet to exceed the 10,000-ton mark. She had a d.w. tonnage of 8,978 and a service speed of 15 knots. Her main dimensions were length overall 504 ft (482 ft b.p.), breadth mld 58 ft and depth mld 43 ft 7 in., the load draught being 32 ft. Her twin screws were driven by two sets of D.R.-geared turbines, each of which comprised a high-pressure and low-pressure unit. The s.h.p. was 5,500. Steam was provided by two double-ended and two single-ended boilers which were oil-fired and had a working pressure of 215 p.s.i. The ship had three continuous decks, with an extra one in the forward hold. Each of her six hatches was served by two derricks. Conforming to Bibby fashion, the *Yorkshire* carried first-class passengers only; 305 in number, their cabins were all arranged on the well-known Bibby tandem system, each having its own porthole. The full-width dining saloon, oak-furnished and with seats for 260, was on the upper deck, just forward of amidships. The Adam-style drawing room, with large sliding windows, was at the forward end of the boat deck. Just aft, and separated from it by a glass screen, was the lounge, domed and in Jacobean style. The smoke room and veranda were also on this deck, but further aft.

The *Yorkshire* was launched on 29 May, 1919, and ran trials on 2 September, 1920. Thereafter she was employed on the Company's regular service from Liverpool to Gibraltar, Marseilles, Port Said, Port Sudan, Colombo and Rangoon. The homeward voyages ended at London for most, at least, of her career it was customary for Bibby ships to pick up the Channel pilot, as shown, in Torbay. Britain's second passenger ship to be sunk in the Second World War, she was in convoy, when, on 17 October, 1939, she was torpedoed in position 44·52 N, 14·31 W (approximately 250 miles off Cape Finisterre). Of her complement 58 were lost, among them 33 passengers, but the rest, numbering 220 were rescued by the American freighter *Independence Hall* and duly landed at Bordeaux.

26   s.s. HUNTSMAN, 1921, Great Britain

For the larger cargo ship, extra size meant more holds and hatches, likewise more derricks to work them. Over a period of many years derricks had usually been mounted on masts, the alternative use of king-posts being for some reason generally frowned on. Among British cargo liners the *Huntsman* marked the end of an era, for she was the last of her type to be given the classic four-masted rig. Among passenger ships this style lasted longer, the Bibby Line, also of Liverpool, taking delivery of its last four-master, the *Derbyshire*, as late as 1935.

The origins of the Harrison Line go back to 1826 when George Brown set up business at Liverpool, as a ship broker. Thomas Harrison was taken into partnership in 1839, and his brother James in 1848; the present title Thos. & Jas. Harrison was adopted in 1853. By that time the firm had a fleet of quite considerable size, and in 1884 titular ownership of this was transferred to the specially formed Charente Steam-Ship Co. Ltd., Harrisons' thereafter acting as managers. Incidentally, it was their earlier interest in the Charente trade which gave the new company its name.

At the time of the *Huntsman*'s construction, the Harrison Line (as it was generally known) maintained services from the U.K. to U.S. Gulf ports, the West Indies, the east and west coasts of the U.S.A., South America, South and East Africa and India. Apart from a very few which could burn either oil or coal, its ships were coal-fired and relied on natural draught—hence their tall funnels. Good quality coal was readily obtainable at their home port Liverpool, while abroad the ships relied mainly on Calcutta or Natal coal, which were, however, softer varieties.

The range of homeward cargoes was great, but sugar, coffee, cotton and tobacco perhaps deserve mention. Since the 1890s, the Harrison fleet was mainly composed of ships of around 4,000 to 5,000 tons gross, together with a few of a much larger sized four-masted group. One of the latter, the *Huntsman*, had a gross tonnage of 8,196, her deadweight on a draught of 27 ft 6 in. being 11,960 tons. She and her sister, *Diplomat*, of a few months earlier, were built by C. Connell & Co. Ltd., Glasgow. Single-screw ships, each had three D.R.-geared turbines, steam being provided by two D.E. and two S.E. boilers, which supplied steam at 200 p.s.i. The result was a service speed of about 12–13 knots, slightly greater than the previous but otherwise similar ships which had reciprocating machinery. The *Huntsman*'s main dimensions were 482 ft b.p. (502 ft overall) × 58 ft breadth mld and 35 ft 10 in. depth mld. Besides her two continuous decks there was a third (orlop) one in No. 1 hold. She had a Lascar crew and British officers.

Launched on 5 July, 1921, she left the Clyde on 18 November on her maiden voyage to Galveston, the next two being to Buenos Aires and the North Pacific Coast respectively. Her travels thereafter were widespread, typical voyages over the years being Calcutta–U.K.–Galveston, U.K.–Mauritius/Calcutta and Calcutta–South Africa–River Plate.

The *Huntsman* was the first Harrison ship to be lost during the Second World War. In October 1939, when in the South Atlantic, she was captured by the German pocket battleship *Admiral Graf Spee* and subsequently sunk, her master and crew being transferred to the prison ship *Altmark*. The lucky exception was her Radio Officer, who was kept on board the *Admiral Graf Spee*. The latter's raiding activities ended in mid-December with the Battle of the River Plate, which forced her to seek sanctuary at Montevideo where her prisoners were promptly released.

27 m.v. ABA, 1918 (rebuilt 1921), Great Britain

The name of Elder Dempster has long been associated with the West African trade. Despite heavy losses incurred during the First World War, the Company's fleet in 1920 still numbered 70 ships, excluding small local service vessels. But of their crack passenger ships which maintained the main line from Liverpool, only two, the 6,300-ton *Abinsi* and the 7,700-ton *Appam* remained. These were owned by two sister concerns, the former by the African S.S. Co. (which had been under Elder Dempster management since 1891) and the latter by the British & African S. Navigation Co. Ltd., which had been acquired in 1900.

To bring the passenger fleet up to minimum strength, two extra ships were needed, the outcome being the purchase of an existing cargo ship, the *Glenapp*, which duly became the British & African-owned *Aba*, and the construction for the African Co. of the 7,800-ton m.v. *Adda*, which entered service in 1922. The *Aba* is shown on plate 27 as she appeared just after her reconstruction and, in the inset, as originally completed. Her background was unusual, for she had been originally ordered by the Russian Tsarist Government from the Clydeside yard of Barclay, Curle & Co. Ltd. The outbreak of the Russian revolution caused work on the ship to be suspended. However, this was resumed in 1918 when she was bought by the Glen Line. The diesel machinery ordered for her was then installed and later that year she entered service as the 7,374-ton *Glenapp*. Then devoid of funnel and with a long, low superstructure, she was mainly used on the Atlantic, ferrying American troops to France.

On her purchase by Elder Dempsters she was reconstructed by Harland & Wolff, Glasgow to something like her original design. In this guise, as the world's first diesel-propelled, ocean-going passenger liner, she ran trials on 16 August, 1921. Exactly three months later on Wednesday, 16 November, she left Liverpool on her maiden voyage to West Africa. As a result of the alterations her gross tonnage was raised slightly, to 7,937, but the net measurement fell fractionally from 4,623 to 4,596 tons. As originally completed her load draught was 30 ft 5 in., but this was cut to 24 ft 3 in. corresponding to a new reduced cargo capacity of about 4,108 tons. Her main dimensions, length 450·5 ft b.p., breadth 55·8 ft and depth of hold 36 ft 6 in. (depth mld 40 ft) remained unaltered. Her original machinery, which gave a speed of about 14 knots, was retained. This comprised two 8-cylinder, 4 stroke S.A. Harland-built, B & W-type diesels. These had cylinders of 750 mm diameter and 1,100 mm stroke and drove twin screws at 120 r.p.m. At this speed the total output was 4,800 b.h.p., the highest then achieved on any motorship. Her oil fuel capacity was 750 tons and this, sufficient for a round voyage, was carried in her double bottom and taken on at Liverpool. All auxiliary machinery was electricially driven.

The *Aba* was given what was described as luxurious accommodation for about 220 first-class and 105 second-class passengers. For a while she also carried 35 third-class. The first-class staterooms, on the upper and shelter decks, included a few singles, but were mainly three-berth. Above, on the bridge deck, there were two three-room suites. The first-class dining saloon was unusually fine. It extended the full width of the ship and for much of its area had double the normal headroom. It was panelled in white with Wedgewood plaques and small tables provided seating for 220 persons.

The *Aba* proved very successful in service and for some years operated with the m.v. *Adda* of 1922 and the older steamers *Abinsi* and *Appam*, the places of these two being taken over by the *Accra* and *Apapa* of 1926–27. In August 1922 the ship carried out a notable salvage operation. On receiving an S.O.S. from the disabled Portuguese destroyer *Guadiana* the *Aba* went to her aid and succeeded in towing her 422 miles to Las Palmas in weather so bad as to prevent the launching of any lifeboats. As a hospital ship during the Second World War, the *Aba* survived many attacks. In February 1941 she was slightly damaged when bombed at Tobruk, also in April 1941 while anchored in Suda Bay, Crete; again a month later when she was machine-gunned at Canea. A day later, on 17 May, she received more damage when twice bombed while she was on passage to Haifa. In April 1944 she incurred severe damage during an air raid on Naples. After repairs she served as a troopship. In 1946, her last year of service, she made a number of trips between Southampton and Hamburg and longer voyages to Port Said and Matadi.

In January 1947 the *Aba*, still owned by Elder Dempster's (by then known as Elder

Dempster Lines Ltd.) arrived at Birkenhead to lay up in the Bidston Dock. A few months later she was sold to the Bawtry S.S. Co. Ltd. (John Livanos & Sons, Ltd.) of London, who renamed her *Matrona*. On 30 October of that year, while still in the Bidston Dock undergoing alterations, she capsized and sank, ending up horizontally with her keel facing the quay. During the next few months the ship's funnel and masts were cut away while divers sealed the hull. Meanwhile, 3,500 tons of concrete were poured into a trench along the quay to form a base for 14 winches. Eventually, in June 1948, these winches each hauling a 9 in. wire rope righted the *Matrona* in a matter of 20 minutes. Later declared a constructive total loss, she was towed to Barrow-in-Furness and there scrapped. So ended the career of the world's first motor passenger liner.

In the course of her career she was repainted in many different ways. As the *Glenapp* she was initially grey all over, but later given a black hull with white bulwarks and white ribbon. As the *Aba* she started (as shown) with all black topsides. Later the top strake of the forecastle was painted white. Next the full height of the forecastle was so painted, likewise the midship bulwarks. During another period (as seen late in 1931) she was painted in this same fashion, but the black was replaced by a light grey. In war she was first painted in the traditional hospital ship colours with white hull, green band and red crosses, but she ended her days painted a light overall grey.

28 (left) s.s. CHARTERED, 1921, Great Britain

For the maintenance of its gas supplies, both for industrial and domestic needs, London was long dependent on ships such as the *Chartered*. Week in, week out, these brought coal from ports on the north-east coast, mainly those of the Tyne-Tees area, since Durham coal was the most popular.

In terms of ownership these colliers fell into several categories. Firstly there were those owned by the gas companies, which were designed for one route only and to suit their own particular wharves. This also applied to the ships of the electricity undertakings, but with these there was often a greater degree of flexibility as to loading and discharge points. Another group comprised the vessels owned by firms long established in the coal trade, such as Wm. Cory, Stephenson Clarke, France Fenwick and Hudson. These were designed for their owners' own trades, but being very well suited, were often chartered by the utility undertakings. In these groups, but especially the first two, there were both the 'down-river' colliers and the so-called 'flatties' which, with their lack of superstructure, were able to pass under London's many low bridges and serve up-river discharge points. Outside all these, there was a reserve of older, generally smaller ships, less specialised and more of the tramp type, which were nevertheless quite well suited for use if and when the need arose.

The owners of the *Chartered*, the Gas, Light & Coke Company, came into being in 1912 and from the start entrusted the management of its ships to Stephenson Clarke & Company Ltd. As far as the larger Thames colliers were concerned, the breakaway from the old engines-amidships layout began slightly earlier, the probable prototype being Stephenson Clarke's 240 ft long *Abbas* of 1911. Soon enlarged versions were built for both fleets and within a few years their design became accepted by owners and collier builders alike as the basic, near standard, type for the trade. The *Chartered* was thus one of a series of very similar ships.

Her builders were John Crown & Sons, Ltd., of Sunderland while her machinery was supplied by the North Eastern Marine Engineering Co. Ltd. She had a gross tonnage of 2,021 and carried a deadweight of 2,950 tons (cargo 2,800 tons) on a draught of about 19 ft. Her length b.p. was 270·4 ft, breadth mld 38 ft and depth mld 20·5 ft. Characteristic features were a 163 ft long quarter deck and a 28 ft forecastle. To suit her for grab discharge she had large, 25 ft wide hatches and her four holds were clear of any obstruction. To compensate for one-way lack of cargo the *Chartered* was fitted to carry a large amount of water ballast. Her fore and after peak tanks could take 149 and 77 tons respectively, a midship tank 252 tons and her double bottom another 506 tons. She had two cargo winches but, like most colliers, carried no derricks, although her masts were fitted to take these should the need arise. Her machinery, of triple-expansion type, had cylinders of 20½, 33 and 54 in. diameter and 39 in. stroke and took steam at 180 p.s.i. from two S.E. boilers. The daily coal consumption was about 15½ tons and the bunker capacity 176 tons. The service speed at 1,325 i.h.p. was about 10 knots.

Like all of her type, the *Chartered* was designed for rough usage and to make a quick turn-round. Cargo was loaded by shute from railway waggons shunted along mast-high staithes which ran parallel to the ship's berth. Then came a passage lasting about 36 hours or so and then, in the Thames, discharge by grab into more trucks. Such was the general pattern of her career from the time of her completion in October 1921 up to the war. In 1940 she was one of several colliers requisitioned by the Admiralty for use as Mine Destructor Vessels. In that year she was commissioned as H.M.S. *Burlington*, but in quick succession she became H.M.S. *Soothsayer* and H.M.S. *Fairfax*. As the last named she was used as a Repair Ship, her end coming in 1945 when she was scrapped at Briton Ferry by T. W. Ward Ltd. As to her original name, this was derived from the fact that her owners, the Gas, Light & Coke Co., had been incorporated under Royal Charter and, to distinguish them from others, were often referred to as the 'Chartered Company'. The funnel device was ingenious, the red triangles and two black bars being symbolic of flames rising above the bars of a grate. This design was retained when, after nationalisation, the Company became the North Thames Gas Board.

28 (right) s.s. CORCHESTER, 1927, Great Britain

It is easy to forget the past magnitude of Britain's coal trade and the effect this had on the composition of her merchant fleet. An analysis of the latter for 1927—the year when the *Corchester* was built—shows that she was one of some 250 steamers of between 1,600 and 4,700 tons d.w. which were either wholly or partly engaged in the carriage of coal. Besides these which traded in coastal or nearby waters, there were also myriads of smaller coasters below 1,600 tons d.w./1,000 tons gross, also the larger deep-sea tramps, for most of which coal was the main export cargo.

The business of Wm. Cory & Son was founded in 1785 and within a century it had become the leading firm in the London coal trade. In its fleet list (which includes a number of early vessels in which the Company or its nominees held a considerable interest) the *Corchester* is shown as ship No. 108. At the time when she entered service she was one of 20 steamships owned by Cory Colliers Ltd. (Wm. Cory & Sons, Ltd.), of London, all designed for the coastal or Thames coal trade. Besides these the Company owned a number of Thames-side wharves and had a very large fleet of lighters, also tugs to handle them.

The *Corchester* had a gross tonnage of 2,374 and was built by S. P. Austin & Son, Ltd., of Sunderland. Although she had no exact sisters, she was very typical of many then in service. A self-trimmer of single-deck type, she had four holds and hatches and was designed to carry about 3,500 tons d.w. on a modest draught of only 18 ft 11 in. Her length b.p. was 285 ft, breadth mld 41 ft 6 in. and depth mld 21 ft 1 in. Forward of the well deck she had a 31-ft forecastle and, extending from the bridge-front aft, a 165-ft-long quarter deck. Her machinery, supplied by George Clark Ltd., Sunderland, gave a speed of 10 knots and comprised a set of triple-expansion engines with cylinders of 21, 35 and 57 in. diameter and 39 in. stroke. Steam was supplied by two S.E. boilers with a working pressure of 180 p.s.i.

The ship was launched on 4 March, 1927, and entered service the following month. Her only major break from the coal trade came in the war, when she was requisitioned for use in the Mediterranean, carrying petrol in cans. While, at Naples, she narrowly missed being hit by bombs. She was returned to her owners in December 1945 and continued on her old run between the Thames and the north-east coast of England until 1956. Her end came on 19 February when, near the Haisbro Light Vessel (off Cromer) and on voyage from London to the Hartlepools, she sank after collision with the Ellerman steamer *City of Sydney*.

The *Corchester* is shown passing another Thames collier, the *Chartered*. The latter, with her engines-aft layout, represented the new in design and the *Corchester* one soon to be discarded. Indeed, only two more Cory colliers were built with engines amidships. Three which followed them in 1929–33 had engines aft and basically resembled the *Chartered*. Thereafter all built for the Cory fleet had engines aft and cruiser, not counter, sterns.

29 s.s. AUTOMEDON, 1922, Great Britain

The turbine-driven cargo liner *Automedon* was one of a group of eleven built in 1920–23 for Alfred Holt & Company which, despite outward similarity, relied on different types of machinery. The Company's first turbine ship, the *Diomed*, built 1917 and torpedoed a year later, had single-reduction gearing and was followed in 1920–22 by a pair with the more efficient, but then less well proven, double-reduction gearing. So as to evaluate the performance of one against the other and in relation to the old, long familiar triple-expansion engine, all three types featured in the group to which the *Automedon* belonged. Thus the *Machaon* of 1921 had triple-expansion engines, the *Adrastus* and *Dardanus* single-reduction geared turbines and all the rest double-reduction. In subsequent vessels, built prior to the switch-over to diesel, the bias—a very slight one—was towards the D.R. type.

Of the several hull layouts to feature in the Company's fleet this century, that with three islands had become easily the best known and accepted as the classic Blue Funnel shape. As regards their steam-driven ships, the *Automedon* and her sisters represented this type at its peak of development. They were, incidentally, the first in the fleet to have rounded, not bar, stems. However, the potential of the diesel engine was already apparent. Indeed, the next Holt ship to be delivered by Palmers (who built the *Automedon*) was the *Medon*, the first of a long series of Blue Funnel motorships, still with the familiar, three-island layout, but naturally differing in detail.

Of this eleven-ship group, the first five, the *Machaon, Eumaeus, Phemius, Troilus* and *Glaucus*, measured 459 ft × 56 ft, but for the next six the beam was increased by two feet. These ships were named *Automedon, Autolycus, Meriones, Rhexenor, Adrastus* and *Dardanus*. The orders for the eleven were spread over seven different yards, Palmers S.B. and Iron Co. Ltd. being responsible for the *Automedon* and *Meriones*.

The *Automedon*, which was launched at Jarrow on 4 December, 1922, ran trials on 2 March, 1923, and attained about 15½ knots. Her gross tonnage was 7,628, net measurement 4,782 and d.w. tonnage approximately 9,400. Overall she measured 476 ft 6 in. (459 ft b.p.) × 58 ft × 35 ft 3 in. to the upper deck. The load draught was 28 ft 1 in.

She had two continuous decks and six holds, of which one, with a capacity of 114,800 cu. ft, was insulated for perishable cargoes. Like all Blue Funnel ships, she was built to an exceptionally high specification and had unusually elaborate cargo-handling gear. As to accommodation, her engineers were berthed in a deckhouse on the bridge deck and the officers and Captain in the bridge house. The seamen and firemen had their quarters in the poop. The 'Marconi house' was on the boat deck. Provision was also made for the accommodation of native passengers in the 'tween decks and forecastle. Her single-screw, double-reduction, geared turbines, supplied by Palmers, were of Parsons impulse reaction type and at 6,000 s.h.p. gave a service speed of about 14–14½ knots. The two main boilers were of double-ended, superheated type and had forced draught. A single-ended, auxiliary boiler using natural draught was also fitted, its working pressure being 220 p.s.i. The bunker capacity was just over 800 tons and the daily coal consumption about 85 tons.

All eleven ships saw long service on various of the Company's services, two of them spending part of their careers with the associated Glen Line. But only three of them, the *Machaon, Glaucus* and *Adrastus,* survived the Second World War. The *Automedon,* bound from Liverpool via Freetown and Durban for Penang, was in the Bay of Bengal (position 04·18 N., 89·20 E.) when, on 11 November, 1940, she was sunk by the German raider *Atlantis.* Her Master was one of those killed during the shelling. The rest, taken aboard the *Atlantis* and subsequently transferred to the captured supply ship *Storstad,* eventually reached Europe, all but the few who escaped during the train journey being taken to a German P.O.W. camp.

30   s.s. JERVIS BAY, 1922, Great Britain

There have been various State-owned passenger lines, but that operated in the 'twenties by the Australian Government proved to be the greatest loss maker of its kind the world had yet seen. Profits made with cargo ships during the war—when few could fail to make them—prompted the Commonwealth Government Line of Steamers, as it was called, to venture into passenger shipping. The *Jervis Bay* was one of five emigrant and cargo carriers built for the U.K.–Australia trade. They were ordered when prices were at their peak and cost the then exorbitant figure of over £1 million apiece, the reputed figure being about £1,300,000.

Raw management was soon faced not with boom conditions but a growing trade depression, also the avowed aim of the Australian seamen's union to capture control of the line and abolish the right of management to have any say in the manning of the fleet. The ships were soon bedevilled by strikes, both ashore and afloat and these, coupled with various ugly incidents, did nothing to encourage popularity. Losses mounted year by year and in 1928 the figure was given as nearly £12 millions.

The *Jervis Bay,* which was the last of the five to be completed, will be remembered not so much for her blighted early career as for her extremely gallant last fight with a German raider, a fight which could only end in death and earned her Commander, Capt .E. S. Fogarty Fegan, a posthumous Victoria Cross. Three of the *Bay* ships were built by Vickers, Ltd. at Barrow: the *Moreton Bay, Hobsons Bay* and *Jervis Bay.* Two others, the *Largs Bay* and *Esperance Bay*, came from the Clydeside yard of Wm. Beardmore & Co.

In her original state the *Jervis Bay* had a gross tonnage of 13,839 (later 14,184) and a displacement of 23,230 tons. Her main dimensions were length overall 549 ft (530 ft b.p.), breadth mld 68 ft and depth to shelter deck 43 ft 6 in. The load draught was 33 ft. She had six decks, of which three were continuous. Most of her cargo space was insulated for the carriage of meat, etc., and of her six holds and 'tween decks, the only ones not insulated were Nos. 1 and 6 and the decks above. Cargo gear included two electric cranes and 23 derricks, one of them being of 35 tons capacity.

The ship had twin screws and four Parson-type, D.R.-geared turbines. These developed 9,000 s.h.p. at a propeller speed of 90 r.p.m. Steam at 220 p.s.i. and 150° F. was supplied by three D.E., and two S.E., oil-fired boilers. These consumed about 90 tons daily from bunkers which held just over 3,400 tons. The service speed was 15 knots. Accommodation was provided for 732 third-class passengers in 2-, 4- and 6-berth cabins, a number of those on C deck being removable, the space otherwise being used for cargo. The first class, limited to suites for 12, was reserved for government officials.

The *Jervis Bay* was launched at Barrow on 17 January, 1922, and she left there early in September for Liverpool, London and her maiden voyage. Within a year there had been reorganisation ashore and from 1923 the service was advertised as the Australian Commonwealth Line, and continued as such until 1928. By then trading losses and a declining reputation caused by irregular sailings and unruly crew behaviour resulted in the fleet being sold. The *Jervis Bay* and her sisters then became the property of the White Star Line, which was then headed by Lord Kylsant. The line, kept as a separate entity, now became known as the Aberdeen & Commonwealth. The first class was abolished, various improvements made and the ships given British, not Australian, crews. The ships' hulls previously all black, were repainted, as shown, in the traditional Aberdeen green, the old Aberdeen Line houseflag, with its six-pointed star, also being adopted.

In the early 'thirties, after the Kylsant group had disintegrated, the Aberdeen & Commonwealth Line was bought jointly by the P. & O. and Shaw Savill Lines, the latter acting as managers. In these later years the *Jervis Bay* carried tourist- instead of third-class passengers, the figures being first 635 and then 542. Although her colours were unchanged, the old 'Australis' type davits had been replaced by new. The bridge now reached to the forward king-posts, while the wings of the forecastle had been lengthened by over 30 ft. As always, she used the Suez route. London was still her terminal, but passengers were handled at Southampton. Outwards she called at Malta, Port Said, Aden and Colombo, thence to Fremantle and ports on to Brisbane.

Then came the war. In August 1939 the *Jervis Bay* was taken over for service as an Armed Merchant Cruiser and sent to the Tyne for conversion where, for fighting power, she was given eight 6-inch guns. Early in November 1940 she was escorting an Eastbound convoy of 38 ships across the Atlantic when, at about 17.00 hrs on 5 November, it was attacked by the German pocket battleship *Admiral Scheer*. In an endeavour to protect the convoy, which had been ordered to scatter, the *Jervis Bay* went into action. Quite outgunned, her steering gear was hit early on and in an hour all guns were out of action and the ship on fire. About two hours after the engagement had ended she sank, still with colours flying. But through her action—and that of the *Beaverford* (q.v.)—the raider was able to sink only six of the 38 ships. Of the *Jervis Bay*'s complement about 180 were lost, while the 65 survivors owed their lives to the gallant action of a Swedish cargo ship, the Brostrom-owned *Stureholm*, which turned back after dark to look for them.

The name *Jervis Bay* lives on, now borne by a large container ship, likewise the last of a series of six built for the U.K.–Australian trade. She too, suffered from early troubles. Ordered from Clydebank, she was delivered about a year later than her sisters which came from a German shipyard. Small wonder that of the group which followed all were ordered from that country.

31   s.s. DORIC, 1923, Great Britain

The *Doric* was built for the Liverpool–St. Lawrence service of the White Star Line, whose seldom used, but nevertheless official, title was the Oceanic Steam Navigation Company. To appreciate the ship the better she needs to be seen not only as a single unit but also in a wider context as the third of a series of four, some of which featured at different times in various of the fleets controlled by the American International Mercantile Marine. Of all these several fleets it should be remembered that the White Star held premier position.

The design was of pre-war origin and the first ship built was the Dominion Line's (later White Star) *Regina*, which entered the Canadian passenger trade in 1922. The second one, the *Pittsburgh* was used on various Atlantic routes, but not with the *Doric*. The latter, which came out in 1923, was of similar dimensions, but the fourth one, the *Laurentic* of 1927, was fractionally longer but much more beamy. Two others, of basically similar design need mention. These were the slightly smaller *Volendam* and *Veendam* (1922–23), of the Holland–America Line. Both of these had twin screws and geared turbines. Like the rest they were built by Harland & Wolff, but at Govan, not Belfast. The *Regina*, *Pittsburgh* and *Laurentic* were all triple-screw and had combination (reciprocating and L.P. turbine) machinery, but the twin-screw *Doric* had the distinction of being the only turbine-driven passenger ship ever built for the White Star Line.

She had a gross tonnage of 16,484 and carried a deadweight of 14,230 tons on a draught of 33 ft 11 in. This corresponded to a displacement of 28,480 tons. Her overall length was 600 ft 6 in., (575 ft b.p.), breadth mld 67 ft 6 in. and depth mld 45 ft 6 in. She had four continuous decks. The nine holds (served by eight hatches) had a cargo capacity of 439,148 cu. ft. Two sets of S.R.-geared, Brown-Curtis turbines developed 9,000 s.h.p. They took steam at 215 p.s.i. from six coal-fired boilers and gave a service speed of $15\frac{1}{2}$–16 knots.

The *Doric* was fitted to carry 583 cabin-class and 1,688 third-class passengers. Probably the most noticeable feature of the main public rooms was the general lightness of touch as regards colour and decor, a great degree of elegance being achieved. Heading the array of cabins were two three-room suites on the bridge deck, the bedrooms of which, in Louis XVI period, had pearl grey walls with white mouldings. For third-class passengers there were 2-, 3- and 4-berth cabins 'fitted with the finest of bedding and wash cabinets of the most approved type'. It was also stated that the orchestra played daily in the third-class quarters and that a piano and a gramophone, with a large selection of records, was provided in the third-class dining saloon. In a further enlightening piece it was stated that the ship carried 'conductresses to care for and assist unaccompanied ladies', also that matrons were permanently employed 'whose duty it is to have special regard for the comfort of women and children'.

The *Doric* was launched on 8 April, 1922, and on Friday, 8 June, 1923 she left Liverpool on her maiden voyage to Quebec and Montreal, calling en route at Belfast to pick up an Irish contingent of passengers. She remained on this run for the greater part of her life. Initially it was advertised as the White Star–Dominion Line, but with the death of the Dominion Line it became known simply as the White Star Canadian service. The *Regina* served with her, both as a Dominion and then as a White Star ship, until 1929.

By 1930 the *Doric*'s accommodation had been modified to take 320 cabin-, 657 tourist- and 537 third-class passengers. She spent the winter of 1932 laid up at Liverpool, but in the following April she was away to start a new career as a cruise ship. She continued in this capacity, first as a White Star and then as a Cunard-White Star liner until

September 1935. On the 5th of that month, while homeward bound from a Mediterranean cruise, she was in collision off the Portuguese Coast with the 2,166-ton cargo steamer *Formigny*. Although the latter was able to proceed, the *Doric*, badly damaged, had to put in to Vigo. Later, when back at Tilbury, she was sold to John Cashmore, Ltd. for about £35,000 'as lies' and on 7 November she left port for Newport, Mon., where she was broken up.

32 s.s. MINNEWASKA, 1923, Great Britain

London's participation in the North Atlantic passenger trade was never very large, emphasis instead being on services to the East and Australasia. That there was room for one London-based trans-Atlantic line was proved by the Atlantic Transport Co. Ltd. when, in 1903–7, they commissioned four ships which combined considerable passenger accommodation (first-class only) with very large cargo capacity.

Although its vessels flew the Red Ensign, the Company was American-owned and formed part of that great organisation, the International Mercantile Marine. Long interested in the North Atlantic trade, its earliest ships had carried cargo and cattle, the passenger aspect being something which developed more gradually. The construction of these four big ships, the *Minneapolis*, *Minnehaha*, *Minnetonka* and *Minnewaska* lifted the Company from the realms of relative obscurity and put it in a forefront position. The service, advertised as 'The Comfort Route', proved exceedingly popular with both passengers and cargo shippers, but the war exacted very heavy toll, all four being sunk, plus several older, smaller units.

The Atlantic Transport Co. were firm believers in large ships and the two which they ordered as replacements were the biggest cargo carriers ever built to trade from London. Like their predecessors, they were 600 ft long b.p., but their breadth and depth were much greater, the former by 15 ft. As before, Harland & Wolff were entrusted with their construction. The previous *Minnewaska* had a gross tonnage of 14,317, but the new one was 21,716 tons, the figure for her sister, the *Minnetonka*, being even greater at 21,998. Their deadweight tonnage was 19,890 and cargo capacity 17,000 tons. Alike as to dimensions, their overall length was 625 ft (600·8 ft b.p.), breadth 80·4 ft, depth of hold 49·4 and load draught 36 ft 9 in. Their hulls had 14 watertight bulkheads and four continuous decks, with a fifth one forward of the machinery. The capacity of the ten holds was vast, over 1 million cu. ft, but little of it was insulated, only four of the 'tween deck spaces. The cargo-handling gear was exceptionally elaborate, six pairs of king-posts being needed to work the derricks and with them 36 electric winches.

Accommodation was provided for 369 first-class passengers. The cabins, approximately 140, were arranged on three decks. Those on the lower promenade deck had either private or shared bathrooms and—the two suites excepted—were fitted with a cot bedstead, a folding upper berth and a sofa, also a wardrobe and electric heating. Those on the decks below were arranged in tandem fashion. The standards throughout were very high, but not over-luxurious and, at the fares charged, were really good value.

The ships had twin screws and these were driven by two Brown-Curtis, S.R.-geared turbines of 18,000 s.h.p. which gave a service speed of about 16½ knots. Steam was provided at 215 p.s.i. and 100° F. superheat by 12 oil-fired, water-tube boilers. Hailed as the largest ship to have been built at Belfast since the war, the *Minnewaska* was launched on 22 March, 1923. On Monday, 27 August she arrived at London, dressed overall, after doing 17 knots on her trip from Belfast. That Saturday she left on her maiden voyage to New York, the *Minnetonka* doing likewise in the following May. For the coming years this was to be the pattern, a Saturday departure from each end with a Monday arrival, nine days in all.

Great cargo capacity brought its own problems and from the time of arrival in port all holds had to be double-manned. Grain continued to form a large part of the Eastward cargo—(generally about 10,000 tons per voyage) and this was discharged into lighters. Soon, however, other smaller cargo liners, and tramps too, started to cut in on this trade. Rates fell as a result and soon it became difficult to fill the ships. Together the two maintained fortnightly sailings, calling en route at one of the French Channel ports. Two others were also used for a while, these being the war-built, 17,000-ton *Minnekahda* and a smaller transferred veteran of 1901 which had been renamed *Minnesota*. They had lower-grade accommodation, but made the overall service a weekly one.

Within a few years, as trade depression worsened, it became obvious that the two ships were too big for the trade. Further gloom came from the knowledge that the fortunes of the controlling I.M.M. were waning fast. In 1932 the London service ceased. The *Minnewaska* and *Minnetonka*, with their accommodation re-graded as tourist, were then transferred to the Antwerp–New York service of the Red Star Line, which was another member of the I.M.M. group. That winter they spent laid up at Antwerp, while the rest of the Atlantic Transport fleet, four cargo ships, lay off Southend awaiting sale. The two *Minne*s resumed sailings during the 1933 season, but that Autumn they were finally withdrawn. The *Minnewaska*'s last scheduled voyage was from New York on 28 September, and London on 11 October. Her sister followed about a fortnight later and was likewise laid up at Antwerp. In November 1934 they were both sold for scrap, to Douglas & Ramsey, Glasgow, on behalf of Smith & Co., Port Glasgow and P. & W. MacLellan Ltd., of Glasgow respectively. Initially the *Minnewaska* had cost £1,100,000 and the *Minnetonka* £1,250,000, but the price realised was only about £70,000 the pair.

33 (left)   m.v. MARGRETIAN, 1923, Great Britain

Among Cardiff-owned ships, the *Margretian* was an oddity and for her owners something of a disaster. Yet in several ways she was a pioneer, also the first motorship to be owned in a port essentially tied up with tramp shipping and coal exporting. If her hull layout was novel and ahead of its time, it was widely borrowed from in later years. Eventually, when mechanical reliability had been achieved, the ship gave excellent service, even in ripe old age.

Her owners, Owen & Watkin Williams & Co., differed from most local firms in that instead of tramping they operated a service, known as the Golden Cross Line, between the Bristol Channel and ports in the Mediterranean. At the time of the *Margretian*'s completion in 1923 their fleet comprised three elderly steamers, the *Arvonian*, *Menapian* and *Menevian*, each of a little under 3,000 tons gross.

The *Margretian* of 2,565 tons gross and 4,740 tons d.w., was built at Bristol—under Lloyd's Special Survey to 100A1 class—by Charles Hill & Sons Ltd. Their third motorship, she followed close after the very successful *Dumra* and *Dwarka* which were the British India Line's first motorships. She had an overall length of 314 ft (297·8 ft b.p.) her breadth being 43·6 ft and depth of hold 21·5 ft. Her depth moulded was 24 ft and load draught 22 ft 10½ in. Of shelter-deck type, she had two continuous decks and, above, a 26-ft-long forecastle. To serve her five holds and hatches she had 10 steam winches and 11 derricks. Like most early motorships, she had twin screws. As to her machinery, this comprised a pair of the newly designed, Beardmore-Speedwell type engines with crankcase-compression. Of 2-stroke, single-acting design, each unit had 6 cylinders of 18 in. diameter and 24 in. stroke. The combined output was 1,200 b.h.p.

The ship was launched in May 1923 and in mid-September she ran trials in the Bristol Channel, touching 11 knots. Already laden, she sailed immediately for Genoa. Records of her early voyages are lacking, but by March 1927 she was laid up at Cardiff. Soon afterwards she was advertised for sale 'with machinery partly dismantled'. Late that year she was bought by Stewart & Esplen Ltd. of London and renamed *Gresham*, her owners for the next few years being the Gresham Shipping Co. Ltd. of the same London address. On Christmas Day, 1928, the ship arrived at Grangemouth to receive new engines. Fitted in December 1930, these comprised a pair of 6-cylinder, 4-stroke S.A. M.A.N.-type engines, again of 1,200 b.h.p. Early in 1931 she resumed trading, mainly to the Levant, but only for two years, after which she was laid up at Blyth. Idle there for four years, she left for West Africa in August 1936, but had to be towed in to Lisbon with machinery disabled. More trouble occurred on a subsequent voyage and in March 1937 she was sold to a Norwegian firm, the Partrederiet Brovigtank (Th. Brovig), of Farsund. Thereafter, as the *Balla*, she operated with remarkable success in the Gulf of Mexico. Apart from only the most occasional visits to Europe, she spent the rest of her life there, her most frequent voyage being to New Orleans and the Mexican port of Progreso.

One brief break in service came in the summer of 1948 when she was again re-engined, this time given an American-built pair of M.A.N. diesels. Early in 1961 she was sold to the Transportacion Maritima Mexicana of Mexico City and renamed *Guadalajara*; her port of registry was changed from Farsund to Vera Cruz. However, this brought no apparent change of route and under their ownership the vessel lasted until 1967 when she was scrapped locally in Mexico.

33 (right)   s.s. USKHAVEN, 1923, Great Britain

If the Cardiff-registered *Margretian* represented the novel and the unorthodox, the Newport-owned *Uskhaven* represented the conventional. Both were built in the same year and were very similar as to dimensions, but there likeness ended. Her owners, the Uskside S.S. Co. Ltd., had been formed in 1913 by Richard W. Jones & Co., a firm which had been in business at Newport, Mon., since 1880. Just prior to the delivery of the *Uskhaven* the fleet comprised the *Uskmouth* and *Uskside*, both comparable in size but built during the war, in 1916 and 1917 respectively. In 1924 a fourth vessel was added, the *Uskbridge*, which, except for the lack of a separate donkey boiler funnel, was a repeat of the *Uskhaven*.

Although primarily engaged in the coal trade, the *Usk-* ships were quite outstanding for their smart appearance, having white-painted islands, superstructure and masts, when the use of dirt-concealing brown was very common for such vessels. Cardiff's tramp ships were of various size groups, but the emphasis was on the larger vessels, then of around 7,000 to 8,000 tons d.w., their basic run being to the River Plate with coal and back to the U.K. with grain. Generally they were of the well-proven single deck, three-island type. While the *Usk-* ships were similar in layout, they were of the so-called handy size (around 4,500 tons d.w.) and they traded rather to the Mediterranean, frequent homeward cargoes being grain, ore or esparto grass.

The *Uskhaven* was built on the Firth of Forth by the Burntisland Shipbuilding Co. Ltd., a small firm then only a few years old, but which was becoming known for its 'Economy' type tramps—ships very well designed and robust, but without unneccessary 'frills'. She was in fact the first of six *Usk*- ships to be built there during the years 1923–29. After the first pair, these showed a very slight progressive increase in size. This was followed by a step-up to 314 ft overall for a later pair which came from Burntisland in 1937 and 1940. These, named *Uskside (II)* and *Uskport*, were the first in the fleet to have cruiser sterns.

The *Uskhaven* herself was 308 ft long o.a. (297·7 ft b.p.), her beam and depth of hold being 43·9 ft and 20·9 ft respectively. Of 2,464 tons gross and 4,464 tons d.w., she had four holds and hatches and a like number of derricks and steam winches She was conventionally powered by a set of steam, triple-expansion engines, the cylinders being 22, 36 and 60 in. in diameter and the stroke 39 in. She had two coal-fired, Scotch boilers working at 180 p.s.i. She also had one donkey boiler, the uptake for which was separate from the main funnel. Contemporary descriptions referred to her cargo capacity (as distinct from total d.w. tonnage) as being 4,350 tons and to her large hatches and clear holds specially suited for the carriage of coal.

The ship was launched practically complete on 19 April, 1923, and ran trials on 30 May, when she attained over 11 knots. Typical voyages over the next few years were to Genoa, Oran, Sfax, Susa, Lisbon, Reggio and Messina. In April 1932 she was laid up at Grangemouth. That autumn she was sold for about £12,500 to Constants (South Wales) Ltd., who in January 1933 re-sold her for £15,300 to a German firm, W. Traber & Son of Hamburg. Renamed *Marion Traber*, she traded mainly in the Baltic and North Sea until she was wrecked in October 1939.

34 (left)   m.v. CANIS, 1888 (rebuilt *c.* 1918), Norway

The *Canis* which was bought in 1922 by the Bergen Steamship Company (Det Bergenske Dampskibsselskab) was typical of many elderly sailing ships which were converted either during or just after the First World War into full-powered, motor- or steam-driven vessels. In all, she lasted sixty years, her re-construction coming at about the mid-way point.

As the three-masted, iron-hulled barque *Andrew Welch* she was launched into the lower Clyde from Russell & Co.'s Kingston Shipbuilding Yard on 30 August, 1888. According to a contemporary description, she had a tonnage of 845, dimensions 195 ft × 34 ft × 18 ft 9 in. and was intended for Captain Marston, of San Francisco. However, later Registers give her as being 185·6 ft × 36·1 ft × 17·5 ft, with a moulded depth of 20 ft 4 in. They also show that for many years she was one of a large fleet of sailing ships managed by Welch & Co., of San Francisco. Another source suggests that in her case they did so on behalf of a Boston firm, C. Brewer & Co., who were the actual owners.

In 1916 she was sold by Welch & Co. to a Swedish concern, L. Lignell & Co., of Gothenburg, who renamed her *Olga*. In January 1918 she stranded badly and was later sold to Sophus Kahrs, (A/S Sophus Magdalon) of Bergen. The ship was then virtually rebuilt and given a 4-cylinder, 2-stroke, S.A. Polar motor of 590 s.h.p. As a result of this work her gross tonnage was raised to 934 and her d.w. to 1,450 tons (bale capacity 62,400 cu. ft), this corresponding to a load draught of 18 ft 4 in. She bore the name *Sophus Magdalon* until 1922 when she joined the Bergenske fleet and received her final name, *Canis*. As such she was used on the Norwegian coastal trade, particularly between Oslo and Trondhjem. In 1923 she was again in trouble and this time sank after hitting a rock. Salved and put back into service, she continued working for the Company until 1948 when she was sold for scrap. On occasion even the best edited books trip up. As an instance of the odd, and often confusing, errors which can arise, one Register for 1920 shows Sophus Kahrs as possessing two ships: (1) the 's.s.' *Olga*, built 1888, 893 tons gross, and (2) the 'aux. m.v.' *Sophus Magdalon*, built 1888, 934 tons. These two were of course, one and the same ship.

34 (right)   m.v. CAPABLE, 1918 (converted 1924), Great Britain

Inevitably, the shortage of tonnage which existed during the war and immediately afterwards provided great scope for the ingeniously minded. Although for the bigger, square-rigged, sailing ships there was limited opportunity for profitable employment, the position for power-driven ships was very different. Thus, among the neutral countries in particular, there were a number of once discarded sailing ships which, stripped of their canvas and converted into full-powered motorships, were proving very useful profit-earners—if only on a short-term basis.

In British coastal and adjacent waters smaller-sized schooners were still a common sight. Besides the many veterans were others of modern construction which may now be seen as the forerunners of the Dutch motor coasters and Scandinavian 'paragraph' vessels of later decades.

This plate shows vessels of these two categories. On the left is the *Canis*, one of the older, iron-hulled deep-sea windjammers which had been converted during the war. On the right is the much smaller *Capable*, an example of a then quite modern steel-hulled auxiliary schooner after being rebuilt as a full-powered motor vessel, and one well suited for the British coastal trade. Even though two of her masts had been removed, so destroying her former symmetry aloft, her hull lines and pronounced sheer revealed her Dutch origin. These features in modified form were to become characteristic of almost countless Dutch motor coasters as then unbuilt. Over the years the *Capable* has acquired an added interest in being one of the earliest sea-going units in what has since become Britain's largest fleet of coasters, that owned at Greenhithe, Kent, by F. T. Everard & Sons, Ltd.

As the *Grana*, a three-masted schooner of 186 tons gross and 128 tons net, she was built by a small Dutch yard, that of the Gebruder Zwolsman, of Ylst . Her deadweight was 216 tons and with a load draught of only 10 ft she could enter many small ports and creeks denied to the conventional, deeper-draught steam coasters. Her registered length (approximating to length b.p.) was 108·6 ft, breadth 23 ft and depth of hold 10·1 ft. For auxiliary power she had a little 2-cylinder, Plenty oil engine of 26 n.h.p. In 1920 she was sold by the A/S Mercur (C. B. Nielsen) of Skien, Norway to Mr. Fred T. Everard. Two years later there was an internal transaction and the vessel was thereafter owned by F. T. Everard & Sons Ltd.

In 1924 she became the *Capable* and was rebuilt as shown, with a single mast and one hold and fitted with a new 4-cylinder, 2-stroke, S.A. Plenty oil engine of 200 n.h.p. which gave a speed of some 7 to 8 knots. In this form and with a gross tonnage of 216 she served Everards' for 11 years until 7 December, 1935, when she became the property of Mr. John D. Sullivan, of Southend, Essex. Still named *Capable*, she continued in service until 5 June, 1940, when she was sunk by a mine at a point 130° and 2·8 miles off Horsesand Fort, Spithead.

35   s.s. AVILA, 1927, Great Britain

The *Avila* and her four sisters were the first passenger ships to be owned by the Blue Star Line. The origins of this fleet date back to 1910 when Vestey Bros., already well known in the meat trade and cold storage business, went into ship-owning. By purchases they gradually built up a considerable fleet of refrigerated ships. Although some of these were engaged on other services, Vesteys' main interest lay in the River Plate trade. On this, homewards, they had their own meat cargoes, but being outside the South American Freight Conference their ships had to make the long outward voyage in ballast. Their admission being blocked by certain Conference members, Blue Star replied by building a fleet of five 15½-knot passenger ships—the 'A-class'—whose fine accommodation won great favour with South American travellers. Through these ships Blue Star eventually gained the admission they sought.

The orders for the quintet were divided between Cammell Laird of Birkenhead and John Brown, of Clydebank. The former were responsible for the *Almeda*, *Andalucia* and *Arandora* and the latter for the *Avila* and *Avelona*. In February 1927 the *Almeda* opened the new service from London to the Plate, via Lisbon, Rio de Janeiro, Santos and Montevideo. By the end of the year sailings were fortnightly. The *Avila* was launched on 22 September, 1926 and ran trials off Skelmorlie in March 1927. A ship of 12,872 tons gross, her main dimensions were length overall 530 ft, (510 ft b.p.) × 68 ft mld × 37 ft 3 in. mld to upper deck. The load draught was 27 ft 6 in. Of her seven decks four were devoted to passengers. She had nine transverse bulkheads which reached to the upper deck and divided the ship into ten watertight compartments. Her cargo space, served by six hatches, was given over to the carriage of chilled and frozen meat and totalled 424,000 cu. ft. As to the propelling machinery, two sets of Parsons combined impulse and reaction turbines drove twin screws through S.R. gearing. Each engine comprised one high-pressure and one low-pressure turbine, the astern turbine being incorporated in the L.P. turbine casing. Steam at 200 p.s.i. was provided by three D.E. and three S.E. boilers which were fitted to burn either coal or oil. The total s.h.p. was 8,000 and the designed trial speed 16 knots.

The special feature both of this ship and her sisters was the high standard of the accommodation, described at the time as at least the equal of anything afloat. The cabins, for approximately 152 first-class passengers, included an unusually large proportion of singles and doubles, as well as a number of en-suite rooms with private bathrooms. The presence of these 'A' ships and their well deserved success must have been particularly galling to the Royal Mail S.P.Co., whose new and much vaunted 22,000-ton *Asturias* and *Alcantara* proved, in their initial motorship form, to be both slower than expected and prone to excessive vibration. Similarity as to style of naming between the two fleets caused some confusion and in 1929 this was remedied by the addition of *Star* to the names of the five, the *Avila* becoming the *Avila Star*, etc. Due to the depression which soon set in, passenger traffic declined and this led to the withdrawal in 1929–30 of both the *Arandora Star* and *Avelona Star*, the former being used thereafter as a cruise ship and the latter as a purely cargo carrier with one funnel removed.

Late in November 1934 the *Avila Star* left London for the Tyne, to be reconstructed by Swan Hunters'. The main feature was a new, taller and longer Maierform bow, which increased her length by 39 ft. The well decks were also enclosed and the base of the superstructure extended aft to just beyond the mainmast. As a result the gross tonnage was increased to 14,443 and the cargo capacity to 537,800 cu. ft. The ship was also converted to oil burning and this made possible the removal of one boiler. In March 1935 she was back in London ready to resume service. The remaining two, the *Almeda Star* and *Andalucia Star* were then treated in very similar fashion.

The war brought the destruction of all five ships. On 5 July, 1942, the *Avila Star* was homeward bound and some 90 miles to the East of San Miguel, in the Azores, when she was hit by two torpedoes and sank an hour later. Although three boat-loads of survivors were picked up a couple of days later, those in the fourth boat were not rescued until

20 days after the sinking. The remaining boat was never heard of again. Out of 199 persons on board the *Avila Star*, 73 perished.

36 m.v. PACIFIC RELIANCE, 1927, Great Britain

The *Pacific Reliance* was the first of an important group of seven motor cargo liners which were built in 1927–29 for Furness Withy & Co. Ltd., London. Of impressive shape, even if somewhat stiff-looking, they were designed for the Company's service to the Pacific Coast of North America. Numerically their largest class of motor ships, they operated with three older, diesel-driven ships. One of these was the *Pacific Commerce*, of 8,960 tons d.w. and 10½ knots, which had been built in 1922 as the *Dominion Miller*. The others, built in 1924, were the 11½-knot *Pacific Shipper* and the *Pacific Trader*, both of some 9,500 tons d.w. These were all of conventional, split-superstructure layout, with counter sterns, the first one being flush-decked and the others having a short, topgallant forecastle. The new design was refreshingly different in detail and introduced a profile new to British ships. The most noticeable differences apart from the cruiser stern, were the extra hatch and king-posts right forward, also the unbroken superstructure, part of which was built around No. 4 hatch, which was trunked to the deck above.

A short while earlier Furness Withy had provoked a somewhat scandalised outcry from British shipbuilders by ordering a series of Prince liners from Germany—and not all the *Pacific* ships came from British yards. Four, the *Pacific Reliance*, *Pacific Enterprise*, *Pacific Pioneer* and *Pacific Exporter*, were built by the Blythswood Shipbuilding Co. Ltd. of Scotstoun. But the *Pacific President* and *Pacific Grove* were ordered from the Deutsche Werft Kiel A. G. and the final unit, the *Pacific Ranger*, of 1929, from Burmeister & Wain, Copenhagen. Ownership was divided between the parent company and two subsidiaries, the Gulf Line and the Norfolk and North American Steam Shipping Co. Ltd., the last named having the *Pacific Reliance* and *Pacific Enterprise*. Of all these, the German-built vessels were longer by 15 ft, while they and the Danish-built one could be distinguished by their bridgehouses, which were one deck taller than on the British, a small item but one which made for a better view over the bows.

The *Pacific Reliance* was of 6,717 tons gross and carried 10,023 tons d.w. on a draught of 17 ft 6 in. Her length overall was 451 ft, (435·9 ft b.p.) breadth mld 60 ft and depth mld 42 ft. She was of open shelter deck type, with two continuous 'tween decks and of these, the lower one (six compartments in all) was insulated for the homeward carriage of fruit. She had twin screws and these were driven by two 8-cylinder, 4-stroke, S.A. Harland–B. & W. type diesels of 4,000 i.h.p. which had been built by Kincaid. The daily fuel consumption was about 20 tons and the designed service speed in loaded condition was 13 knots. The ship was launched on 28 June, 1927, and, after running trials, loaded at Glasgow, Manchester and Liverpool before starting on her maiden voyage. Thereafter her normal run was to the Panama Canal, up the coast to Vancouver, her most northerly port, and then back to the U.K., starting with London.

Wartime losses were heavy and the *Pacific Reliance* was the first of three of this group to be sunk in 1940 alone. Of the seven, only two of the Blythswood ships survived the war. One of these, the *Pacific Enterprise*, continued in service until 1949 when she was wrecked. The other, the *Pacific Exporter*, remained with the Company a year or so longer, when she was sold to the Italian Costa Line to start a new career as the *Giacomo C*.

37 s.s. KEDAH, 1927, Great Britain

The *Kedah* was built at Barrow-in-Furness by Vickers, Ltd., a company generally associated with the construction of warships and large passenger liners. Against such vessels she appeared somewhat insignificant. Even so, she was intended to be the prestige ship of a large and well-known fleet and, in the event, she more than lived up to all expectations. In addition, in the later years of war, she seemed to be possessed of a charmed life. In many ways her design was akin to that of a cross-channel ship. But although she had many of the same characteristics—high speed, fine lines and light draught—she was designed to operate in tropical waters, not just on a short route, but one which involved a distance of about 350 miles.

Her owners, the Straits Steamship Co. Ltd., of Singapore, old associates of Alfred Holt & Company's Blue Funnel Line, possessed a large and varied fleet which carried passengers and cargo between the many small ports and harbours along the coast of Malaya, others also operating on longer routes. The *Kedah* was expressly designed for the passenger and cargo service between Singapore, Penang and Belawan. She had a gross tonnage of 2,499 and carried a deadweight of 1,170 tons on a draught of 14 ft 8 in. Her overall length was 330 ft, breadth mld 50 ft 3in. and depth mld (to shade deck) 25 ft 6 in. She had two continuous decks and three holds with a mail room further aft. For cargo handling she had six steam-driven deck cranes, each of 2-tons capacity.

Amidships she had accommodation for about 80 first-class passengers. For them there were three public rooms, grouped vertically beneath the bridge, the two lounges being above the dining saloon. Aft of these, on two decks, there was an array of two-berth cabins, while another block was located at the after end of the boat deck. The Captain's accommodation was by the navigating bridge, that for the engineers and officers being on the top of the after deckhouse. The *Kedah* also carried up to 960 deck passengers, access and ventilation to the spacious main deck being provided by a series of double doors and large openings. She had twin screws and was propelled by four Parsons turbines. These developed 5,800 s.h.p. at 2,400 r.p.m., S.R. gearing reducing the propeller speed to 220 r.p.m. The four boilers were of Babcock & Wilcox water-tube type.

The ship was launched in July 1927 and on trials that Autumn she did 19 knots under easy conditions, while her maximum was well over 20. She proved extremely popular in service—even if she was extravagant in fuel. Sailing from Singapore at 11.30 hrs on Thursdays, she would arrive at Penang at 8.30 hrs next morning. She also did weekend trips to Belawan, returning to Singapore on Tuesdays at 13.30 hrs. The Company's largest ship, she was granted as a special favour, something marked on the charts of Singapore as '*Kedah*'s Anchorage', and conveniently within sight of her owners' office.

In 1939 she was requisitioned and armed to become a Naval Auxiliary. She was one of the last convoy to leave Singapore in February 1942 and there, as H.M.S. *Kedah*, she returned in 1946 to be de-requisitioned. This followed a brilliant war career, owing partly to her speed and manoeuvrability, but also to the abilities of her Captain. The ship , then in a poor state, was brought home to England and there sold to become the Palestinian-registered *Kedmah*. As such she was the Zim Line's first passenger ship, ownership being through a subsidiary, the Kedem Palestine Line. While being towed to Antwerp for a major overhaul, she broke adrift from her tug and was nearly wrecked on the Cornish coast. Subsequently she was used in the Mediterranean by Zim until 1952, when she was bought by the London firm of Harris & Dixon. Renamed *Golden Isles*, she was put on their Sterling Line service between Marseilles, Malta, Cyprus and the Lebanon. On her first return to Marseilles she received a great ovation, for she brought back the 186 crew members of the wrecked French liner *Champollion*. After a final two-year (1954–55) spell on the Marseilles–Haifa run (on Zim charter) she was sold late in 1956 to John Cashmore, Ltd. The tug *Turmoil* was used to tow her from Genoa to Newport, Mon., where she was scrapped.

38 s.s. BEAVERFORD, 1928, Great Britain

In 1928 the Canadian Pacific North Atlantic cargo service was transformed by the introduction of a magnificent group of five cargo liners. Twin screw, 14-knot, turbine ships of approximately 10,000 tons gross, they represented a very great advance on the 10- to 11-knot freighters previously employed. With the arrival of this new tonnage, five of the older units were sold, the *Brandon, Brecon* and *Bosworth* (war-built vessels of 6,600 tons gross) and the somewhat smaller *Balfour* and *Berwyn*.

The *Beaver* ships, which were among the finest of their type afloat, were built for service between London and the St. Lawrence, with calls at Hamburg, Antwerp and Havre. During the summer they went as far as Montreal, but in the winter they turned about at St. John, N.B., For obvious reasons they had ice-strengthened hulls. When they were being designed, the diesel was becoming increasingly popular, but it was decided that for the relatively short Atlantic route, steam still appeared the better proposition. Besides their turbines the ships were given the latest in coal-fired, steam-raising plant while, to assess their relative merits, two types of water-tube boilers were chosen. Two of the group were therefore given Babcock & Wilcox boilers with hand-firing and the other three (among them the *Beaverford*) Yarrow-type boilers and mech-anical stokers. As a group the five *Beavers* proved to be the most efficient coal-fired ships of their day.

The *Beaverford* and *Beaverhill* were built by Barclay Curle & Co. Ltd., of Scotstoun, Glasgow, the *Beaverburn* by Wm. Denny & Bros. Ltd., Dumbarton and the *Beaverdale* and *Beaverbrae* (the two with manual firing) by Armstrong Whitworth & Co. Ltd., Newcastle. They were owned by the Canadian Pacific Rly. Co., but managed by Canadian Pacific Steamships Ltd. The main hull dimensions were length on waterliner 512 ft, breadth mld 61 ft 6 in. and depth mld 40 ft 6 in. The load draught was 29 ft 11 in. and the corresponding deadweight about 10,600 tons. The gross tonnage of the *Beaverford* was 10,042. She and her sisters had two continuous decks and six holds, of which all but no. 6 had an extra 'tween deck. The total cargo capacity was about 570,000 cu. ft, of which 80,000 cu. ft (in Nos. 4 and 5 holds and lower 'tween decks) was insulated. No. 3 lower hold could alternatively be used as a deep tank. The most distinctive feature of the *Beaverford* and her sisters was the array of twin king-posts and derricks, of which 27 were fitted, including one of 45-tons capacity. All of the accommodation was above the hull, in the superstructure. The officers and engineers had their cabins on the port and starboard sides of the bridge deck, with their respective saloons at the forward end. The Master's accommodation was above and that of the crew below, on the upper deck.

Six Parsons turbines of 8,000 s.h.p. drove twin shafts through S.R. gearing. Four water-tube boilers supplied superheated steam at 250 p.s.i. In the *Beaverford, Beaverhill* and *Beaverburn* these were fitted with Erith-Roe mechanical stokers—the first in the British Merchant Service . Two single-ended, Scotch boilers were also installed, mainly for dealing with the auxiliary machinery and for use in port. The bunker spaces, immediately forward and aft of the boiler room, held 2,500 tons.

The *Beaverford* was launched on 27 October, 1927, and on 21 January she left the Clyde on her maiden voyage. Thereafter she and her sisters operated from London, their normal berth being in the Surrey Commercial Docks. From there, on average, they made ten round voyages per year. In February 1940 the *Beaverford* was requisitioned for the carriage of war supplies and other priority cargoes. Late that year she had the ill-fortune to be one of the Eastbound Atlantic convoy which was attacked by the German pocket battleship *Admiral Scheer* on the evening of 5 November, 1940. As is well known, the escorting Auxiliary Cruiser *Jervis Bay* deliberately drew the enemy's fire, so providing time for the convoy to scatter. After the *Jervis Bay* had been sunk, the *Beaverford*, despite her meagre armament, held the *Admiral Scheer*'s attention for several hours until inevitably she too met a like fate, sinking with the loss of all 77 of her complement in position 52·26N, 32·34W.

As to the others of this class, the *Beaverburn* had previously been torpedoed in the North Atlantic, in February 1940. The *Beaverdale* suffered a similar end in January 1941, while the *Beaverbrae* went down two months later after air attack. The *Beaverhill* continued in service until November 1944, when she stranded off the New Brunswick coast and subsequently became a total loss.

39 s.s. PARRACOMBE, 1928, Great Britain

The *Parracombe* had no great claim to distinction, but she was representative of a large number of open shelter deck type tramp steamers built in Great Britain during the 'twenties and early 'thirties. Her split superstructure—with bridgehouse separate from the funnel and engine casing—was typical of that period. She, it will be noted, had a flush deck, but many of her contemporaries, though otherwise similar, had a short raised forecastle; later ones would have had a cruiser stern. Such a tramp would have been a rarity in pre-war years. Certainly she would have been rather smaller and of a single-deck, three-island type with bluff, vertical stem, but otherwise not so different from the *Benrinnes*, shown on plate 21.

The *Parracombe*'s beak-like stem projection was unusual. Generally referred to as of semi-clipper type, it was favoured by only a very few owners, notably the well-known Pyman family. Almost certainly she was the penultimate ship to be built with this feature, the final one being the *Welcombe*. As to the funnel marking, a black disc on a white band, this in pre-war years had featured on a large number of tramps, all owned by various of the Pyman concerns—Pyman Bros. Ltd., London, George Pyman & Co., West Hartlepool, Pyman, Bell & Co. Ltd., Newcastle, J. W. Pyman & Co., Cardiff and J. S. Pyman of London. Of these, listed in descending order according to size of fleet, Lloyd's Register for 1920 showed only the Newcastle firm—and with its fleet shrunk to one vessel. Such had been the ravages of war. Soon that firm too dropped out of shipowning. However Pyman Bros., Ltd., of Newcastle re-entered the field and in 1928 took delivery of the *Parracombe* and then, two years later, of the similar-looking but fractionally larger *Welcombe*. These were the last merchant ships to be owned by any of the Pyman family.

The *Parracombe* came from a yard long known for the construction of tramp steamers —Wm. Gray & Co. Ltd., of West Hartlepool. Her gross tonnage was 4,698, net 2,848 and she could carry 8,815 tons d.w. on a draught of 24 ft 10 in. Her main dimensions were length b.p. 406 ft 6 in., breadth mld 54 ft and depth mld to upper deck 27 ft 6½ in. The hull was divided by six water-tight bulkheads and her holds had a steel, centreline bulkhead and wooden shifting boards for grain-carrying. Her cargo handling gear comprised ten derricks and steam winches. She was propelled by the conventional type of triple-expansion engine. This, supplied by the Central Marine Engine Works, had cylinders of 26½, 44 and 73 in. diameter and 48 in. stroke and took steam at 180 p.s.i. from four single-ended, coal-fired boilers, one of which was an auxiliary.

The ship was launched on 22 November, 1927, and ran trials on 11 January, 1928. It seems that no reference to her speed ever appeared in print, but she probably did about 10 knots loaded. Thereafter she spent the rest of her career in the general tramp trade. She was joined in 1930 by another from the same builders, the *Welcombe* of 9,208 tons d.w., which measured 421 ft × 55 ft × 28 ft. In June 1940 Pymans' sold these, their last vessels, to the Stanhope Steamship Co. Ltd., of London, of which J. A. Billmeir & Co. Ltd. were the managers. The prices paid were approximately £80,000 and £90,000. Wartime restrictions prevented any changes of name. Soon, however, both were lost by enemy action. The *Parracombe*, bound from the U.S.A. to Britain with a full cargo of grain, was torpedoed on 4 April, 1941, in mid-Atlantic, taking with her 20 out of her crew of 41. Less than a month later it was the *Welcombe*'s turn. While making what was described as the first unescorted passage from the United Kingdom to Malta, with a cargo of government stores, she was attacked by Heinckel aircraft. Out of her crew of 47, 30 were lost.

40 s.s. SOUTHERN EMPRESS, (converted c. 1928), Great Britain

In the first quarter of this century it was the Norwegian whaling fleet which held premier position, even though its ships were generally small and elderly. A typical whale factory ship, used during the early 'twenties, was the s.s. *Pythia*, 4,401 tons gross, which, on her annual voyage to and from the Antarctic, generally called at Cape Town. There, a quarter of a century earlier, she had been well known as the mail and passenger liner, *Raglan Castle*, one of Donald Currie's famous Castle Line.

The whaling industry received fresh impetus when, during the 1922–23 season, new and very prolific whaling grounds were discovered in the Ross Sea. This brought the need for more and larger factory ships, able to work independently of shore bases. A technical breakthrough which followed in 1925 was the invention of the stern ramp. This was of major importance, since it obviated the tedious and dangerous business of flensing the whales as they lay floating alongside the factory ship. The first vessel to be given this feature was a converted engines-amidships freighter.

At that time (in the 'twenties) the Eagle Oil & Transport Co. was starting a fleet-pruning policy which led to the sale of several of their big 15,000-ton d.w. tankers. The *San Gregorio* was bought and converted by the Norwegians to become the world's largest whaler. However, the problems of incorporating a stern ramp into a ship with machinery aft proved daunting, so instead she was given a bow ramp which was protected by side doors. Even though this proved unsatisfactory, the use of such a large ship proved well justified. Two more Eagle tankers were therefore bought by Norway and converted, although initially they contrived to work without a ramp.

In Britain, Lever Bros (later to become part of Unilever) bought two other Eagle tankers through a subsidiary of theirs, the Southern Whaling & Sealing Co. Ltd. of Liverpool. The first of these, the *San Jeronimo* (plate 18) was taken over in May 1928 and the *San Patricio* a year later. Reconstructed, they became Britain's largest whalers, named respectively the *Southern Empress* and *Southern Princess*. Much alteration was needed to fit them for their new work. Probably the most important visible addition was the long and lofty superstructure which carried the flensing deck above. This vast space, with the 'tween deck below, was used to house the factory equipment (including 56 press boilers), the ship's own vastly increased crew and, when required, those of her attendant whale catchers. Stores sufficient for the whole flotilla had also to be carried and, of course, fuel too. The initial conversion did not involve the stern, but later the engine and boiler room area was remodelled and the ship given twin funnels, so providing centreline space for the stern ramp. Surprisingly, these changes had little effect on the gross tonnage, the final figure being 12,308, as against the original 12,028.

The vessel had been well maintained and she continued to give good service in her new guise. As a whale factory (or whale oil refinery as they were then called) the general pattern of service was an autumn departure for the Antarctic with a call at

Cape Town and another call there when homeward bound in the spring. Then, after her whaling personnel had been landed, cargo discharged and the ship's own crew paid off, she would undergo a long refit to prepare her for the next season. The war brought the destruction of all but a very few of the world's big factory ships. Both the *Southern Empress* and the *Southern Princess* (which had been sold about 1939 to Chr. Salvesen & Co. of Leith) were among those which were lost. The former, while carrying a cargo of fuel oil from New York to the Clyde, was some 400 miles South of Cape Farewell when, on 13 October, 1942, she was torpedoed and sunk by a U-boat. Of those on board 48 were lost. Her sister was on a similar voyage when sunk in March 1943. (For early career see *San Jeronimo*, 1914, plate 18)

41 m.v. HIGHLAND CHIEFTAIN, 1929, Great Britain

The name of Nelson, as applied to the U.K.–South American meat trade was long synonymous with *Highland* ship names, although what motivated this choice has never been discovered. The Company, known in full as H. & W. Nelson, Ltd., owned through the Nelson Steam Navigation Co. Ltd. an impressively large group of ten 13-knot sister or near-sister ships, all built 1910–11. Basically meat carriers with a gross tonnage of 7,000 plus, they also had extensive passenger accommodation and on that trade represented the main opposition to the Royal Mail Steam Packet Co. The lesser inevitably came under the control of the greater, this in 1913. From then on no replacements were ordered and by the early 'twenties the *Highland* passenger fleet had shrunk to six through two wartime losses and two strandings.

Of the several R.M.S.P. services to South America the most prestigious was maintained by the 'A'-named liners operating out of Southampton. From Liverpool there was another, of intermediate category, maintained by the 11,000-ton D-class refrigerated cargo/passenger ships of 1911–12. These had supplanted the Lamport & Holt 'V'-ships (such as *Vauban* Plate 16), and most of them enjoyed long careers, based on the Mersey while the *Highland*s continued from the Thames. The Blue Star Line's entry into the South American meat and passenger trade in the late 'twenties could not be stopped by non-admission into the appropriate conference. The newcomers were too big and eventually consolidated their position. In terms of passenger accommodation the Blue Star ships (see *Avila*) offered the best in first-class travel while as cargo carriers they could hardly be bettered. Homewards they carried their owners' own cargo, but outward they competed with both the elderly R.M.S.P. D-ships and the *Highland* steamers.

Such briefly was the background scene which led up to the construction of the *Highland Chieftain* and her several sisters. Not dissimilar in speed to the new Blue Star ships, their accommodation was intended to be complementary to that of the crack R.M.S.P. Southampton-based liners. Solid comfort was the theme for the first class, that provided for the lower categories being adequate but not glamorous. So, on the London–Plate trade it was the Blue Star accommodation which received the bouquets, although the *Highland* ships were slightly the bigger cargo carriers. The main group of five, headed by the *Highland Monarch* entered service 1928–30. One was wrecked within a year, so a sixth was built in her stead, to enter service in 1932 as the *Highland Patriot*. There was just time for her to make one round voyage in Nelson livery before she and the rest were absorbed into the unified fleet of Royal Mail Lines. The old colours were then discarded in favour of black hulls and plain buff funnels.

One ship, the *Highland Hope*, was built at Govan, the rest by Harland & Wolff's main establishment at Belfast. The *Highland Chieftain* was the second in the series. She had a gross tonnage of 14,131 and carried a deadweight of 9,070 tons on a draught of 28 ft

1 in. Her length was 523·4 ft (544·5 ft o.a.), breadth mld 69 ft, and depth mld 43·7 ft. Twin screws were driven by two 8-cylinder, 4-stroke, D.A. Harland-B. & W. diesels (680 mm × 1,600 mm). These had an output of 10,000 b.h.p. and gave a speed of about 15 knots. Accommodation was provided for 135 first- and 66 intermediate-class passengers. Up to 600 steerage could also be carried, for besides the emigrants from Spain and Portugal there was also a seasonal, two-way flow of labour between those countries and South America. The public rooms in the first class were mostly old English and Tudor in style and the cabins, on the shelter and bridge decks, were mainly two-berth. Those in the intermediate class were two- and four-berth. Beneath the shelter deck (well deck level) there were three other decks with an extra orlop deck in all but two of the six holds. These had a cargo capacity of over 507,000 cu. ft and five of them, together with most of the 'tween decks, were insulated for the carriage of chilled meat.

The *Highland*s were the first of the squat-funnelled motor liners to be based on London and their profile was made the more distinctive by the Royal Mail policy of having the bridgehouse and the officers' quarters separated from the passenger areas. As built, the ships had a 101-ft long forecastle, as shown, but during their post-war refits, this was extended to link up with the bridge, and the space gained was used to enlarge the crew's accommodation.

The *Highland Chieftain* was launched on 21 June, 1928 and left Belfast for trials—and London—on 26 January, 1929. The past importance of passenger shipping to Harland & Wolff is emphasised by the fact that two days previously the firm had launched the *Ulster Monarch* at Belfast and the *Highland Hope* at Govan. Initially the *Highland Chieftain* operated with the *Highland Monarch*, *Highland Brigade*, *Highland Hope* and *Highland Princess*, their departures being fortnightly. The voyage to the Plate took three weeks and included calls at Vigo, Lisbon and Las Palmas. However, regularity of schedule was broken in November 1930, when the *Highland Hope* became a wreck on the Farilhoes rocks, some 60 miles north of Lisbon. Her replacement, the *Highland Patriot*, entered service in the Spring of 1932. Also short lived, the *Patriot* was the only *Highland* ship to be lost during the war, although two others were badly damaged.

The London–Plate service was resumed in November 1947 and was maintained on a four-ship basis for eleven years. In October 1958 the *Highland Chieftain* was sold to a whaling concern, the Calpe Shipping Co. Ltd., and became the Gibraltar-registered *Calpean Star*. As such, she had a brief and luckless career, her final misfortune coming in June 1960. While in tow off Montevideo she had an engine room explosion and then grounded, her wreck thereafter becoming part of the local scene. Of the others, the *Highland Monarch* was scrapped at Dalmuir in 1960. The *Highland Hope*, sold in 1959 to John S. Latsis of Athens, was renamed first the *Henrietta* and then the *Marianna* before being broken up.

The *Highland Princess* also went to Latsis at the same time. Very briefly she too bore the name *Marianna* before being resold to become the Czechoslovakian *Slapy*. Sold again in 1960, she has since operated as the *Guanghua*, her flag being that of Communist China. Subsequently the place of the *Highland* ships was taken by a new 20,000-ton trio, the *Amazon*, *Arlanza* and *Aragon*, but in 1968 the passenger service died.

42 s.s. VASILEFS CONSTANTINOS, 1914, Greece

In 1912, Embiricos Bros., managers of the National S.N. Co. Ltd. of Greece, suffered the loss of their 6,000-ton *Macedonia* which, after being commandeered by the Greek Government, was sunk by a Turkish warship only a few months after her completion. Still determined to expand their transatlantic passenger fleet, they ordered two 9,000-ton passenger liners from Cammell Laird & Co. in 1913. They also bought two 4,000-ton, ex-British vessels, and in 1914 took over two 6,000-ton liners from a rival concern.

The First World War upset the Company's plans, for of these two new liners only the first one, *Vasilefs Constantinos*, was delivered to them. The acute shortage of shipping resulted in her twin, the *Vasilissa Sofia* (*Queen Sofia*) being bought by the British Government. Completed in 1917 as the troopship *Leasowe Castle*, she was torpedoed a year later.

The *Vasilefs Constantinos* was launched on 9 June, 1914; a handsome, twin-screw ship of 9,272 tons gross, she was 470 ft in length b.p., and 58 ft in breadth mld. Her depth moulded was 35 ft 6 in. and her load draught 24 ft 2 in. Cammell Laird & Co. also supplied her propelling machinery. This comprised two sets of quadruple expansion engines with cylinders of 27½, 39, 56 and 80 in. diameter and 54 in. stroke. Her 8 main boilers had a working pressure of 220 p.s.i., these and the donkey boiler all being of the single-ended type and coal-fired. Contemporary descriptions give the vessel's speed as 18 knots.

She was designed for service between the Eastern Mediterranean and New York, primarily to carry emigrants, and she was fitted to take 1,800 of these on the main and upper decks. She also had accommodation for 60 first-class passengers, in two- and four-berth rooms, and an unrecorded number of second-class. Standards for both appear to have been high and one of her special features, unique on board ship, was a Greek church, located on the shelter deck.

She had three continuous decks, and the life-saving equipment included Welin davits, 19 lifeboats and one 11-knot motorboat, also a number of semi-collapsible McLean-type boats. Lloyd's Register gives her completion date as December 1914, but because of wartime censorship as to ship movements little is known of her early years. She was apparently idle for some time, but about 1917 was requisitioned by the French Government and for about two years operated under the Tricolor. However a photograph taken at Piraeus in 1919–20 shows her still named *Vasilefs Constantinos* but back under the Greek flag, her appearance being as shown on plate 42.

Some time later she was given a black hull. The name *King Constantine* being hardly popular, the ship was rechristened *Megali Hellas*, and started operating between Constantinople, Piraeus and New York. Sailings were augmented by the purchase, on the part of a British associate, the Byron Steamship Co. Ltd., of several ex-German liners.

In 1924 the *Megali Hellas* was transferred to this fleet and renamed *Byron*, London becoming her new port of registry. Owing to U.S. restrictions on the inflow of emigrants and the heavy operating costs of the other ships, profits declined and led to the gradual disposal of older units. In 1928 the *Byron* reverted to National Steam ownership and was re-registered at Andros. Thereafter the voyages were generally between Jaffa (Haifa), Piraeus, New York and Boston. Eventually sold for £29,000, she was scrapped at La Spezia early in 1937. Not until 1953 was another large liner built for Greek ownership, the well-known *Olympia*, which is still in service.

Of the *Vasilefs Constantinos* one collector's piece exists—an official Cammell Laird postcard: a coloured artist's impression which shows the ship—unnamed but quite unmistakably her—with owners' houseflag and funnel design clearly visible. Its interest lies in the fact that the ship has three, not two, funnels. That she ever had three is extremely unlikely, and the only possible explanation is that the card was produced at the owners' request, the third funnel being to impress would-be migrants.

43 s.s. PATRIS II, 1926, Greece

Despite her modest size—her gross tonnage was only 3,902—the *Patris II* held an important place in the development of Greek Mediterranean passenger shipping.

Hitherto, with only one exception – that of the 2,000-ton Embiricos steamer *Syria* (later *Andros*) of 1914 – all other Greek passenger ships so employed had been elderly units bought second-hand. The *Patris II* was designed for regular service between Marseilles, Genoa, Piraeus, Alexandria, Cyprus and Beyrout and right up to the time of her sale she remained the crack ship of the Greek Mediterranean passenger fleet.

Officially, for the first couple of years or so, she was owned by the Byron Steam Ship Co. Ltd. of London. In fact this was merely the British offshoot of Embiricos Bros., to whose other and older firm, the National Steam Navigation Co. Ltd. of Greece, the *Patris II* was later transferred. The ship was built and engined by Swan, Hunter & Wigham Richardson, Ltd. and was launched into the Tyne on 19 October, 1925. She ran trials exactly three months later, on 19 January, 1926. Of 6,000 tons displacement, she was 336 ft in length b.p., her breadth being 47·5 ft and draught about 20 ft. Twin screw, triple-expansion engines and oil-fired boilers gave her a service speed of about 14 knots. For cargo-handling she had eight 5-ton winches while, of her holds, part of No. 3 was refrigerated for the carriage of fruit, vegetables and meat. She had accommodation for approximately 100 first-class and 150 second-class passengers, provision also being made for deck passengers. Among her special features were eight *cabines-de luxe* while, as was then fashionable, her first-class public rooms had period-style decor.

In Greece, the year 1933 was one of political upheaval and largely because of the change of regime the fortunes of the Embiricos family slumped; by 1935 when the *Patris II* was sold, there was left remaining only one ship from their two once-sizeable fleets. The new owners of the *Patris II* were the Rederi A/B Svenska Lloyd (Swedish Lloyd), Gothenburg. By them she was renamed *Patricia* and had her accommodation modified to take some 112 first-, 80 second- and 52 third-class passengers. In this form she was used on the Company's London–Gothenburg mail service, operating with two larger turbine vessels which had come from the same shipyard—Swan Hunter's—in 1929.

After the outbreak of the Second World War this service had to be suspended and the two newer ships, the *Suecia* and *Britannia*, were accordingly laid up. The *Patricia*, however, was sold in 1940 to the Swedish Navy. Without change of name she was converted into a depot ship for submarines. To provide the extra accommodation needed not only for her own crew but those of her nine submarines—a total of 500 men —about 600 tons of steel were used. The cost of buying and converting such an elderly vessel (the total was estimated at £387,500) was the subject of some local criticism, but in her near-static role she has lasted well, still being in commission in 1970. Shipping history is full of strange twists and years later—in 1966—her two latter-day running mates, the *Suecia* and *Britannia*, were sold to Greece for use on an east–west Mediterranean service virtually that for which the *Patris II* had been built.

44 s.s. KARIMOEN, 1911, Holland

In pre-war years, twin masts were not generally found on British ships, the main exceptions being those of the Blue Funnel Line, but they became widely used by certain Dutch companies, mostly those which traded to the East. There, the resultant increase in derrick outreach was of particular value when cargo-handling operations were carried out in open roadsteads with an array of local craft alongside. In this and other respects the *Karimoen* was representative of many Dutch cargo liners built for service between Holland and what were then her possessions in the East Indies. In common with many of these she was also fitted out to carry pilgrims to and from Jeddah.

She was the lead ship of a class of five delivered to the Nederland Line (Stoomvaart

Maatschappij Nederland), Amsterdam, during the years 1911 and 1912. William Hamilton & Co. Ltd., of Port Glasgow, were responsible for both the *Karimoen* and *Karimata*, while the Northumberland Shipbuilding Co. Ltd. built the *Kangean*. The other two, the *Kambangan* and *Krakatau*, were built in Holland by the Rotterdam Dry Dock Co. and Fijenoord yard respectively. The main dimensions of the *Karimoen* were length o.a. 445·5 ft, length b.p. 430·8 ft, breadth mld 55 ft, and depth mld to shelter deck 37 ft 3 in. Her displacement was 14,500 tons and she could carry 9,556 tons d.w. on a draught of 28 ft 4 in. The gross measurement was 6,910 tons. She had two continuous decks beneath the shelter deck and her five holds were served by six hatches, 22 derricks and a similar number of steam winches. Her single-screw, triple-expansion machinery, of 4,500 i.h.p., was made by Dunsmuir & Jackson Ltd., Glasgow. It had cylinders of approximately 27½, 48 and 82¾ in. diameter and 53 in. stroke and took steam from two D.E. and two S.E. boilers at 215 p.s.i. The coal bunker capacity was just over 1,100 tons.

The *Karimoen* was launched on 30 June, 1911, and when she ran trials on 29 August she achieved a satisfying 14 knots, 2½ more than her designed service speed. She saw long service on the Eastern trade, but the recession of the early 'twenties caused her to be laid up at Amsterdam for a quite considerable time. Further employment on her old route followed, periodic calls at Jeddah being linked with the movement of pilgrims. In 1929–30 the Company took delivery of new cargo tonnage in the form of the *Poelau* and 'T' classes and, as the old year 1930 gave way to 1931, the *Karimoen*, *Karimata* and *Krakatau* were sold to become the *Waalkerk*, *Westerkerk* and *Wissekerk* of the United Netherlands Navigation Co., the two remaining ships subsequently going to breakers. During the course of 1931 the three 'W'-ships made a brief appearance on the Holland–Africa Line's service to the Cape and East Africa, but the *Waalkerk* was very soon withdrawn and laid up, again at Amsterdam. In 1933 she made a final come-back on the Eastern run, to make several extended voyages to Dairen for the Holland–East Asia Line, but in the Spring of 1934 she was sold to Dutch breakers and subsequently scrapped at Hendrik-Ido-Ambacht.

45 s.s. SPAARNDAM, 1922, Holland

At the time when the *Spaarndam* and her sisters were ordered, Europe was still suffering from the ravages of war and America enjoying an unparalled boom. For years emigration had been suspended and the lists of would-be passengers growing ever longer. So these four ships were built to meet an urgent need which, in the event, proved to be of relatively short duration.

In part compensation for the loss of a 32,000-ton liner ordered from Britain but which, because of the war, was never delivered, the Holland America Line had been awarded 60,000 tons of shipbuilding material. This was put towards the construction of a new fleet of ships ordered in Holland, the most numerous of which were the eight 6,800-ton (gross), B-class cargo liners. The *Spaarndam* and her three sisters *Edam*, *Leerdam* and *Maasdam* were originally intended as freighters of a rather larger design of which two, the *Gaasterdijk* and *Grootendijk*, were subsequently built. Instead, the designs of the four were modified to suit the requirements of the Company's Cuba–Gulf of Mexico service which had been reopened in 1919. The 'tween decks were fitted out to take emigrants, while part of the superstructure was raised one deck to provide extra cabin space. Further, to emphasise their passenger ship status, an extra, dummy, funnel was fitted. In this amended form the ships were able to carry some 174 cabin-class and 800 third-class passengers.

The *Maasdam Edam* and *Leerdam* were all delivered in 1921, each by a different shipyard, Fijenoord, Rotterdam, Royal de Schelde, Flushing and the New Waterway S.B. Co., Schiedam. The last named also built the *Spaarndam*, which was launched on 11 January, 1922. A single-screw steamship of 8,857 tons gross, she carried a deadweight of 11,400 tons on a draught of 30 ft 2 in. Her length overall was 466 ft, length b.p. 450 ft, breadth 58 ft and mld depth 40 ft. She had three continuous decks and six holds, the latter being served by 32 derricks. As was the case with her sisters, John Brown & Co. Ltd., Clydebank, supplied the propelling machinery. This comprised three steam turbines with D.R. gearing, also four S.E. boilers which were oil-fired and had a working pressure of 215 p.s.i. Their daily consumption was given as 37·5 tons and the total bunker capacity 1,790 tons. The service speed at 4,200 s.h.p. was about 13 knots.

On her maiden voyage the *Spaarndam* left Hamburg on 16 July, 1922, from Antwerp three days later and Vigo—after embarking emigrants—on 24 July. Exactly a month later she arrived at New Orleans after other calls which included Havana and Vera Cruz. In general this voyage pattern held good for several years, but some time prior to 1928 the number of cabin-class passengers carried was cut to 11 and that of the third-class raised to around 950. In December 1930 falling trade caused the *Spaarndam* to be laid up and for some years she remained idle at Rotterdam, joined for brief periods by one or more of her sisters as they skipped a voyage or two.

In 1934 it was decided to abolish the third-class accommodation but raise the number of cabin-class passengers to 28, these being given 14 outside cabins. At the same time the dummy funnel was removed. The *Spaarndam* was the last to be altered and it was 1935 before she returned to service. She and her sisters then operated with various of the B-class freighters, both on the Cuba–Mexico–Gulf service and, on occasion, to East Coast ports such as New York and Baltimore, also calling at London.

In November 1939, when almost at the end of a voyage from New Orleans to Rotterdam and Antwerp, the *Spaarndam* was passing through the British Contraband Control in the Thames Estuary when she was sunk by a magnetic mine. One of the first victims of this new weapon, she settled on a sandbank and caught fire. Four crew members and one passenger died, but the rest were safely rescued by a pilot boat. In June 1941 the *Maasdam* was torpedoed in the North Atlantic, but the other two remained with the Company until 1954 when they were sold to Far Eastern breakers.

46 s.s. KLIPFONTEIN, 1922, Holland

If only by their very appearance, the later generations of United Netherlands *-fontein* liners became such a well-known and accepted feature of the South African trade that one is apt to overlook the earlier vessels with which the foundations of their service were laid. The *Klipfontein* of 1922 was the first so named and the final ship to be built for the Hollandsche Zuid-Afrikaansche Stoomv. Maats., of Amsterdam, who opened the service.

The idea of starting a regular line between Holland and South Africa originated during during the First World War when, as a temporary measure, the Dutch East Indies mail steamers were diverted from the Suez to the Cape route. The outcome was the formation in 1919 of the H.Z.A. Chartered tonnage was first used and the initial sailing from Rotterdam was made by the *Rijndijk* in December 1919. The Company then bought three modern 5,000-ton steamers and with them initiated the *-fontein* style of naming. These were the *Jagersfontein* and *Rietfontein*, both of Japanese origin, and the Clyde-built *Randfondtein* which was bought immediately after her delivery to Norwegian owners in 1920. One elderly Elder Dempster ship was also acquired but, proving unsatisfactory, she was soon sold. A subsidy having been granted by the Dutch Government, two more new ships were bought in 1921-22. These were the 5,544-ton *Klipfontein*, the only turbine steamer in the fleet, and the *Springfontein* of 6,406 tons gross. Although the latter was the largest of all she was perhaps the less interesting in being a modified version of the Blue Star Line's *Empirestar*.

In her layout the *Klipfontein* was an early example of what was to become a very popular design of the 'twenties and early 'thirties. Characteristics of this were a short, topgallant forecastle, a split superstructure and five hatches. In her case the break in the superstructure was minimal, owing to the fact that the bridgehouse was extended forward and aft to provide the accommodation for her 34 passengers. The ship had a displacement of 13,545 tons and carried a deadweight of 8,710 tons on a draught of 26 ft 2 in. Her length b.p. was 402·4 ft, breadth 58·3 ft and depth of hold 26·4 ft. She had three decks and four holds (No. 2 hold had two hatches) and these were served by 10 steam winches and 10 derricks, one of which could handle 40-ton loads. The *Klipfontein* was built by the Rotterdam Dry Dock Co., but her two turbines were supplied by Metropolitan Vickers of Manchester, and these drove the single screw through D.R. gearing. At sea her three boilers used about 47 tons of coal per day. Her bunker capacity was 2,130 tons. The speed at 3,000 s.h.p. was 12½ knots.

The advent of the *Klipfontein*, whose launch took place on 8 February, 1922, brought the fleet up to six. Sailings were approximately monthly and, for a while, calls were made at S.W. African ports. Subsequent financial difficulties, largely the result of German competition, caused the management of the Company to be taken over by the United Netherlands Navigation Co. With the world depression the losses continued and in 1932 the Holland Zuid-Afrika Lijn—as it had become known—went into liquidation. Its fleet and service were bought by the other firm while, at the same time, the title of what had become a two-way, round-Africa service was restyled the Holland Afrika Lijn. In 1934 the delivery of the 10,000-ton motor-liners *Bloemfontein (II)* and *Jagersfontein (II)* led to the sale of first the *Rietfontein* and then—in 1935—the *Klipfontein*. Bought by Fratelli Rizzuto of Naples, the latter became first the *Gloriastar* and then, in 1935, the *Gloriastella*. As such she was sunk by an air attack off Benghazi on 17 September, 1940. Raised in 1949, she was scrapped at Spezia in the following year.

As to the colouring of the *Klipfontein*, she and the other early ships originally had grey hulls and black funnels, but for most of the time she was painted as shown. Of the house flag worn then, a description too vague for accurate portrayal referred to a springbok's head on an orange ground, with the circumscription 'Eendracht maakt Macht; Union is Strength', the motto of the Union of South Africa. For the final period under United Netherland ownership, the *Klipfontein* had a black-painted stack with orange band. Later the name *Klipfontein* was revived for a ship of 1939, one which remained with the company until 1953.

47   m.v. BALOERAN, 1929, Holland

Of all the ships portrayed in this book the *Baloeran* was the last to be built. Launched in 1929, she did not enter service until the following year. Seen historically, she and the *Dempo* of 1931 represented the penultimate stage in the development of the Rotterdam Lloyd passenger and mail liner. In their outward appearance these two could not be mistaken for anything built either before or afterwards, a pair unique in their distinguished shaping and dignity in relation to size. With passengers their reputation could hardly have been higher, although Suez Canal pilots thought otherwise.

Their opposite numbers in the rival Nederland fleet were the 19,000-ton, two-funnelled, *Johan Van Oldenbarneveld* and *Marnix Van St. Aldegonde* of 1930, a pair whose ponderous sounding names seemed in keeping with their impressive if somewhat inelegant external appearance. The Nederland pair, thus slightly larger, had a speed of 16¾ knots and carried over 100 more first-class passengers, the former's capacity being 338 first-, 281 second- and 64 third-class. But the earlier ships in both fleets were smaller. As regards the Rotterdam Lloyd (the additional word 'Royal' was not added until 1947) the sequence leading up to the *Baloeran* had been the 11,406-ton *Slamat* of 1924 (their last passenger steamship), and the motor liners *Indrapoera* (1925, 10,678 tons) and *Sibajak* (1927, 12,040 tons). Against these the *Baloeran* had a gross tonnage of 16,981, her net measurement being 10,062. She displaced 21,000 tons and carried a deadweight of 8,740 tons on a draught of 28 ft 4½ in. Her total cargo capacity was 335,857 cu. ft. The overall length was 574 ft (550 ft b.p.), breadth mld 70 ft and depth mld to upper deck 44 ft. She had twin screws, driven by two 10-cylinder, 2-stroke S.A. de Schelde-Sulzer diesels. These developed 14,000 b.h.p. at 102 r.p.m. and gave a maximum speed of 18½ knots. The *Baloeran* carried 234/252 first-class, 280/253 second-, 70 third- and 48 fourth-class passengers. Provision in the form of sofa berths was also provided for 48 children in the first-class. The crew (including 172 Javanese stewards) numbered 335.

One quite unique external feature was the step-in of the superstructure each side. This doubtless reduced Canal dues, besides giving a degree of shade to the top-grade cabins. The *Baloeran* was also one of the very earliest of the big liners to have her masts—quite divorced from derrick handling—placed so close to the funnel. Apart from two derricks worked from the bridge-front, electric cranes were used for cargo-handling, two for each of the four holds. One somewhat odd feature was the placing of the swimming pool on the forecastle. The accommodation for the several classes was divided vertically, the mainmast representing the approximate point of division between the first- and second-classes, this down through several decks. The third-class was right aft and rather lower and the fourth-class forward, under No. 2 hatch and the forecastle. The first-class cabins, for one and two persons, were all outside rooms and had no upper berths. They were spread over the bridge and upper decks amidships, a dozen more being above, on the promenade deck. Prominent features in the silvery grey topsides of the hull were the large closely spaced portholes of the first-class (forward) and second-class dining saloons whose sizes, incidentally, called for one and two sittings respectively. These were on the second deck which, at its after end, became the middle one of three devoted to the third-class cabins. The forward end of the promenade deck was glazed and inside this screen was the nearly circular, first-class saloon. Above it was another full-width promenade space and, one deck up and just before the funnel, the first-class sports deck. The two main second-class social rooms were at the base of the mainmast.

The *Baloeran* was launched at Rotterdam by the Fijenoord Shipbuilding Co. (Maatschappij voor Scheeps-en Werktuigbouw Fijenoord) on 29 August, 1929, and entered service in the Spring of 1930. The *Dempo*, like the *Baloeran*'s machinery, was built at Flushing, her launch taking place on 26 July 1930. Right up to the war the two ships operated on the Europe–Far Eastern service. Study of the Company's sailing list for 1938–39 shows three-weekly departures from Rotterdam, the sequence being *Baloeran*, *Sibajak*, *Dempo* and *Indrapoera*, in that order, with the *Slamat* operating independently. On one representative voyage the *Baloeran* left Rotterdam on Wednesday, 8 June, 1938, and arrived at Batavia (now Djakarta) on 7 July, having called en route at Southampton, Lisbon, Tangier, Gibraltar, Marseilles, Port Said, Suez, Colombo, Sabang, Belawan and Singapore. The *Baloeran* left Batavia on 20 July and arrived at Rotterdam on 16 August, sailing again on 31 August.

The two ships last met at Cape Town in September, 1939, the *Baloeran* then being homeward bound. Both became war losses. The *Baloeran*, damaged in May 1940 during the German raids on Rotterdam, was later taken over by the German Navy to become the hospital ship *Strassburg*. On 1 September, 1943, she hit a mine off Ymuiden and a fortnight or so later any faint hopes of salving her were destroyed by the work of British M.T.B.s The *Dempo* became an Allied troopship and was one of a Mediterranean convoy bound from Italy to North Africa when, on 17 March, 1944, she was sunk near the Algerian Coast, fortunately without loss of life.

48 s.s. SAN GUGLIELMO, 1911, Italy

The role of the *San Guglielmo* as an emigrant ship reflected Italy's long-term problems of poverty and over-population. From that country there was a steady outward flow of emigrants and this led to a rather larger than normal proportion of passenger ships. Below their top-grade accommodation most of these had extensive 'tween deck accommodation for would-be settlers. Prior to the year 1914 it was customary for many of Italy's passenger ships to be built in Britain, but this long sequence finally ended in 1925 with the belated delivery of a large prestige ship for the Lloyd Sabaudo.

The *San Guglielmo* was one of the last Italian emigrant ships to be built in Britain prior to the First World War and she represented this type at its pre-war best. Her owners. the 'Sicula Oceanica' Societa di Navigazione, had been founded in 1906 by the Fratelli Pierce, Guglielmo and Giorgio, who were then already well established as shipowners, At first the Company was based on Messina, but later it moved to Naples, even though the parent firm stayed on. The *San Guglielmo* was the third of a two-funnelled series to be ordered from the U.K. and these were used on the Company's New York and South American services. The first of these was the 6,392-ton *San Giorgio*, a 14-knot, 405 ft long ship delivered by Laing of Sunderland in 1907. A few months that same shipyard delivered the 430-ft long *San Giovanni*. Then, after an interval, came the yet longer *San Guglielmo*, which was launched into the Clyde by D. & W. Henderson & Co. on 29 March, 1911.

Like the others she was twin screw, but had a better turn of speed, 15 knots. Her length b.p. was 490 ft, breadth mld 56 ft and depth mld 36 ft 3 in. She was given two set of triple-expansion engines with cylinders of 25, 41 and 68¼ in. diameter and 48 in. stroke. Steam at 200 p.s.i. was supplied by six coal-fired S.E. boilers. The hull was of shelter deck type and the 74 ft long forecastle and 54 ft poop were joined by an unbroken deck, open beneath. Her derrick equipment was elaborate. In addition to those worked by a pair of forward king-posts, she had eight others (an unusually large number) mounted on the foremast and six on the mainmast.

Contemporary descriptions stressed the point that her equipment included an installation of Marconi wireless telegraphy, suitable for long distances. She carried 2,000 passengers in three classes. The first-class accommodation, on the promenade deck, included the usual range of public rooms, also several suites with bedroom, bathroom and living room. Besides these there were several rooms described as for the Italian Royal Commissioner. The second-class accommodation was on the promenade and shelter decks. The third-class passengers numbered about 1,800 and had their quarters in the 'tween decks and under the poop. For them there was a notably large dining saloon, over 130 ft long.

The three ships *San Guglielmo*, *San Giorgio* and *San Giovanni* made up a small, but well-balanced fleet, which was apparently well patronised. A yet larger passenger liner of about 12,000 tons gross, the *San Gennaro*, was ordered from an Italian yard during the war, but in 1917, before she was completed, the Sicula Oceanica Company lost its identity. Together with several other lines, it was absorbed into a new concern, the 'Transoceanica' Societa Italiana di Navigazione, which was formed at Naples by the N.G.I. (Nav. Generale Italiana), to whom the *San Gennaro* (renamed *Colombo*) was delivered. However, the *San Guglielmo* saw little service under the new regime, for on 8 January, 1918, she was torpedoed and sunk in the Gulf of Genoa. Many years later, in January 1932, the N.G.I. was, in turn, merged with two other trans-Atlantic lines to form the Italia Line.

49 s.s. SUWA MARU, 1914, Japan

For very many years the only Japanese passenger liners to be seen in Europe were those of the Nippon Yusen Kaisha. Except for some early units, the image which they presented was a remarkably unified one, since all those built for this service between 1908 and the mid-'twenties conformed to one basic style of profile. Known for their smartness, the N.Y.K. ships looked the better when the Company forsook its original all-black funnel, and to it added a broad white band and on this superimposed two slim red ones. Apart from a very gradual progression in size, there was little to distinguish one N.Y.K. passenger ship steamer from another, but of them all the *Suwa Maru* and her sister *Fushimi Maru* were the largest to be used on this trade.

The Nippon Yusen Kaisha (Japan Mail Steamship Co. Ltd.) which has its head-quarters at Tokyo, opened this service between Japan, Great Britain and the Continent in 1896, using the 5,000-ton *Tosa Maru*. Mails, passengers and cargo were carried and the itinerary included a very large number of ports. An ambitious building programme followed and this permitted fortnightly sailings. Although all the ships used were of three-island type, some had four masts and others—like the 6,000-ton *Awa Maru* of 1903—two only. She was joined in 1908 by three K. class ships of just under 8,000 tons, of which the *Kamo Maru* was the first. Five years elapsed before the next ones, the 9,800-ton *Katori Maru* and *Kashima Maru*. Then, in 1914, the year when the Great War started, the Company commissioned the *Suwa Maru*, *Fushimi Maru* and *Yasaka Maru*, these sisters being the first to exceed the 10,000-ton mark. The career of the *Yasaka Maru* was brevity itself, for in December 1915 she was sunk by torpedo in the Mediterranean. But the other two had long and successful careers.

The *Suwa Maru* had a gross tonnage of 10,672. Her displacement was 21,020 tons and d.w. cargo capacity 12,700 tons, the corresponding draught being 29 ft. The length b.p. was 516 ft, breadth 62·6 ft and depth mld 37·5 ft. She had six holds and two continuous and a third partial deck, this featuring in three of the holds. A twin screw ship, she was fitted with two sets of triple-expansion engines, with cylinders of 28, 47 and 79 in. diameter and 51 in. stroke. Steam was supplied by seven S.E. boilers working at 200 p.s.i. These used about 130 tons of coal per day, out of bunkers which could take just over 4,000 tons. The service speed was about 15½ knots but less, it would seem, in later years. Accommodation was provided for about 120 first- and 50 second-class passengers, also over 300 steerage or third—these presumably only when out East. Heading the first-class accommodation was one three-room suite, but in both the first- and second-classes the majority of the cabins were two-berth. All had electric fans. One permanent feature, then somewhat rare, was a large swimming pool on the upper deck.

Both she and the *Fushimi Maru* were built and engined by the Mitsubishi Shipbuilding & Engineering Works, the short-lived *Yasaka Maru* coming from the Kawasaki Dockyard. The *Suwa Maru* was launched at Nagasaki on 29 March, 1914, and delivered that September. During the First World War the Company diverted its European line ships from the Suez to the Cape route and later, in 1917, transferred its crack ships, including the *Suwa Maru* and *Fushimi Maru*, to trans-Pacific trade. By 1922, they were running once again to London and the Continent, together with four of a new, but slightly smaller class, all four of which had H names. These six formed the backbone of the London service right up to 1939. In November of that year the m.v. *Terukuni Maru* (one of two squat-funnelled ships built 1930) was sunk after hitting a mine in the Thames Estuary. As a result of this disaster the N.Y.K. passenger service was suspended —for good. Within a few years, as a follow-on to the Japanese attack on Pearl Harbour, her merchant fleet, then used for other purposes, was decimated. Both the *Suwa Maru* and the *Fushimi Maru* were torpedoed in 1943 by American submarines. The former was sunk near Wake Island on 28 March, and the latter near Japan on the first day of February.

50   s.s. ARABIA MARU, 1918, Japan

Among the world's shipbuilding nations Japan was a latecomer. Impetus to expand on any scale only came with the First World War, during which many new shipyards were established. Under a wartime agreement Japan was supplied with large quantities of steel from America, her yards paying for this with new standard-type cargo ships. This brought Japan much needed supplies for the expansion and rejuvenation of her merchant fleet, much of which was then very elderly. Largest of all the merchant ships built during that period for home ownership were the several passenger/cargo liners of the *Arabia Maru* class, the last of which were delivered in 1920. The only merchantmen of larger size ever built there had been a handful of fast passenger and mail ships commissioned in 1911–14 for trans-Pacific service and the Nippon Yusen Kaisha line to Europe. But of their own particular category the *Arabia Maru* and her sisters were the largest and finest under the Japanese flag.

At the time of their construction most Japanese ships were owned by small companies. A fleet of 24 was considered large and above that figure there were only the K. Line, which in 1920 owned 48, the giant Nippon Yusen Kaisha (102) and, greatest of all, the owners of the *Arabia Maru*, the Osaka Shosen Kaisha, which, in that year 1920, had 124 steamships. Seen in retrospect, her profile—with its raised forecastle and poop and basically low superstructure—has an interest of its own, since it belonged only to that period and was only found under the Japanese flag.

The *Arabia Maru* was the fourth in her series. The first ready was the 9,482-ton *Hawaii Maru* of 1915, the only one to be built by the Kawasaki Dockyard Co. Then came the sequence built at Nagasaki by the Mitsubishi Zosen Kaisha, the *Manila Maru* (1915), *Africa Maru* and *Arabia Maru* (both 1918). The final pair, *Arizona Maru* and *Alabama Maru* (both 1920), differed slightly in having a longer forecastle and an extra pair of king-posts. As built the *Arabia Maru* had a gross tonnage of 9,500, but this was later reduced to 9,414. She carried a deadweight of 11,500 tons on a draught of 28 ft 3 in., this corresponding to a displacement of about 17,475 tons. She and the others measured 475 ft b.p. × 61 ft breadth × 40·7 ft depth of hold.

Twin screws were driven by triple expansion machinery, with cylinders of 27, 44½ and 75 in. diameter and 48 in. stroke. Five S.E. boilers supplied steam at 200 p.s.i. In their original state as coal-burners the ships had a bunker capacity of over 2,700 tons and used about 85 tons per day. But in 1924 all six were converted to burn oil. References as to power and speed vary greatly. The builders of the *Arabia Maru* quote a maximum of 8,153 i.h.p. and a trial speed, obviously in ballast condition, of 16·26 knots; in service it was probably about 13–14. There were three continuous decks, with an extra one in the forward hold. Six holds and hatches were served by 17 derricks and 16 steam winches. Although basically a cargo carrier, the *Arabia Maru* had accommodation for 42 first-class passengers, as well as 314 (later 125) third-class. The latter had their quarters on the main deck where, starting from amidships, four dormitories extended aft, over the last three holds.

The *Arabia Maru* was laid down in May 1917 and launched on 30 March, 1918. Thereafter things speeded up and the ship was delivered exactly a month later. Like her sisters, she was immediately put on the North Pacific trade, the main ports served being Kobe, Shanghai, Yokohama, Hong Kong, Tacoma, Seattle and Vancouver. In the mid 'twenties the Company broke fresh ground by starting a service between Japan and the River Plate, via Colombo and ports in East and South Africa. The *Arabia Maru* and others of her class were transferred to this, their sailings alternating with those of several newly built motorships. The *Alabama Maru*, the final ship in the series, was the first to be lost, this by stranding in 1930. The rest were all sunk during the Second World War, two in 1942 and the others in 1944. The *Arabia Maru*, then acting as a transport, was some 100 miles East of Manila when, on 18 October, 1944, she was torpedoed by a U.S. submarine.

51   s.s. BRANT COUNTY, 1915, Norway

In most ships there is an element of conformity and linkage with her period and trade. But no so with the *Brant County*, whose two slim, closely spaced funnels represented a reversion to a much earlier style. Of all the ships regularly employed on the North Atlantic, where she spent nearly all her life, no other could boast quite such a profile. With but the fewest exceptions, notably the *Howick Hall* (plate 11), this close spacing of funnels on cargo ships had been associated with just one firm. This was the D.A.D.G. (Deutsch-Australisch D.G.) or German Australian Line who, years earlier, just before and after the turn of the century, had built a number of cargo liners with this 'twin woodbine' profile.

That the *Brant County* was laid down to D.A.D.G. account is known, but why they should revert to an arrangement discarded years earlier remains something of a mystery. The censorship associated with war leaves many questions unanswered. The *Brant County*'s date of construction is given as 1915, but whether this was the year of her launching or completion is not known. More probably it was the former. Her intended name was *Mulhausen*, which conformed to D.A.D.G. policy, yet she was completed as the *Lennep*, apparently named after a Dutch fiction writer of the nineteenth century. Such a choice suggests that there had been ideas of a sale to Holland. To turn to the known facts, the ship was built and engined by the Akt. Ges. Neptun of Rostock. Her main dimensions were length b.p. 419·9 ft, breadth 54·1 ft and depth of hold 26·3 ft. The load draught was 24 ft 11 in. She had two decks and five hatches and was propelled by a set of triple-expansion engines with cylinders of approximately 30, 48¾ and 80¾ in. diameter and 55 in. stroke. The four, single-ended boilers had a working pressure of 213 p.s.i. The coal bunker capacity was 845 tons, with reserve space for a further 1,070 tons. Her speed, it would seem, was never shown in reference books, but her passage times suggest an average of 11/12 knots. Her d.w. tonnage was 7,937. As to gross measurement, this was originally 4,972, later 5,289 and finally 5,001.

As the *Lennep* she was surrendered to Great Britain in 1919 and managed on behalf of the Shipping Controller by F. C. Strick & Co. Ltd. In March 1921, while lying at

Swansea, she was one of a batch of some 70 ex-German ships offered for sale to British nationals. Bought by Coull & Sons, Newcastle, she was renamed *Brant County* and re-sold that year to become the largest ship of the Bergen Steamship Co. Ltd. (Det Bergenske Dampsskibsselskab). Her red, white and black funnel markings were not theirs, but were linked with a venture started by Canada Steamship Lines, Ltd., Montreal who, in May 1921, announced the opening of a regular cargo liner service between the St. Lawrence and Europe; the Continental ports eventually settled on being Hamburg, Rotterdam, Antwerp and Le Havre. The new company was advertised as the Inter-Continental Transport Services Ltd. but—if memory serves—it became known familiarly as the County Line. The ships used, generally renamed after Canadian counties, were chartered from Norwegian firms like Mowinckel, Westfal Larsen, Bergen Steamship, L. W. Hansen and Olaf Orvig. On this service the *Brant County* spent the rest of her career. On 11 March, 1943, while carrying 670 tons of explosives, she was torpedoed in mid-Atlantic when U-boats attacked her convoy which was bound from Halifax to the U.K. Small wonder that 35 of those on board lost their lives.

52 s.s. STAVANGERFJORD, 1918, Norway

Few North Atlantic liners have given quite such excellent and long sustained service as this ship, which spent the whole of her 45-year-long career with the company for whom she was built. As is normal for such vessels, her accommodation was many times modified to suit current trends. What was less usual was the manner in which engine room alterations were able to add appreciably to her original speed.

She was the third ship to be built for the Norwegian America Line (Den Norske Amerikalinje A/S). It was in June 1913 that this company opened its service between Christiania (Oslo), Bergen and New York with the *Kristianiafjord*, a newly completed liner of 10,669 tons gross. She was joined a few months later by her sister *Bergensfjord* and results were such that in January 1915 an order was placed for the *Stavangerfjord*. As for the earlier pair, the shipbuilders chosen were Cammel Laird & Co. Ltd., of Birkenhead. Because of the strain imposed on shipyards by mounting war losses at sea, the Admiralty caused the contract to be cancelled, but rescinded their decision after strong representations had been made by the Norwegian Government. Soon after her launch—on 21 March, 1917—disaster befell the *Kristianiafjord* which, in mid-July, stranded and became a total loss near Cape Race, fortunately without loss of life. Slightly larger than the first pair which measured 512 ft b.p. × 61 ft, the *Stavangerfjord*'s main dimensions were length b.p. 532 ft 6 in. (553 ft o.a.), breadth mld 64 ft. and depth mld 32 ft 6 in. Her gross tonnage was 12,977 (subsequently raised to 13,156 and finally 14,015) and displacement approximately 17,300 tons. The load draught was 27 ft 3 in. and the corresponding deadweight 7,300 tons. For cargo she had six holds and corresponding 'tween deck spaces. Twin screws were driven by quadruple expansion machinery of 9,500 i.h.p. This had cylinders of $26\frac{1}{2}$, $37\frac{1}{2}$, 53 and 76 in. diameter and 56 in. stroke and took steam at 220 p.s.i. from 8 S.E. boilers. As a coal-burner the ship carried 3,560 tons and consumed about 165 tons daily, but some years later, in 1924, she was converted to oil. Initially her speed was given as $15\frac{1}{2}$ knots, but in later years the figures quoted were as high as 17.

When new, the *Stavangerfjord* carried 88 first-, 318 second- and 820 third-class passengers. In the early 'thirties her accommodation was remodelled to take 145 cabin and 200 tourist, the third-class remaining as before. Various minor changes were made in later years and by the time she was nearing the end of her career her capacity had been cut to 88 first-class, 182 cabin- and 411 tourist-class. One useful engine-room change made in the 'thirties was the installation of an exhaust L.P. turbine with D.R. gearing and hydraulic coupling.

Right through the 'twenties and 'thirties the *Stavangerfjord* operated with the older *Bergensfjord*, although she did make the occasional North Cape cruise. In June 1938 the Company commissioned a fine new motorliner, the 18,673-ton *Oslofjord* and as a result during the following winter it was possible to withdraw and modernise the *Stavangerfjord*. One external change made then was the replacement of her old tall, thin funnels (which reached to crosstree level) by slightly shorter, stouter ones. At the time of the Norwegian occupation her running mates *Bergensfjord* and *Oslofjord* were safe on the other side of the Atlantic. The former became an Allied troopship, and although she survived the war she did not return to N.A.L. service. Nor did the *Oslofjord*, whose brief career ended in December 1940. Meanwhile the *Stavangerfjord* had arrived at Oslo in December 1939, there to be caught by the invading forces who used her as billets for the Wehrmacht.

Soon after the war had ended she was used as a repatriation ship. Once this was finished she was overhauled and put back on the New York run. On this she operated alone until 1949, when the new *Oslofjord (II)* was put in service. When two years later another new ship, the *Bergensfjord (II)*, was commissioned, the *Stavangerfjord* was given another major refit. In 1963 she was finally withdrawn and in mid-December she left Oslo for Hong Kong. She arrived on 4 February, 1964, and was there broken up by the Shun Fung Iron Works.

53   m.v. SARDINIA, 1920, Norway

With the *Selandia* and *Suecia* of 1912, the Scandinavians established a world lead in the operation of diesel-driven, ocean-going cargo liners. These nations had besides long been the homes of many fruit-carrying steamers, small vessels which relied on a good turn of speed and extra, well-ventilated holds for the carriage of their perishable cargoes. Their employment was perforce confined to shorter routes, such as the Mediterranean and Canary Islands, from which they would return with fruit to Northern Europe and Britain. Many others operated in the Caribbean on long-term charter to American firms such as United Fruit. Although in Scandinavia the application of diesels was extended to include some tankers and tramps, there was a considerable interval before this type of machinery was fitted in fruiters. The Norwegian-owned *Sardinia* of 1920 was thus among the forerunners of the present great Scandinavian fruitship fleet. Even so, some further years elasped before such ships were given refrigerating plant and it was after this that large-scale construction got under way.

The *Sardinia* was one of several ordered from a Dutch yard, that of J. & K. Smit, by Otto and Thor Thoresen A/S, of Christiania (now Oslo). The latter were managers of two separate fleets, one (mainly fruiters) which had 'S'-names and which were owned by the Otto Thoresen Line and those which wore the different livery of the Thor Thoresen Line and had names ending in *-fos*. The first of the series was the engines-aft *San Miguel* which was soon joined by the rather larger twins *Sardinia* and *San Andres*. The *Sardinia*, which was launched in October 1920 and delivered early in 1921, had a gross tonnage of 2,060 and carried 3,000 tons d.w. on a draught of 19 ft 3½ in. Her length overall was 315 ft (302 ft b.p.), breadth 42 ft and depth 20 ft 4 in. A single-decker, she had four holds and five hatches, these being served by ten winches and derricks. Accommodation was provided for eight passengers. She had a single screw which was driven by what was then the largest type of Werkspoor engine. This was of 4-stroke, single-acting type and had 6 cylinders of 670 mm diameter and 1,200 mm stroke. Its output at 110 r.p.m. was 1,650 b.h.p., this giving a speed of 11 knots in loaded condition.

Initially the *Sardinia* operated with a new steamship of similar size, the *San Jose*, on a regular service between Las Palmas and London. However, in 1921, the Otto Thoresen Line, its title and its ships were bought by Fred. Olsen & Co., also of Christiania. As built the *Sardinia* had her very thin funnel painted plain yellow, but the Fred. Olsen house flag was now painted on it—and also on the hull forward, where it replaced the Thoresen design. Sometime later the Company became known as the Spanish Line (D/S A/S Spanskelinjen), then Den Norske Middelhavslinjen. The *Sardinia* remained with them until 1957 when she was sold for service under the Liberian flag. Her new owners were a Panamanian-registered concern, the Cia. de Nav. Epos S.A., which was operated by A. Scufalos of Montevideo. A year later, somewhat belatedly, she was renamed *Georgios S*. In 1961 she was again sold, this time to the associated Cia. de Nav. Pelagos, who gave her the name *Stefanos*. Another year went by and she again changed hands, being bought by a firm headed by M. Scufalos of Piraeus, who renamed her *Egli*. This name she bore only briefly, for in February 1963, while bound from Thessaloniki to Alexandria, her cargo of pyrites shifted causing the ship to heel over and sink.

54 s.s. CUNENE, ex-ADELAIDE, 1911, Portugal

This ship has a two-fold claim to interest. First as an example of a cargo liner design very popular in Germany during the years prior to the First World War, secondly as one of the many ships lost to that nation through wartime seizure by former neutrals, the intake of which helped to start new merchant fleets. For the German merchant fleet the years which led up to the First World War were ones of great expansion. An aggressive trade policy resulted in the construction of many fine cargo liners and others, quite apart from those built for the furtherance of trade between Germany and her overseas possessions.

At the end of the war and under the Treaty of Versailles Germany was stripped of all merchant ships of 1,600 tons gross and over. However, even before that she had lost many which, at the outset, had sought refuge in neutral ports, only to be seized when their host nations came into the war. On the other side of the Atlantic, the American intake was about 90 ships, while of the various Latin American countries Brazil gained about half that number. In Europe, Italy seized about three dozen vessels and the Portuguese rather more, the latter's merchant fleet being greatly rejuvinated in the process. In the 'twenties and after, there were therefore many cargo ships and others which had seen only brief service under German ownership but which were to have long careers under other flags. In this respect the steamship *Adelaide* was very typical, her initial five years under German colours being followed by nearly forty years as the Portuguese-owned *Cunene*. She was also interesting because of her layout and general shaping, since parallels to these showed in the *Brant County* (*see* plate 51).

For many years national design characteristics showed very strongly in German-built vessels. This applied to basic layout and also the shaping of equipment and detail. Once one became familiar with these, German origin was obvious, whatever colours the ship might be wearing. In this respect the *Adelaide*/*Cunene* was likewise representative of an important and essentially German style. Of all the various 'hallmarks' incorporated in her appearance, the very short, forward well deck was one, also the casing at the funnel base. So, too, was the shaping of the bridgehouse which, despite its large size, had no lifeboats. Instead, the boats were arranged three aside on the fidley (the after mass), an arrangement which was peculiarly German. Another design feature associated with that period and one especially favoured by the ship's original owners, the D.A.D.G. (Deutsche Australische Dampshciffahrts Ges.), was the positioning of the funnel, etc., slightly forward of amidships. Thus, contrary to usual practice, the majority of the hatches were aft, not forward, of the machinery space. While this probably aided trim, it also resulted in an unduly long propeller shaft.

The ship's original owners, the D.A.D.G., alternatively the German–Australian Line, were then one of Germany's major shipping companies. Their main services were from the Continent to South Africa, Australia and Java, also to the Straits, India, etc. It was formed in 1888 and lasted until 1926 when its fleet was absorbed into that of the Hamburg America Line. The *Adelaide* was one of a group of four, all with Australian names, which were built and engined in 1911–12 by the Flensburger Schiffbau Ges. She had a gross tonnage of 5,898 (5,875 when *Cunene*) and carried 8,825 tons d.w. on a draught of 25 ft 3 in. Her length b.p. was 450 ft, breadth mld 58 ft and depth mld 29·5 ft. She had two continuous decks with a third one in the forward hold. She had a single screw and triple-expansion machinery of 4,000 i.h.p. Steam at 185 p.s.i. was supplied by four S.E. coal-fired boilers. Their daily consumption was around 58 tons and the bunker capacity just over 2,400 tons. The service speed was about 12 knots.

The *Adelaide*'s brief career as such ended in 1916 when the ship, then at Loanda, was seized by the Portuguese Government and renamed *Cunene*. She remained under government ownership until 1925 when, after a long period of idleness, she was taken over by the then four-year old Sociedade Geral de Commercio, Industria e Transportes, of Lisbon, and with them she remained for the rest of her life. Mainly she traded to South America, both the East and West coasts, but she also made the occasional voyage to Portuguese African ports. In her later years, however, she was generally used on the Gulf trade. Her final voyage ended on the last day of 1954 when she arrived at Dunston-on-Tyne to be broken up. By that time she had outlived the last of her sisters by fourteen years.

55   s.s. INFANTA ISABEL, 1912, Spain

The *Infanta Isabel* was the first of two handsome Spanish transatlantic liners which were built on the Clyde in 1912–14. Their owners, Pinillos, Izquierdo y Cia. of Cadiz, had long been established in the trade between Spain and the Americas and since 1890 had spent much money with Clydeside builders. An early and well-known series built there had been the three two-funnelled, *Manila*-class ships of 1895. Then had followed a long Connell-built sequence, which culminated in the completion in 1908 of the 5,600-ton sisters *Barcelona* and *Cadiz*. Their design formed the basis of the much larger *Infanta Isabel* and *Principe de Asturias* which, however, were built by Russell & Co. of Port Glasgow. The latter, incidentally, represented the end of an important phase: not only was she the last passenger ship to be built for the Pinillos Line but—of greater significance—she was the final Spanish passenger liner to come from British builders, orders thereafter being given to newly emergent Spanish shipyards.

The *Infanta Isabel*, which was built to the highest specification of Lloyd's Register, had a gross tonnage of 8,182 and was designed to carry saloon passengers, emigrants and cargo. Her main dimensions were length b.p. 459·5 ft, breadth mld 58 ft, and depth mld 32 ft. Fully laden at 5,300 tons d.w. she had a draught of 26 ft 1 in. Beneath the shade deck she had three continuous decks, with a fourth one in the forward hold. Her twin screws were driven by a pair of Rowan-built quadruple-expansion engines, with cylinders of 24½, 35, 50 and 72 in. diameter and 51 in. stroke. These took steam at 215 p.s.i. from three D.E. and two S.E. boilers. Always a coal-burner, she had bunker space for nearly 2,000 tons. She was launched at Port Glasgow on 29 June 1912, and was delivered in the early Autumn.

Like the rest of the Pinillos fleet, the *Infanta Isabel* was intended for use between Barcelona, other Spanish ports and the Americas. Although the war which soon followed brought greatly increased profits and traffic to neutrals, the Company's fortunes were hit by two very severe losses. The first happened one night in March 1916, when the *Principe de Asturias*, the newest in the fleet and then bound from Barcelona and Las Palmas for Buenos Aires, hit a rock and sank within five minutes, taking with her over 400 of her complement. The second tragedy came in 1919, when the *Valbanera*, a 13-year-old ship of 5,099 tons gross, foundered with the loss of 488 lives. From then on the *Infanta Isabel* was the centrepiece of a small and otherwise elderly fleet. Voyage reports show that during the early 'twenties she operated between Spanish ports, Havana, Galveston and New Orleans. However, largely as a result of the earlier disasters, the Company went into liquidation. About 1925 the *Infanta Isabel* and three other vessels were taken over by the Cia. Transoceanica de Navegaceon of Barcelona, but only to be soon dispersed. In August 1926 the *Infanta Isabel* was sold to Japan and later the following month she left Hamburg on her final voyage from a European port. This lasted eight weeks and it was only after her arrival at Kobe that her new owners, the Osaka Shosen Kaisha, changed her name. She then became the *Midzuho* (later *Mizuho*) *Maru* and joined two other recent purchases from Europe on the Company's Formosa Line, the three running regularly between Kobe and Keelung. Years later, during the Japanese war with China, the ship was used as a troop transport. She was classified as a hospital ship during the Second World War; whether she was used in that capacity is not known, but in September 1944 she was torpedoed and sunk by a U.S. submarine when off the North coast of Luzon.

56 s.s. REINA VICTORIA-EUGENIA, 1913, Spain

This liner, of 10,136 tons gross, was the first of a pair delivered in 1913 to the Compania Trasatlantica, of Barcelona. She was built on the Tyne by Swan, Hunter & Wigham Richardson, Ltd and ran trials in February. Those of her Clyde-built sister, the 10,348-ton *Infanta Isabel de Borbon*, followed a month later. Compared with the Company's previous ships, the two represented a tremendous advance, both as regards size and appointments, and until the early 'twenties they remained Spain's most important merchant ships.

At the time of their construction the Cia. Trasatlantica owned nearly 20 steamers. Generally these were of considerable age; most of them dated back to the 'eighties, one being even older. Prior to the advent of the new pair, the Company's largest and least elderly was the 6,748-ton passenger ship *Alfonso XII* of 1890, originally the N.D.L.-owned *Havel*. The need for new ships was then urgent if the Company was to retain its status as Spain's premier line and meet steadily growing competition from the Pinillos Line. Most of the C.T.A.'s activities were centred in the Central American and Caribbean areas. New York featured in their itinerary, but generally it was merely a port of call. Also of major importance was a service from Barcelona and other Mediterranean ports to South America, and it was for this that the two new ships were designed.

Like so many pairs built by different yards, the two liners showed variation in detail, even though their main hull dimensions were alike. The Denny-built ship differed outwardly in having a shorter funnel and cowl tops to her king-posts. At the time when they were ordered the geared turbine had still to prove itself. For large vessels the use of combination machinery was then still popular, steam for the two wing reciprocating engines being passed through an L.P. turbine, which drove a centre-line screw. Although the Clyde-built ship conformed to this practice, the *Reina*'s builders recommended a quadruple-screw layout as more efficient. Thus her two 4-cylinder, triple-expansion engines were flanked by L.P. turbines of Parsons design which drove wing propellers. Steam was provided by 7 single-ended boilers working at 180 p.s.i.

On 7 February, 1913, the *Reina Victoria-Eugenia* ran trials in a half-loaded condition, her displacement being 10,181 tons. Despite bad weather, she averaged 18·12 knots at 10,840 h.p. (reciprocating engines 7,340 i.h.p., turbines 3,500 s.h.p.). During consumption trials, a week later she averaged, in a fully laden state (13,229 tons displacement) 16·10 knots at 7,917 h.p. her daily fuel consumption working out at 95 tons. Compared with triple- and quadruple-expansion machinery, this was hailed as representing savings of 20 per cent and 25 per cent respectively.

The *Reina* had six decks and her four holds were served by eight 5-ton and eight 7-ton derricks. Her length overall was 498 ft (480 ft b.p.), breadth mld 60 ft and depth mld (to shade deck) 43·9 ft. She was fitted to carry 200 first-, 46 interchangeable, 100 second- and 80 third-class passengers, also 1,640 emigrants. Her officers and crew numbered about 250. As was then usual, the first-class public rooms were in various styles of decor, the most notable being Louis XVI, Georgian and Jacobean.

The First World War brought great profits to the neutrals and for a while both the *Reina* and her sister appear to have been diverted to the New York trade. During the post-war period they saw constant service on the Spain–River Plate run. The two provided monthly sailings, the passage from Barcelona to Buenos Aires taking 18–20 days. Political changes caused both ships to be renamed in 1931, the *Reina Victoria-Eugenia* becoming the *Argentina* and the other the *Uruguay*. However, the service continued unbroken until the summer of 1932, when the two were finally laid up at Barcelona. There, as units of the Republican merchant fleet, both were sunk during air attack in January 1939. Raised that autumn, they were considered fit only for scrap.

57 m.v. INFANTA BEATRIZ, 1928, Spain

The 6,279-ton *Infanta Beatriz* had a special claim to interest in being the first motor passenger ship to be built for Spain. Her owners were the Cia. Trasmediterranea, a large concern which, at the time of her delivery, owned about 60 ships. It had been formed in 1916 by the amalgamation of many small provincial companies, each with a different base port and sphere of operations. The ships thus brought together under single ownership included units from the Maritima Barcelona, Gijonesa, Islana Maritima, Menorquina, Navegaceon e Industria, Tintore, Valenciana and Vinuesa fleets. Together they made up a very mixed collection, mainly elderly and of small size. With this material the newly formed Cia. Trasmediterranea had to take over and rationalise a network of mail, passenger and cargo services which not only linked ports along the coast of Spain but also extended to the Balearic Islands, Africa and the Canaries.

Quite a number of ships were added to the fleet during the first few years, but few of them were of any great size or interest. Among the various elderly vessels modernised was the 1,203-ton *Jatina* (built 1880) which was re-engined in 1922 to become the Company's first motorship. The results paid off, for despite her age she lasted another eleven years. In the late 'twenties the Company's policy underwent radical change and the *Infanta Beatriz* was the highlight of a new and ambitious building programme which consisted solely of passenger-carrying motorships.

The order for the *Infanta Beatriz* and her machinery was placed with Fried Krupp

A.G. of Kiel and she was completed in February 1928. Her design was based on a very successful pair, the *Rio Bravo* and *Rio Panuco* which that yard had built in 1924 for the Germany–West Indies trade. The main outward difference lay in the height of the funnels, those of the new ship being rather shorter. Many years later they were replaced by a single one of greater width. The main dimensions of the *Infanta Beatriz* were length overall 410 ft, (393·3 ft b.p.) breadth 52 ft, and depth of hold 25·4 ft. The load draught was 21 ft 6 in., this corresponding to a deadweight of 5,200 tons. She had twin screws and these were driven by two 6-cylinder, 2-stroke, S.A. Krupp diesels which developed 4,340 b.h.p. at 110 r.p.m. and gave a speed of about 14 knots. The ship was designed for service to and from the Canary Islands and her holds were therefore fitted for the carriage of bananas. Her first-class accommodation was remarkably good. Besides two luxury staterooms it included an unusually large proportion of single cabins, 47 in all, the other 84 passengers in this class having 2- or 3-bed cabins. In the second- and third-classes she carried 38 and 60 respectively. The crew numbered about 90.

In 1931 the Company introduced a new naming policy which affected many of its better ships. In this the names of cities replaced those of personages and so the *Infanta Beatriz* became instead the *Ciudad de Sevilla*. The savage civil war of the 'thirties was nearly over when in January 1939 the ship, then at Barcelona, was bombed and sunk by aircraft. Duly raised and refitted, she saw another long spell of commercial service. About 1960–61 she was again out of commission for some considerable while, this time for further modernisation. This, however, did not affect her external shaping. A final period on the Canaries run ended in 1965 and in the winter of 1965–66 she was sold to breakers at Puerto de Santa Maria.

58 s.s. ATLAND, 1910, Sweden

Of the various types of merchant ships in vogue during the early part of this century, the turret steamer was probably the most revolutionary. Below the waterline its hull was of conventional form, but above that level its shape in section could be likened to a wide jar with the neck occupying just over half the total width—this being flanked by horizontal shoulders.

Once owners had overcome their initial suspicion they found that the turret ship offered many real advantages, notably lower deadweight and cubic capacity, which resulted in lower port dues, an important economic factor. The design also combined great strength with a reduced amount of steel. Vulnerable openings such as hatches were placed higher on the central (turret) deck and this turret proved an excellent feeder for cargo, while the curved gunwales below made for easy stowage of bulk cargoes. Another point in its favour was that water could not lodge on deck in a position where it might tend to capsize the vessel.

The Sunderland shipbuilding firm of William Doxford & Sons was responsible for the design of the 'turret deck steamer' as it was officially styled. The construction of this type formed the greater part of this Company's output from the early nineties up to 1911, when production ceased. Over that period Doxford's delivered 178 turret ships, but besides these there were a very few others built elsewhere under licence, at least one on the Tyne and one in Spain.

The prototype, which had engines aft, measured 280 ft b.p. × 38 ft, and those which followed soon after showed no great difference in size, although some had machinery amidships. Later, however, the turret form of hull was applied to several size groups, the largest and most bizarre-looking being some engines-aft ships which were built for the ore trade. To speed the handling of cargo these were given a great array of twin masts and one, the 440-ft long ship *Grangesberg* of 1903, boasted seven pairs. Numerous twin masts were also a feature of a few large, engines-amidships cargo ships. Again, other turret steamers were built not as single-deckers but with an extra internal ('tween) deck.

In retrospect, however, all these can be seen as the exception to the general style, for the very great majority were two-masted, single-deck ships like the *Atland*. Completed in 1910, and therefore one of the last of the series, she was also one of the most successful. Never sold or renamed, she remained with her original owners right throughout the whole of her 33-year-long career. Her owners, the Tirfing S.S. Co. Ltd., were then, as now, the leading member of the well-known Brostrom Group of companies, whose headquarters are at Gothenburg.

The seventh and largest turret ship to be built for them, the *Atland* was launched on 24 April, 1910, and ran trials on 15 June, when she attained a speed of 12·75 knots. She was built to British Corporation classification and had a gross tonnage of 5,029 (latterly 5,203) her d.w. capacity on a draught of 27 ft 2 in. being 8,000 tons. Her length b.p. was 388·9 ft, breadth 52·4 ft and depth mld 29 ft. Doxfords supplied both the hull and machinery, the latter comprising a set of triple expansion engines of 2,200 i.h.p. with cylinders of 26, 42 and 68 in. diameter and 48 in. stroke. Her total coal capacity was 1,778 tons and her daily consumption about 32 tons. For cargo she had three holds and six hatches, which were served by 12 derricks and steam winches. Her water ballast capacity was 3,000 tons. Like the Company's other turret ships she was mainly used for the carriage of iron ore, in particular from Narvik. However, war upset the normal pattern of trading and her career ended on 25 March, 1943, when she was sunk in a convoy collision near Peterhead while on a voyage from Freetown and New York to London.

Not long after the *Atland* was built, changes in Board of Trade rules enabled a new type, the open shelter-deck steamer, to be built with large capacity and low tonnage and so, in 1911, the construction of turret steamers ceased.

59   s.s. TIVIVES, 1911, U.S.A.

The association between the Belfast shipbuilding firm of Workman Clark & Co. and the United Fruit Co. of Boston started in 1903 and continued for nearly thirty years. The outcome was some of the most handsome passenger and cargo ships ever built. While the prime function of these vessels was the carriage of bananas from ports in the Central American/Caribbean area to the U.S.A., this type of voyage had obvious passenger appeal. So, after the first three ships, which carried up to 18 passengers apiece, the great majority of those which followed were given a considerable amount of first-class accommodation.

Although air competition eventually killed this side of the United Fruit Co's business, their ships were indeed the ancestors of the present international fleet of cruise liners now operating in that area. In terms of aesthetics pride of place went to a series of ships, numbering over a dozen, which were built during the years 1908–11, subsequent classes never quite equalling their good looks. Within this main group experience in service naturally led to minor improvements and, as a result, the final ships built in 1911, the *Tivives* among them, were probably the most handsome.

Her main dimensions were length overall 394 ft (378·8 ft b.p.), breadth 50·3 ft and depth of hold 29·1 ft. Her cargo space comprised eight insulated compartments, the fruit being kept in condition by cooled air driven through ducts by electric fans. Cargo could be handled either through deck hatches or side doors in the hull. The main propelling machinery comprised a set of triple-expansion engines of 3,000 i.h.p. and five Scotch boilers which worked under forced draught. The result was a speed of about 13 knots. Her gross tonnage was 5,017 and her d.w. capacity approximately 4,500 tons, this on a draught of 24 ft 10 in. Accommodation was provided for over 100 first-class passengers. A number of the staterooms were arranged for use as family suites, while she also had two *cabines-de-luxe*. Public rooms, besides the dining saloon and entrance hall, comprised a music room, lounge and smoke room.

The *Tivives* ran successful trials off Belfast on 27 October, 1911, and then proceeded to Holyhead to embark passengers for her first voyage to the West Indies. Despite actual American ownership she, like all others of her class, was registered at Glasgow in the name of the Tropical Fruit S.S. Co. Ltd., of that port. This arrangement continued for some years and resulted from the framing of American legislation which denied U.S. registration to any but home-built ships. During later service under the Stars and Stripes, minor changes were made to the title of the owning company; in 1920 this was known as the United Fruit Co. Line, but by 1939 it had become the United Fruit S.S. Corporation.

The *Tivives* and her sisters were primarily associated with the West Indies trade but, for a period in the 'thirties, some were used on two Pacific routes, one from the U.S. west coast to the Far East, the other between San Francisco and Central America. In their later days some at least carried cargo only and had part of their superstructure removed but, as a whole, the class lasted well. The *Tivives* was sunk by enemy action in October 1943. She was then on bare-boat charter to the U.S. War Shipping Administration, as were three others which were lost in similar fashion. For these the Company was later paid $2,150,000 in compensation. Active service for the seven which survived the Second World War ended in 1945 when they were traded in to become part of the Government laid-up fleet, this against a new construction subsidy awarded to United Fruit. So passed the last of what had been one of the world's largest groups of passenger- and cargo-carrying sisters, and certainly the best looking.

60 s.s. MATSONIA, 1913, U.S.A.

Judged by pre-1914 Pacific standards, the *Matsonia* was a large ship, even although she could hardly be compared with the crack passenger liners operating between the Pacific Coast and the Orient, and Australasia. For her own particular trade, that between Hawaii and the U.S.A., she was by far the most ambitious yet built, combining as she did large cargo capacity with accommodation for over 300 passengers. Historically, her main claim to interest lay not in size alone, but in the fact that she was one of the first passenger liners and certainly the finest of pre-war years to have her machinery aft. For ships of such tonnage this was a new and isolated development, although the British Yeoward Line vessels (see *Avoceta*) were examples of how this style, as applied to a smaller size group, had been developed from ships of virtually coastal type.

The Matson Navigation Co. of San Francisco, the owners of the *Matsonia*, were primarily interested in the carriage of sugar, that of passengers being regarded as a useful and profitable sideline. The *Matsonia* was their fourth large ship with engines aft. This series started with the 5,928-ton *Lurline* of 1908. Basically a freighter, but carrying 66 first-class passengers (figures for 1922), she originally had a three-island type profile not unlike that of a tanker. The second stage in development came with the *Wilhelmina* of 1908 and the *Manoa* of 1913. In these, which carried 147 and 100 first-class passengers respectively (again 1922 figures) there was no after well deck, but a greatly enlarged bridge structure which, however, stopped short of the aftermost hatch. The *Matsonia* and the 4-ft longer *Manoa*, which followed in 1917, represented this theme in its final stage of development. Both were flush-decked and had a very long superstructure which started well forward and continued unbroken almost to the stern. By way of postscript, two more large, engines-aft ships were built for Matson in 1921, the four-masted, 480 ft long *Manukai* and *Manulani*. These, however, were freighters, with the minimum of superstructure, and carried only six passengers.

The *Matsonia* and her machinery were products of the Newport News Shipbuilding and Dry Dock Co. Her main dimensions were length b.p. 480 ft, breadth mld 58 ft, depth mld 45 ft and load draught 30 ft 6 in. She had a single screw and 4-cylinder, triple-expansion machinery with cylinders of 35, 62 and (2) 81 in. diameter and 66 in. stroke. Steam was supplied by nine oil-fired boilers, 3 single-ended and 6 of water-tube type. The speed at 9,000 i.h.p. was about 15 knots. The gross tonnage was 9,728 (later 9,402), displacement 17,500 tons and deadweight 9,900 tons.

The ship was completed in November 1913 and had just over four years of commercial service before being taken up for use as a transport. As such she was armed with four 6-in. guns. She was returned to her owners in September 1919 and subsequently refitted, her post-war passenger accommodation being for 251 first-class and 78 third-class. She then saw a long continuous spell of work on the Hawaii–San Francisco trade, each passage taking about six days. This ended in September 1932, when she arrived at San Francisco to start what proved to be a long lay up. In 1937 she took a new name, *Etolin*, after being bought by another San Francisco firm, the Alaska Packers Association. She remained with them until August 1940 when she was chartered by the U.S. Army for service, once again, as a transport. Although sold again in 1944, this time to become government property, she continued trooping until April 1946 when she was laid up. After long years of idleness she was finally sold by the U.S. Department of Commerce to the Bethlehem Steel Company, her career ending on 12 March, 1957, when she arrived at Baltimore to be broken up.

61 s.s. AMERICAN MERCHANT, 1920, U.S.A.

This vessel was one of a group of five sisters which for 15 years maintained a weekly service between New York and London. Over a shorter period a further two operated on a complementary service to Liverpool. Although very successful, they were undeniably the ugliest of all passenger-carrying ships then operating on the North Atlantic. That they should have been built at Hog Island was apt, since a tendency to hog (or droop at the ends)—either actual or real—was one of the most pronounced features of their strange, double-ended style of profile.

Their background was interesting, since they had been designed in the latter part of the war as transports, but also made suitable for eventual peacetime use as freighters. Twelve of these Hog Island B-type (Design 1,024) ships were built, all by the American International Shipbuilding Co. of Hog Island, Penn. The original contract, as placed by the United States Shipping Board, Emergency Fleet Corporation, was for 70, but the others were subsequently cancelled. Of those built, one was delivered to the U.S. Navy, the rest to the U.S. Army. These Hog Island B-ships were the smallest of the three American troopship types built then, the *President Harding* and *President van Buren* (plates 63 and 62) being representative of the others.

The *American Merchant* was of 7,430 tons gross and 8,133 tons d.w. and had a cargo capacity of 355,260 cu. ft. Her main dimensions were length overall 450 ft, breadth mld 50 ft and depth mld (to upper deck) 40 ft. The load draught was 31 ft. She was of shelter-deck type with three continuous decks and seven holds, the last named being served by

18 derricks and winches. A single screw was driven by two General Electric, D.R.-geared turbines of 6,000 s.h.p. Steam for these was supplied by six oil-fired, water-tube boilers. Her daily fuel consumption was about 80 tons or so, and her bunker capacity 1,750 tons. In her early days on the London service she carried 12 tourist-class passengers, but this figure was soon raised to 78.

The *American Merchant* (whose original name was *Shohokin*) was laid down in November 1918 and commissioned on 30 October, 1920. Later a different style of naming was adopted for the group and she became the *Aisne*. She started her commercial career in 1924. This resulted from the sale by the U.S. Shipping board of the *President van Buren* and her four sisters, which had previously maintained the New York–London service. Their places were taken by the *American Merchant*, *American Banker* (ex-*Cantigny*), *American Farmer* (ex-*Ourcq*), *American Shipper* (ex-*Tours*) and *American Trader* (ex-*Marne*). The new service, known as the American Merchant Lines, was operated for the U.S.S.B. by J. H. Winchester & Co. To start with, the funnel was all black—save for the houseflag, which was a red and blue burgee, divided diagonally with, superimposed, the white letters AML. A better effect was soon achieved by having the flag on a white band.

In 1929 the U.S. Shipping Board sold the American Merchant Lines and the United States Lines to P. W. Chapman & Co., but each fleet kept its separate identity. Forced to foreclose two years later, the Shipping Board then sold the two to the newly-formed United States Lines Co. of Nevada. The *American* ships were then absorbed into the main fleet and were thereafter painted as shown. Over a period of years their appearance was altered somewhat, by the removal of the two after lifeboats (one aside), also by the fitting of bulwarks on the bridge deck and along the after part of the boat deck. Later the white paint was carried lower; on the sides of the forecastle and poop this was given an upward slope, so as to suggest sheer.

Regularity of sailing continued until the outbreak of war in 1939. Then the American Neutrality Act caused the suspension of the United States Lines' services to Great Britain, France and Germany. To overcome this it was suggested that the ships be put under the Panamanian or Norwegian flags. Instead, in 1940 the *American Merchant* and her sisters (including the two from the Liverpool route, also one *President* liner) were sold to a specially formed Belgian concern, the Société Maritime Anversoise S.A. All were given *Ville* names, the *American Merchant* becoming the *Ville de Namur*. The finale came quickly, for in the course of 1940 all but one of the ships were sunk. The *American Merchant* was sunk by torpedo on 19 June while bound from New York to Europe and with her were lost 25 of her crew. The only one of the *Ville*s to survive the war was the *Ville d'Anvers* (ex-*American Banker*), a ship which bore several names and eventually ended her career as the *Arosa Kulm*.

Phoenix-like, the *American*-style of naming was revived in 1946 and has since been applied to scores of freighters owned by the United States Lines.

62   s.s. PRESIDENT VAN BUREN, 1920, U.S.A.

Of the vast output of standard ships built in America during and just after the First World War, the very great majority were purely cargo carriers. Besides these were certain others which had been intended as troop transports but which were completed too late for use as such. Most were modified for commercial service while still under construction, but later units were built from the keel upwards as passenger-cargo liners.

All save a few were given American State nicknames, such as *Old North State* (that for Carolina) and the like. However, it was soon realised that these were hardly suitable for liners intended for world-wide trading. Some indeed were faintly ridiculous, for what non-American passenger would appreciate the significance of *Blue Hen State*? A new system was therefore adopted and all but four were given the names of American presidents. As such they became internationally known.

Deliveries to the United States Shipping Board commenced in the winter of 1920–21. In October 1920 this 10,533-ton, lead ship of a class of seven was completed as the *Old North State*, and later became the *President van Buren*. This group comprised what was familiarly known as the '502' design, this being their length in feet b.p. Larger ships of the '535' series (length o.a., not b.p.) followed in 1921–22.

The two groups were easy to distinguish, the smaller vessels being of three-island type, the larger ones having no forecastle or poop, the midship structure thus appearing even larger. There was also considerable difference as regards machinery and speed. The '502' ships were all built and engined by the New York S.B. Corp. of Camden N.J. Their main dimensions were length o.a. 522 ft 5 in., length b.p. 502 ft, breadth mld 62 ft, depth mld to A deck 42 ft, and load draught 31 ft 9 in. Each had three continuous decks, eight holds and nine hatches. The bale capacity was 466,000 cu. ft and refrigerated cargo capacity 52,300 cu. ft. The deadweight capacity was approximately 12,000 tons.

The main machinery, of 6,850 i.h.p., comprised two sets of 4-cylinder, triple-expansion engines—the cylinders were of 24, 40½, 54 and 54 in. diameter and 45 in. stroke, and normally operated at about 105 r.p.m. The six Scotch boilers worked under forced draught at 220 p.s.i. Each measured 15 ft 8 in. × 11 ft 6 in., and together they had a heating surface of 16,000 sq. ft. The bunker capacity was 3,476 tons and the daily oil consumption in the region of 92 tons. The ships needed a crew of approximately 115. Like many of that period, the ships had no sheer amidships and also none on the forecastle and poop. Instead these islands were given sloping bulwarks.

In 1921 the *Old North State*, as she was still called, and two sisters, were put on a new one-class service between New York and London. Their operators, the short-lived United States Mail Steamship Co., soon ran into financial difficulties and this forced the U.S. Shipping Board to take over this and other North Atlantic services. Coinciding with this change a new trade name was introduced, that of United States Lines.

In 1922 their passenger accommodation, previously for 78 first-class, was altered to take a greater number of cabin passengers by the fitting of extra berths. The single fare from London to New York was fixed at £30. Also in that year the *Old North State* was renamed *President van Buren*, her running mates becoming the *President Adams* and the *President Monroe*. A few months later, when two more ships—the *President Garfield* and the *President Polk*—were added, the London service was put on a weekly basis.

This, however, lasted only a short time, for in the autumn of 1923 all five were sold to the Dollar Line who, in the following year, put them on a new round-the-world service. On this the ships sailed westwards only, and continued to do so after the fleet's takeover by the American President Line in 1938. Two years later the *President van Buren* relinquished her name to a new ship, and became the *President Fillmore*. Not long after, she commenced a new phase of war-time service, first as an Army transport and then from 1943 to 1946 as the Army hospital ship *Marigold*. After release she resumed her previous name and became one of the vast fleet owned by the U.S. Maritime Commission. Two years later she was sold to the Kaiser Company and scrapped at Oakland, Calif.

63   s.s. PRESIDENT HARDING, 1921, U.S.A.

Of all the American passenger ships which operated on the North Atlantic during the 'twenties and 'thirties, none saw such long continuity of service as the *President Harding* and the *President Roosevelt*. So alike as to be virtually indistinguishable, these two began their trans-Atlantic careers in 1922, and it was 1939 before the partnership was broken. The *President Harding* was one of the so-called '535' (535 ft) class ships. Of these she and ten others were built by the New York Shipbuilding Co. of Camden, N.J. and the other five by the Bethlehem Sparrow's Point Shipyard. As originally conceived during the war, these ships were to have been built to the slightly smaller '502' design, as represented by the *President van Buren* (plate 62), and the order for their construction was placed with the Newport News Shipyard. Soon afterwards it was realised that they would be ready too late for war service. The order was accordingly cancelled and new contracts placed elsewhere for re-designed, more ambitious vessels better suited for commercial use.

The resultant '535' class ships were the largest merchantmen to be built or designed in America during the First World War. The *President Harding* and *President Roosevelt*, which served the United States Lines so well, were the only ones of this larger class to operate on the North Atlantic. Their main dimensions were length overall 535 ft, breadth mld 72 ft and depth mld (to A deck) 50 ft. They carried a deadweight of 13,000 tons on a draught of 30 ft 6 in. and had a bale capacity of around 455,500 cu. ft. As built, the *President Harding* had a gross tonnage of 14,187, which was subsequently reduced to 13,869. The machinery was far more sophisticated than that of the '502' class, the twin screws being driven by D.R.-geared Westinghouse turbines of double-flow type. Steam at 265 p.s.i. and 750° F. superheat was supplied by 8 Babcock & Wilcox oil-fired, water-tube boilers. The designed service speed was originally given as $17\frac{1}{2}$ knots at 12,000 s.h.p., but some years later the *President Harding* was credited with speeds of up to 19 knots. Certainly voyage reports show that while with the United States Lines she made the Atlantic crossing to Germany, with various calls, in 9 days. The two ships carried 320 first- (later cabin-) class and 324 third-class passengers and during their peacetime careers they appear to have been very popular, especially with those who preferred unostentatious travel.

When the *President Harding* entered the North Atlantic trade at the beginning of 1922 it was not under that name, but as the *Lone Star State*—the nickname for Texas. However, before the summer of 1922 was over she had been re-christened, first the *President Taft* and then the *President Harding*, and it is as such that she will be remembered by the great majority. From the day of her maiden voyage right up to the Second World War the *President Harding* and her sister sailed under the banner of the United States Lines. Behind this trade name there was first Government (U.S. Shipping Board) ownership, then that of two quite distinct companies. These changes occurred in 1929 and 1931 and the most noticeable outward result was that after the first of these the German terminal was switched from Bremerhaven/Bremen to Hamburg. With the outbreak of war and the passing of the Neutrality Act the Company's sailings to the belligerent countries ceased. Early in 1940 the *President Harding* and several smaller ships were transferred to a specially formed Belgian subsidiary, the Société Maritime Anversoise (Antwerp Navigation Co.). The *President Harding* then took the name *Ville de Bruges*, but her service as such was brief, for on 14 May 1940, she was bombed and set on fire by German aircraft while she was in the River Scheldt, outward bound for New York. As for the *President Roosevelt* (known at the beginning of her career as the *Peninsula State* and the *President Pierce*) she became the U.S. transport *Joseph T. Dickman* in 1941 and kept that name until scrapped in 1948.

64   s.s. MOUNT CLINTON, 1921, U.S.A.

A feature of the early 'twenties was the appearance of a number of new North Atlantic services, both passenger and cargo, many of which were destined to be short-lived. Major factors in this were the surfeit of American ships, both new and ex-German, and, on the other hand, the eagerness of the big German lines—then virtually devoid of tonnage but with plenty of expertise—to get back into business. A contrast to the many old and often quite unsuitable ships put into service was provided by the newly completed *Mount Clinton* and *Mount Carroll* which, to meet a need of the times, were converted to carry large numbers of immigrants. Service in this capacity was brief, but in their designed role as freighters they had long careers.

They were among the first merchant ships to be built in the States after the Armistice for private owners. These were the Shawmut Steamship Co. Inc., of New York, one of the several subsidiaries of the American Shipping & Commerce Navigation Corporation which was to become more widely known as the United American Lines, Inc. The A.S.C.N. were already operating a New York–Hamburg cargo service and the new pair were under construction when the Company and the Hamburg American Line came to an agreement for the re-establishment of certain pre-war H.A.L. services. The Americans were able to provide the large, three-funnelled *Reliance* and *Resolute*, also a much smaller, ex-German ship, the 8,140-ton *Mount Clay* of 1904. To operate with the last named the *Mount Clinton* and *Mount Carroll*—which, as originally designed, had the normal split superstructure of a cargo ship, with two lifeboats aside and a single funnel —were completed as shown.

The pair, which were built by the Merchant Shipbuilding Corp., at Chester, Pa., measured 457 ft overall (440 ft b.p.) × 57 ft breadth mld × 39 ft mld to shelter deck. Beneath their 'tween decks they had five holds which were served by 10 winches and 10 5-ton derricks, plus another of 30-tons capacity. Their designed deadweight was 10,500 tons and load draught 28 ft 9 in. The gross tonnage of the *Mount Clinton* worked out at 7,510. The propelling machinery, a Westinghouse, cross-compound turbine rated at 4,200 s.h.p. at 3,600 r.p.m., comprised two elements which drove a single screw through S.R. gearing. Of the five boilers, one was of water-tube type and the others, normal single ended; their working pressures were 250 and 220 p.s.i. The service speed was 13 knots.

Cabins for 1,500 steerage passengers were arranged on the two upper decks and had two, four and six standee berths. Since the flow of passengers catered for was a Westward one from Europe, these cabins were designed for quick assembly and removal, so that on the Eastward run the space could be used for cargo. Another special feature was the installation of a special kitchen for kosher cooking. Possibly the amount of accommodation needed was over-estimated, for a little later their capacity was given as 585.

The *Mount Clinton* was launched on 8 February, 1921 (four weeks after her sister) and on 26 May she left New York on her first voyage to Hamburg, a passage which normally took 12 days. Thereafter, this third-class steerage service was maintained by the three United American *Mount* steamers and some Hamburg American vessels headed by the new 9,000-ton *Bayern* and *Wurttemburg*. As more German tonnage became available, the *Mount*s were withdrawn, and the *Mount Clinton* made her last Atlantic crossing in 1923. In 1925 the two sisters were sold to the Matson Line, Inc. of San Francisco, the *Mount Clinton* becoming the *Maunalei*. It was then, doubtless, that their dummy after funnel, accommodation and extra lifeboats were removed. Thereafter their careers were linked with the carriage of sugar and pineapples from Hawaii to the U.S.A. In

1948 the *Maunalei* (ex-*Mount Clinton*) was sold to start a new career under the Italian flag. Renamed *Santa Rosa*, registered at Genoa and owned by Piaggio & Ravano, she was re-sold within months to become the *Capo Manara*, still registered at Genoa, but owned by the Compagnia di Nav. 'Stellamaris' S. p. A. Under this name she traded for six years, her career coming to an end late in 1954 when she arrived at Yokohama to be broken up. The *Mount Carroll*, later the Matson-owned *Maunawili*, subsequently became the *Socrates* (in 1946), *Southern Albatross* aad *Pontaratissa* (both in 1955). In 1958 she too went to Japanese breakers.

65 s.s. INDARRA, 1912, Australia

Visually the *Indarra* was by far the most impressive passenger liner that had been built for the Australian inter-State trade. On arrival there she not only joined the élite of such ships but for a while held premier position. She was described there as most palatial, with the appointments and fittings equal to those of an ocean liner. Among the various novelties which impressed were a gymnasium and an open-air swimming pool. Of the passenger ships on her particular route, she alone could boast two funnels while, in relation to hull length, her superstructure was the most impressive. She thus represented this type of vessel in its outwardly most flamboyant form.

Short-term popularity followed, but she was not the success anticipated. Excessive rolling in the Australian Bight was probably the cause. It would seem that the brevity of her stay in that trade was not entirely due to size alone, since several other of comparable or rather larger tonnage were built for rival inter-State lines, this right up to the mid-'thirties. These however were of more discreet height and, in relation to this, rather less pinched as to beam. An atmosphere of apparent misfit dogged this interesting ship, until she went to Japan, where her final owners removed some of her topweight and increased her draught by 14 in.

She was built and engined by Wm. Denny & Bros. Ltd., Dumbarton, for the Australian United Steam Navigation Co. Ltd., a firm whose association with the British India Line was revealed by identical funnel markings. She was designed for the Company's prestige—and most competitive—service between Fremantle (her port of registry) and Sydney. The *Indarra*'s main dimensions were length b.p. 451 ft, breadth mld 60 ft and depth mld 40 ft. As built she had a gross tonnage of 9,735 (subsequently reduced) and carried a deadweight of 7,038 tons on a draught of 26 ft 6 in. She was of awning deck type and had two continuous decks, together with a third one in No. 2 hold. For cargo-handling she relied mainly on silent hydraulically-operated cranes, two of which were allocated to each hatch. For heavier loads, of up to 10 tons, she had derricks mounted on the foremast.

Accommodation was provided for approximately 230 first-, 140 second- and 120 third-class passengers. For the first named there were four public rooms, the dining saloon, music room, smoking lounge and veranda. Twin screws were driven by two sets of quadruple-expansion engines, with cylinders of $26\frac{1}{2}$, 38, 54 and 76 in. diameter and 48 in. stroke. Seven S.E. boilers supplied steam at 210 p.s.i. and for them she had bunker space for over 2,500 tons of coal.

The ship which was launched on 1 July, 1912, ran trials on 6 November and on them attained 16·69 knots. Service on the Australian coast was relatively brief since, like many of the inter-State liners, she was called up for wartime trooping and the like.

During this period she was probably subjected to hard usage and this may have affected subsequent performance. In 1919 the Orient Line, then short of tonnage, chartered the *Indarra* as a temporary measure. Three round voyages between England and

Australia were advertised, but after two she was handed back to the A.U.S.N. as being too slow. In that same year the Lloyd Royal Belge, having decided to enter the Belgium–South America passenger trade, ordered four 10,000-ton, two-funnelled, 16-knot liners, two from Denny and two from Scott's of Greenock. Then, early in August 1920, the *Indarra*, then laid up, was reported as sold to the British offshoot of the L.R.B., Lloyd Royal Belge (Great Britain) Ltd. A Belgian report described her enthusiastically as a 19-knot ship with accommodation for 450 passengers and stated that she was to open the new service to Brazil and the River Plate.

The names provisionally allocated to those on order were *Pays D'Anvers*, *Pays de Bruxelles*, *Pays de Liège* and *Pays de Namur*; names with a doubtless national appeal, but rather at a disadvantage when subjected to international appraisal. In the same vein, the *Indarra* (kept under the British flag) was re-christened *Pays de Waes*, a name which, to the English-speaking world, had even less romantic appeal than the American *Blue Hen State*. The largest of the 92 ships then controlled by the Lloyd Royal Belge, the *Pays de Waes* left Antwerp in mid-September to inaugurate the new service, Prince Leopold being one of her 400 passengers. Before the ship had finished her third round voyage the Lloyd Royal Belge decided to drop the whole project. Orders for the new ships (two of which had been laid down) were cancelled and, after her return to Antwerp in April 1921 the *Paes de Waes* started a long lay-up. Later the Australasian United regained possession of the ship and on 13 February, 1923, she left Antwerp and, after a leisurely seven-day passage, she arrived at Falmouth, where she was again laid up.

In October she was sold to the Osaka Shosen Kaisha and three months later she left Hamburg for Osaka, where she arrived on 1 February, 1924, after an eight-week voyage. There she was renamed *Horai Maru* and given a thorough refit. From this she emerged listed as a ship of 9,192 tons gross and 14½ knots speed, with the after part of her superstructure shortened by the length of a lifeboat and her former cranes replaced by derricks. Inside, her accommodation had been remodelled to take 51 first-, 123 second- and 553 third-class passengers. In the 'thirties the third-class was progressively extended to take 669. Subsequently the *Horai Maru* was used on the O.S.K. Formosa (Kobe–Keelung) service on which, from 1926, the *Midzuho Maru* (ex *Infanta Isabel*, plate 55) was also employed. The ship ended her wanderings on 1 March, 1942, when, as a Japanese transport, she was sunk in the Sunda Strait by a combination of gunfire and bombs from Allied warships and aircraft. Still valuable as steel, her wreck was raised after the war and broken up in Japan.

66 s.s. STAD ANTWERPEN, 1913, Belgium

In the Belgian Government's Ostend–Dover fleet the changeover from paddle to turbine came in 1904 with the introduction of the *Princesse Elisabeth*. A triple-screw vessel of 1,767 tons gross, she was designed for a service speed of over 24 knots, but on trials off Greenock she achieved 26·25 knots, making her the fastest merchant ship afloat. As a result of her success, two more of very similar design were built, the *Pieter de Coninck* and *Jan Breydel*, both of 1910. That the next two, the *Stad Antwerpen* and *Ville de Liege*, should be about 50 ft shorter might seem surprising, but they were in fact designed for winter service when traffic was light and so did not justify the use of the other vessels. In the event they were the last ships with direct-drive turbines to be built for the Belgian Marine, the *Princesse Marie Jose* of 1922 being given twin screws and geared turbines.

In terms of external appearance, the Belgian cross-channel ships have always stood apart, their profiles incorporating certain subtleties of feature which have distinguished them from all others. Most apparent in these early turbine ships were the horizontal cowl tops to their raked funnels and the shallow but very rounded cruiser sterns, always well embellished with 'gingerbread'. The *Stad Antwerpen* was built at Hoboken by the Soc. Anon. John Cockerill and her machinery was supplied by their Seraing establishment. Her gross tonnage was 1,384, the net measurement being 979. She had two continuous decks and measured 300 ft b.p. × 36 ft × 22·9 ft depth of hold. Her three sets of turbines developed 12,000 s.h.p. and steam for them was provided by 8 coal-fired water-tube boilers which worked under forced draught. The passenger capacity was approximately 900, considerably less than that of the previous three. The *Stad Antwerpen* was commissioned in 1913, and the *Ville de Liege* early in 1914, the two replacing a pair of paddlers, the *Ville de Douvres* and *Prince Albert*, which had been built in 1886.

In service their shorter hulls brought rather disappointing results, while the rather deeper fullness of the stern proved a hindrance when going astern as they entered port. So, even though their turbines were faster (600 r.p.m.) than on the earlier ships, the two did not normally exceed 23·5 knots. Both ships were experimentally fitted with Frahms anti-rolling tanks which were situated in the upper part of the hull. Their extra weight, 30 tons, coupled with the use of lighter weight, water-tube boilers created stability problems, so they were soon removed.

During the First World War, the *Stad Antwerpen* was used by the Admiralty between British and French channel ports, carrying troops and wounded. Post-war service on her old run continued until 1934; in October of that year she was sold by auction to D. Assenheimer & Co. for 347,600 fr. and subsequently scrapped, her demise coinciding with the introduction of the new m.v. *Prince Baudouin*.

The *Ville de Liege* lasted many years longer and made shipping history in 1936 when she was rebuilt for further service between Ostend and Dover as the car ferry *London-Istanbul*. In that guise she had side doors and space for 100 cars, but a much reduced number of passengers.

67 s.s. PRINCESS MARGUERITE, 1925, Canada

In her day, this ship and her sister were accepted as being the finest examples of the coastal liner to be found anywhere in the world. She and the *Princess Kathleen*, both owned by the Canadian Pacific Rly. Co., of Montreal, were designed to operate as a pair on the Vancouver–Victoria–Seattle service. The distance involved was about 165 miles, and Victoria (situated near the Southern tip of Vancouver Island) represented the approximate half-way point. Special requirements were high speed, large passenger capacity and also a very high degree of utilisation, since there were both day and night crossings. Their introduction to this run was somewhat overdue for the two they replaced, the *Princess Victoria* (1,943 tons gross) and the *Princess Charlotte* (3,925 tons), had been built as far back as 1903 and 1908 respectively. Two replacements had indeed been ordered in 1913, but on their completion the *Princess Irene* and the *Princess Margaret*, as they were named, were promptly bought by the Admiralty for use as minelayers.

The *Princess Marguerite* and *Princess Kathleen* were 22½-knot ships of 5,875 tons gross and 5,275 tons displacement and both came from John Brown & Co.'s yard at Clydebank. Their main dimensions were length overall 368 ft (350 ft b.p.), breadth mld 60 ft, depth mld to upper deck 28 ft 9 in. and load draught 18 ft. They had twin screws and four S.R.-geared turbines of Brown-Curtis type. These were rated at 14,000 s.h.p. and took steam from four cylindrical and two Yarrow-type water-tube boilers. These consumed about 67 tons of oil per day, the bunker capacity being 590 tons. Out of the 1,400 passengers carried, about 330 were first-class and a special feature of their accommodation was the provision of 17 special rooms, each with private bathroom, also 22 2-berth cabins each with its own shower.

The *Princess Marguerite* was launched on 29 November, 1924 (two months after her sister), and on 25 March, 1925, she sailed from the Clyde on her maiden voyage. Once on station the two were worked surprisingly hard. How hard is shown by a summary of the *Princess Marguerite*'s activities during an 11-month period. During this she spent three days in dry dock, but otherwise operated continuously on the day and night services from 14 May, 1938, to 13 April, 1939. Over that period she steamed more than 81,000 miles and never spent more than 2½ hours in port. Shortly after this, in May 1939, the *Princess Marguerite* was chosen to carry King George VI and Queen Elizabeth from Vancouver to Victoria.

During the war, both ships were used as transports. Their design and speed made them ideal for use in the Mediterranean and it was there, on 17 August, 1942, while on voyage from Port Said to Cyprus, that the *Princess Marguerite* was torpedoed by the U 83. In view of the fact that she had on board 1,000 troops, the loss of life—49—was relatively light. In June 1947 the *Princess Kathleen* returned to the so-called 'triangular' service between Vancouver–Victoria and Seattle, but 12 months later she was switched to the Alaskan run. In August 1951 she was holed after a collision with the *Prince Rupert*, while thirteen months later, while bound from Vancouver to Skagway, she stranded in a gale at Lena Point, about 31 miles North of Juneau. Although no lives were lost, the ship became a total loss.

68   s.s. CARELIA, 1921, Finland

The Baltic and North Sea timber trade provided employment for a large number of small steamers and for these the mast arrangement shown on the *Carelia* was one that became extremely popular. By placing the masts and their winches at the ends of the bridge deck and on the forecastle and poop, the well decks were left clear for the easy stowage of deck cargoes such as timber and coke. This so-called Fredrikstad mast arrangement, named after its originator, a Norwegian shipbuilding firm, made its first appearance well before the First World War. An early ship so fitted which became well known in London was the Norwegian *Borgila* of 1910, latterly one of the Fred. Olsen fleet. It reached its peak of popularity in the 1920s and vessels with this arrangement were built by many (mainly Scandinavian) shipyards. The *Carelia*, likewise a Thames 'regular', was typical of the many rather smaller examples built soon after the war. Her gross tonnage was 1,123 (later reduced to 1,083) and she could carry a deadweight of 1,500 tons on a draught of only 15 ft.

She was built by a small yard, the Maskin & Brobygnads Aktiebolaget of Helsingfors for a local firm, the Atlantic Rederi A/B., who took delivery in 1921. Her length b.p. was 217 ft, breadth 34·5 ft and depth of hold 14 ft. She had a single deck and above this had three islands, a 23-ft-long poop, a 62-ft bridge deck and a 29-ft forecastle. Steam triple-expansion engines and coal-fired boilers gave a speed of about 8 knots. The Atlantic Company's fleet comprised three near-sisterships, the others (from the same yard) being the *Finlandia* (built 1920) and *Ostrobotnia* (1921). In 1925 all three were bought by Finland's largest shipping concern, the Finska Angfartygs A/B (Finland S.S. Co. Ltd.), also of Helsingfors. All three vessels, whose name remained unchanged, gave the Company good service—especially the *Carelia*. Not only did she survive the war, but she continued on until 1963 when she was sold to a Dutch firm and broken up at Hendrik-Ido-Ambacht.

69   Steam Schooner **COMMANDANT DE ROSE**, 1918, France

France, like her Allies, incurred heavy merchant ship losses during the 1914–18 war. To help offset these much new tonnage was ordered from home yards and also from the 'States. However, with America's entry into the war, the U.S. Government requisitioned all the conventional steel-hulled steamers which had been ordered there by countries overseas. But these powers of requisition did not extend to certain wooden ships. Thus of one group ordered, all 40 were delivered to the French Government save for one which was lost on her maiden voyage.

In view of their bizarre design, American non-interest was hardly surprising. Five-masted, wooden-hulled schooners of about 3,500 tons d.w., each was given auxiliary power in the form of two small steam, triple-expansion engines which drove twin screws. The order for these vessels had been placed with the Foundation Company and their construction was more or less evenly divided between the firm's Tacoma and Portland shipyards. All 40 were completed in 1918. Their main dimensions were length overall 280 ft, length b.p. 249 ft 7 in., breadth maximum 45 ft 6 in. and depth mld 24 ft 11 in., the load draught being 23 ft. Special features of their design were a straight but sharply raked stem with virtually no curve at the fore-foot, while the upper part of the stern was a nearly flat transom. There were three holds and hatches. Incorporated in the forecastle and extending aft of the foremast was a large deckhouse which on one side contained the donkey boiler and pumps and, on the other, accommodation. The crew's messroom and galley were in a second deckhouse just aft of the mainmast. The main part of the accommodation was in a full-width house some 50 ft long, this being just aft of the machinery space. The two engines had cylinders of 10, 16½ and 26½ in. diameter and 24 in. stroke and took steam at 225 p.s.i. from two water-tube boilers. The hulls, masts and spars were of Oregon pine and the total sail area was about 16,000 sq. ft.

The example shown, the *Commandant de Rose*, was one of those built at Tacoma. Launched in the summer of 1918, she made one long ocean voyage to France, saw briefest service in the U.K.–Continental trade and was then laid up. By 1923 she had been sold for scrap and by the end of 1925 the very great majority of her group had shared the same fate. The last survivor, the *Gerbeviller*—one of the very few to be sold to commercial operators—went to the breakers about 1931, having spent the last few years as a sailing ship, without machinery. Although most of the early illustrations of these steam schooners show them with grey hulls, the very few existing photographs of them in European waters imply that they were later repainted as shown, with black hulls.

Built of wood to avoid the bottlenecks then associated with steel ship construction, these vessels proved to be a commercial failure. Nevertheless, it is worth recalling that in the 'forties Sweden built a smaller series of more modest-sized, three-masted, steel-hulled schooners. They had diesel, not steam, auxiliary power and proved far more satisfactory.

70   s.s. **ISAR**, 1929, Germany

Over the years 1927–29 the Norddeutscher Lloyd, Bremen took delivery of ten handsome, 14-knot, four-masted cargo liners of 7,000–8,000 tons gross. The leadship, *Aller*, was steam-driven as were six others, and the rest were motorships. These ten were used mainly on the Company's Far Eastern and Australian services.

The group was rounded off by the completion in 1929 of two slightly larger ships of similar layout, with short raised forecastle, four tall masts and eight hatches. Nevertheless, they were immediately distinguished from the rest by having a cruiser, not counter-type stern and, what was completely new for ships of this size, bow lines which were convex, not concave. The stem seen in profile had a pronounced curve and sloped back to join the keel at a point approximately beneath the foremast, but the differences aft were less pronounced. Among the merits claimed for this new design were reduced skin friction and easier water flow, both contributing to either better speed or fuel consumption.

The *Isar* was the first important ship to be built with this now well-known Maierform style hull. In addition, she and her sister had two less obvious refinements aft, a stream-lined propeller hub and an Oertz-type rudder. Another point of interest was the coupling of a low-pressure exhaust turbine to her otherwise conventional single-screw, reciprocating machinery. The *Isar* and the *Donau* were of 9,026 and 9,035 tons gross respectively and carried a deadweight of approximately 12,000 tons on a draught of 28 ft 1 in. Their overall length was 546·5 ft, breadth 63·5 ft and depth of hold 30·7 ft. Besides their triple-expansion machinery they had a Bauer-Wach turbine with D.R.-gearing and hydraulic coupling. Superheated steam was supplied by five S.E. coal-fired boilers. The total horsepower was 6,500 and the service speed 14 knots. The ships had three decks and although essentially cargo carriers they had cabin-class accom-modation for 16 passengers. Both vessels were built by the Deutsche Schiffs-und-Maschinenbau A. G. Vulcan, Hamburg, their machinery coming from the Vulcan Werke. The *Isar* ran successful trials at the beginning of May 1929, her sister a few weeks later. Later in the year the Vulcan yard completed one more ship, a tanker, and then closed down owing to financial difficulties.

The *Isar* saw regular service on the Eastern trade for which she was designed, her voyages being between Bremen, Hamburg, Antwerp, Colombo, the Straits and ports in China and Japan. Homeward calls included Genoa and London. She did, however, make at least one voyage to Australia via the Cape. The *Donau* spent her early years on the North Pacific Coast run and it was 1933 before she joined up with her sister.

The *Donau* was bombed and sunk by aircraft near Oslo in 1945. Raised two years later and sold to Norway, she was later scrapped. The *Isar*, however, survived the war. During the immediate post-war years she was used locally in the Baltic, but in August 1947 she arrived in the Tyne to lay up. There she was bought by the Stanhope Steam-ship Co. Ltd. of London, refitted and converted into the oil-burning *Stanroyal*. As such she returned to commercial service in 1948. She kept that name until 1952 when she became the *Haran*, owned at Istanbul by Hasim C. Mardin. Seven years later she was sold locally, to the Ipar Transport Co. Ltd., who renamed her *Necip Ipar*. This was the final phase in her career and ended with her sale to Turkish breakers in 1965.

71   s.s. ROYAL SCOT, 1910, Great Britain

Throughout the period covered by this book there were several companies which, except for the war years, provided regular passenger sailings between London and East Scottish ports. Of these the London & Edinburgh Shipping Co. Ltd. was one of, perhaps the, most important. At the time of the *Royal Scot*'s completion in 1910, this very old Leith-based firm (founded in 1809) provided three passenger sailings a week in each direction. At London its ships berthed at the Hermitage Steam Wharf, Wapping, on the north side of the Thames and a mile or so below the Tower Bridge. From there the ships left on Tuesdays, Wednesdays and Saturdays, while the sailing days from Leith were Wednesdays, Fridays and Saturdays. Besides these there were other sailings to the Continent.

The Company's main competitor was the venerable Carron Company, of Falkirk, whose origins went back to the eighteenth century. Their black-funnelled ships were based on Grangemouth, also on the Firth of Forth, but well to the west of Leith. At London their Carron Wharf was situated on the north bank of the River, just below Tower Bridge. At that time they too maintained three sailings a week in each direction, with an additional weekly one to Granton. Other competitors in the London–Scottish passenger trade were the Aberdeen Steam Navigation Co. Ltd., whose buff-funnelled steamers sailed twice weekly, and the Dundee, Perth and London Shipping Co. Ltd.

The *Royal Scot* was built at a time when rivalry between her owners and the Carron Company was at its height; in the event she proved to be the last and fastest of the fliers. A ship of 1,726 tons gross and 1,330 tons d.w., she was built and engined by the Caledon Shipbuilding & Engineering Co. Ltd. of Dundee. Launched on 10 May, 1910, she ran trials on 31 August, attaining a mean speed of about 19 knots. Her main dimensions were length b.p. 290·2 ft, breadth 38·2 ft and depth of hold 18·1 ft, the load draught being 17 ft 6 in. She had two continuous decks and a cargo capacity of about 63,000 cu. ft. Her passenger capacity was long quoted as being 100 first- and 120 second-class but, at the time of her sale, the figures listed were 123 first- and 74 second-class.

Initially she operated with the 17-knot, 1,611-ton *Fiona* of 1905, the 1,562-ton *Fingal* of 1894 and the 1,182-ton *Malvina* of 1872. Of these, she alone survived the war. In 1924 she was joined by a new passenger ship, the 14-knot, 2,187-ton *Royal Fusilier* and, four years later, by a virtual repeat, the *Royal Archer*. In 1930 the name *Royal Scot* was given to a new cargo ship carrying 12 passengers only, and the older vessel was re-christened *Royal Highlander*. In October 1932, after being used as a reserve ship, she was sold for some £3,500 to become the Colombian Naval transport *Mosquera*. Thereafter shown as mounting a couple of 3·5-inch guns, she lasted until 1945 when she was sold for scrap.

72 s.s. LONDON QUEEN, 1910, Great Britain

If the *Royal Scot* represented the British coastwise passenger liner in its fastest and, for its period, most highly evolved form, the little *London Queen* came at the lower end of the scale. In her hull layout she was typical of many small coastal and short seas tramps of that time, yet she operated on advertised and regular services and was therefore a true liner, even though in miniature. Her owners had long been engaged in the Channel Islands trade. Although as the London & Channel Islands Shipping Co. Ltd. the firm had only been founded in 1899, the business had been carried on under various names at least as far back as 1873, when sailings were maintained on a fortnightly basis.

The first of the many ships with *Queen* names was the 615-ton steamer *Island Queen* of 1900 and with her the Company built up a great reputation for regularity. By the time the *London Queen* entered service at the beginning of 1911, after delivery at the end of 1910, sailings had become bi-weekly. A limited number of passengers had probably been carried since very early days, but the *London Queen* had accommodation for 20. Fares were exceptionally low and the *Queen*s provided a very cheap means of travel to and from the Islands, or for a round voyage lasting nearly a week. Outwards the ships carried general cargo, but homewards it was always broken granite from the Guernsey quarries which, because of its great hardness, was in constant demand for road-making.

Steel-built and of 599 tons gross, 279 net and 700 tons d.w., the *London Queen* measured 169·5 ft (b.p.) × 28·1 ft × 11·7 ft depth of hold. Her load draught was 12 ft 2 in., 5 in. less than her moulded depth. For deck erections she had a 25-ft-long forecastle and a 10-ft bridge deck (which with the deckhouse above contained the passenger accommodation), while aft of this there was an 84-ft-long quarter deck.

She was built in Holland by Van Vliet & Co. of Hardinxveld, but her triple-expansion machinery was made by Richardsons, Westgarth & Co. Ltd., of Middlesbrough. This had cylinders of 14, 23 and 39 in. diameter and 27 in. stroke, took steam at 180 p.s.i. from one single-ended boiler and gave a speed of about 10 knots.

At the time of her construction, the Company was seeking to develop the passenger side of their trade and in 1912 the *London Queen* was joined by the slightly larger *Channel Queen* which carried 40 passengers. During the war a yet larger one carrying 60 was delivered, but was soon sold for Naval service. The *London Queen* remained on the Channel Islands trade until the mid-twenties. Sold to Norway, she briefly operated as the *Risøy* before starting a new and long career in South America. Bought by the Chilean firm of Braun & Blanchard of Valparaiso, she was renamed *Pilar* and registered not at that port but at Magallanes (Punta Arenas), the implication being that she was used locally in that area. Her Lloyd's Register classification was withdrawn in 1934, but she continued under the same ownership until about 1940. She then became one of a much smaller fleet, that of Martinez, Pereira y Cia. Ltda., also of Valparaiso, which then became her port of registry. As the *Pilar* this remarkable little ship still features in the current edition of Lloyd's Register.

73 s.s. NORMANNIA, 1911, Great Britain

In terms of marine engineering, the *Normannia* made history in being the first cross-channel ship to be propelled by geared turbines. On the various routes across the English Channel the need for high speed was greatest on the short ones from Dover–Folkestone and Newhaven, hence the early adoption of the direct-coupled turbine, which started with *The Queen* of 1903. The Southampton-based fleet of the London & South Western Rly. Co. was employed on much longer crossings (to the Channel Islands, Le Havre, etc.) and was the last of them to break from reciprocating machinery.

The Company's first turbine ships, the 1,500-ton *Caesarea* and *Sarnia*, built for the Channel Islands service in 1910, had triple screws and direct-coupled turbines. The L. & S.W. Rly. then set a world lead for such ships in adopting geared turbines for the next pair, the *Normannia* and *Hantonia*, both of which were launched in 1911. The results were highly satisfactory, the much lower propeller speed being coupled with improved fuel consumption and other gains. The two ships, exact sisters, were built and engined by the Fairfield Shipbuilding & Engineering Co. Ltd. of Govan, Glasgow, and bore consecutive yard numbers, 481 and 482. The *Normannia* was launched on 9 November, 1911, and her sister on 23 December. The latter originally bore the name *Louvima*, but was renamed before entering service.

The *Normannia* had a gross tonnage of 1,567 and a displacement of 1,800 tons. Her overall length was 299 ft (290 ft b.p.), breadth mld 36 ft and depth mld (to promenade deck) 23 ft 6 in. The draught was very light, only 12 ft 3 in. She had a passenger capacity of just under 700 and could carry 123 tons of cargo (16,700 cu. ft) in her two holds. Her twin screws were driven by two sets of Parsons geared turbines. Each comprised two units; an H.P. turbine running at about 2,000 r.p.m. and a combined L.P. and astern turbine running at about 1,500 r.p.m., the S.R. gearing giving a propeller speed of 315 r.p.m. The two boilers, one double-ended and one single-ended, were coal-fired. The bunker capacity was 120 tons and the consumption about 3 tons per hour.

The ship's contract speed was 19½ knots, but during trials off Skelmorlie the *Normannia* achieved a maximum of 20·48 knots at 6,100 s.h.p. while over a six-hour run she averaged

19·7 knots at 5,000 s.h.p. As ever, various experts and engineers of the old school expressed grave doubts as to whether the machinery would stand up to strenuous use demanded of it. But from the beginning of 1912 right up to 1939, the *Normannia* and *Hantonia* maintained an almost unbroken nightly connection between Southampton and Le Havre.

They were the first two-funnelled ships to be built for the L. & S.W. Rly. since the 'nineties and following their success another of almost similar design, the *Lorina*, was built in 1918, but for the Channel Islands run. The line of continuity then passed through the *Dinard* and *St. Briac* of 1924, both for the St. Malo route, to the *Isle of Jersey* series of 1929–32.

The *Normannia* was an early war loss, being sunk by German aircraft on 30 May, 1940, while off Dunkirk where, on the previous day, the *Lorina* had met a like fate. The *Hantonia* survived the war and continued with Southampton as her home port until the summer of 1952, when she was scrapped at T. W. Ward's yard at Grays, just above Tilbury. The *Normannia* is portrayed as built. In January 1923 she and the rest of the L. & S.W. Rly. fleet were taken over by the Southern Rly. Co. and from then on her funnels had black tops. At later dates she was given bulwarks in place of open rails by the bridge, had the after part of the superstructure enclosed and the white paint carried down to deck level. The same applied to the *Hantonia* but in post-war years she looked somewhat different, and unbalanced, through having no mainmast.

74   s.s. LADY CLOÉ, 1916, Great Britain

Despite the existance of many small local railway lines, now long extinct, cross-country travel was often tedious and time-consuming. For the traveller and holiday maker, coastal passenger and cargo ships such as the *Lady Cloé* often provided the easy answer. She was the second of two very similar steamers, each with accommodation for 70 passengers, which were built for the Dublin–London service of the British & Irish Steam Packet Co. Ltd. Her builders were Sir W. G. Raylton Dixon & Co. Ltd. of Middlesbrough, her triple-expansion machinery coming from the nearby firm of Richardsons, Westgarth & Co. Ltd. Her running mate was the *Lady Wimborne*, which had been built in 1915 by the Clyde Shipbuilding & Engineering Co. Ltd. Although basically alike, the earlier vessel had a taller funnel (with deeper black top) and a rather different form of counter stern. Itineraries are seldom maintained over a period of years without seasonal or other changes, but the general voyage pattern of these two ships was Dublin–Cork–Falmouth–Plymouth–Torquay–Southampton–London and vice-versa, their sailings being weekly in each direction.

The gross tonnage of the *Lady Cloé* was 1,581 and her deadweight 1,876 tons. Her main dimensions were length b.p. 260 ft, breadth 38 ft and depth of hold 15 ft. She was of shelter deck type and above her three holds there was a full-length 'tween deck. Her cargo capacity was 94,960 cu. ft and her load draught 16 ft 11½ in. For cargo handling her three hatches were served by five derricks and four steam winches. Her machinery had three cylinders, of 19, 31 and 52 in. diameter and 36 in. stroke and took steam from two single-ended boilers. She had bunker space for 500 tons of coal and at 10 knots her daily fuel consumption was about 18 tons.

The British & Irish Steam Packet Co. was one of the many firms controlled by Coast Lines, Ltd. of Liverpool and in the summer of 1937 the *Lady Cloé*, hitherto registered at Dublin, was transferred to the parent firm to become the Liverpool-registered *Normandy Coast*. For a while at least she continued on her old route, but it has been stated that she also made some runs between Dublin and South Wales ports. Her career ended on 11

January, 1945, when she was torpedoed and sunk by a U-boat in 53·19N, 04·48W, to the south of Holyhead.

Her near-sister *Lady Wimborne* lasted rather longer. Renamed *Galway* in 1938, she became the *Galway Coast* a year later and as such continued as one of the Coast Lines fleet until 1946. In that year she became the *Virtu*, still registered at Liverpool, but owned by the Virtu S.S. Co. Ltd. and managed by Anthony & Bainbridge Ltd. of Newcastle. This phase was of brief duration, for on 27 February, 1948, she stranded on the North African coast between Bardia and Tobruk. Subsequently refloated, she was towed to Tobruk and there broken up.

75 s.s. DARINO, 1917, Great Britain

It is probable that the first merchant ship to be given a cruiser stern was a French cross-channel steamer built in the early 'nineties, she and her sisters being followed by some small ships for the Belgium–U.K. trade. There was certainly no rush to adopt the new feature and in general its application was reserved for the fast and high-powered types. It was in the years shortly before the First World War that two British companies took the lead in applying this feature to smaller, handy-sized vessels. These were the Wilson Line, of Hull and Ellerman Lines, the latter for vessels intended for their Papayanni Line services to Mediterranean and nearby countries. For Ellermans' the first quarter of the twentieth century was a period of great expansion and saw the absorption of many well-known lines. Purchase of the Papayanni Line occurred early this century, that of the Wilson Line (which has retained its separate entity) during the First World War.

Between the various lines there was considerable inter-change of tonnage, the *Darino* providing but one example of this. She was built for Wilson Line account, but from about 1920 or so was listed as an Ellerman ship, with Ellerman & Papayanni Lines Ltd. as her managers. While both fleets contained a number of sister or very similar ships, the emphasis was rather on one-off designs, each of which showed a slight advance on its forbear. This applied to the *Darino*. Although in no way outstanding, she was nevertheless typical of the higher-class, short-seas trader of her day. Built and engined by Ramage & Ferguson Ltd. of Leith, she was completed in October 1917. Of 2,057 tons d.w., she had a load draught of 17 ft 4 in. Her gross tonnage was originally 1,433, but this was later reduced to 1,351. Her length b.p. was 236·3 ft, breadth 36·5 ft and depth of hold 17·1 ft. The depth moulded was 19 ft 3 in. She had two continuous decks, three holds and hatches, with five steam winches for cargo handling. Under the bridge she had accommodation for four passengers. Her machinery was of the conventional triple-expansion type with cylinders of 16½, 28¼ and 48½ in. diameter and 33 in. stroke. These took steam from two single-ended boilers which had a working pressure of 210 p.s.i. and gave a speed of about 10 knots. Her coal bunker capacity was 240 tons and daily consumption about 14 tons.

Records of her peacetime movements show that she traded from the United Kingdom, with London as the most frequently mentioned port, to Lisbon, Oporto and Cadiz. She was never renamed and was still engaged on her old trade when she met her end. This came on 19 November, 1939, when she was torpedoed off the Spanish coast in position 44·12N, 11·07W.

76 s.s. WAR VIPER, 1918, Great Britain

As one of the B-type steamers, the *War Viper* belonged to what was the most numerous of all the standard ship designs built in Britain during and just after the First

World War. The urgent need for the construction of simply designed standard ships became apparent late in 1916 and the initial orders were placed that winter. Of Britain's government-sponsored, new building programme the first to be completed was A-type cargo ship *War Shamrock* which was handed over by Harland & Wolff, Ltd., Belfast, in August 1917. While the A- and B-types had similar 400 ft long hulls, the initial A-design had but one deck. In all just over 50 such ships were built. It was very soon realised that there was greater need for a two-deck version and the emphasis was switched to this. The Armistice came with many B-type ships in various states of uncompletedness and these were eagerly bought by private shipowners, who had them completed to suit their own requirements. Altogether, including these modified vessels, around 150 of the B-type were completed, the last 30 or so being given privately chosen—not *War*—names.

Although deeply involved with the construction of other types, Harland & Wolff contrived to build nine of these 400-ft ships in 1917–18, not including some delivered by their Clyde establishments and others which were completed later for private owners. It should be remembered that these A- and B-types were but part of a wide range of cargo ship designs evolved and built in Great Britain, over a dozen for ocean-going service, plus others for coastwise use.

The *War Viper* is shown as delivered in March 1918, with hinged king-posts forward and aft, a short funnel and side screens extending along the sides of the well decks. Her main dimensions were length overall 412 ft (400 ft b.p.), breadth mld 52 ft, depth mld 31 ft. The load draught was 25 ft 3 in. The deadweight tonnage was 8,110, the gross and net measurements being 5,160 and 3,122. Harland & Wolff were responsible for both the ship and her machinery. The latter was of triple-expansion type, with cylinders of 24, 44 and 73 in. diameter and 48 in. stroke. The boilers, single-ended and three in number, had a working pressure of 180 lb and were oil-fired. The service speed at 2,500 i.h.p. was approximately 11 knots.

In 1919 the *War Viper* was sold to become the *Cabotia* of the Anchor Donaldson Line Ltd., the managers of which were Henderson Bros. of Glasgow. Under their ownership, with black hull and black, white-banded, funnel, she was employed on the North Atlantic, trading to the St.Lawrence and U.S. East Coast, her usual ports this side being Glasgow and Avonmouth. In January 1925 she again changed hands, being bought by Haldin & Co. Ltd., London for their Court Line and duly renamed *Cedrington Court*. By that time her appearance had been modified somewhat: the funnel (now buff, with black top) had been heightened by about two diameters and a light topmast added to the crosspiece which joined the two forward king-posts. The hull, forecastle and poop were now black, but the sides of the centre-castle painted white. In this form the ship spent the rest of her career engaged in worldwide tramping. Her end came on 7 January, 1940, when she was sunk by a mine 2 miles N.E. of the North Goodwin Light Vessel. It is perhaps worth observing that of the Harland-built group of nine to which the *War Viper* belonged, only one reached the shipbreakers' yard; one other was lost (wrecked) in the Goodwin area, and the rest were victims of the Second World War.

77   wooden s.s. WAR MINGAN, 1918, Great Britain

In addition to the great number of standard-type cargo ships which featured in Britain's domestic wartime building programme, many others were built for her by overseas yards. As a matter of expediency, nearly 50 handy-sized, wooden-hulled steamers were ordered by the British Government from shipyards in North America, and these were delivered in 1918 and 1919. In the main their hulls were built of Douglas fir or Oregon pine, so longevity was hardly to be expected. The two largest of these wooden steamers, the *War Mystery* and the *War Marvel*, both of 3,484 tons gross, were built at Orange, Texas. The rest came from various shipyards in Canada, some of which were almost as new as their ships. Altogether the yards involved in this particular wooden-ship programme numbered over a dozen and their individual output varied between two and six hulls. The ships they built were to a common design, even though they varied slightly in detail.

Typical of the rest of this series, the *War Mingan* was one of two completed in 1918 by the Three Rivers Shipbuilding Co. Ltd. of Three Rivers, Quebec. Her gross tonnage was 2,217, deadweight approximately 3,300 tons and total cargo space 130,000 cu. ft. The length b.p. was 251·1 ft, breadth extreme 43·5 ft and depth mld 25·3 ft. The hull, of single-deck type, had a 30-ft-long forecastle and a combined bridge and poop deck which extended 136 ft. It was classified '12A1' by Lloyd's Register, rather higher than some of the others, which only achieved '10A1'. Like all of this Canadian-built group, the *War Mingan* had a single set of triple-expansion engines. This was made by the Dominion Bridge Co. Ltd. of Lachine and had cylinders of 20, 33, and 54 in. diameter and 40 in. stroke. Steam at 185 p.s.i. was supplied by two forced-draught, water-tube boilers. Bunker space was provided for some 200 tons of coal.

The *War Mingan*'s service under the Red Ensign was minimal. In 1919 she was sold by the Shipping Controller to become the Italian *Candiope*, owned at Venice by the Credito Industriale di Venezia and managed by the Societa Esercizi Marittimi. Lloyd's Register for 1920 shows them as having 10 of these wooden ships, but it is very questionable whether their purchase was ever justified. By the end of 1923 this fleet had ceased to exist, the *Candiope* and the rest having all found their way to Italian breakers. Two years later only two out of the whole group were still in service.

78 s.s. JOLLY BRUCE, 1920, Great Britain

As seen in retrospect, interest in the *Jolly Bruce* lies not so much in the ship herself, but in her layout. The bridge-amidships, engines-aft arrangement as shown in the *Topaz* had long been accepted as the norm for handy-sized British coasters of the 145/180-ft range. In essence, the layout of the *Jolly Bruce* was little different, save that she had her bridge aft of, and not over, the cargo space. Also that extending aft from that point, there was a full-height poop, not quarter deck. The afterpart of the hull and the superstructure above it was therefore several feet taller than on the conventional design. Small changes these, but they can now be seen as marking the first stages in the evolution of a new type of vessel which, a decade or so later, was to replace the old. So despite the fact that she was steam-driven, the *Jolly Bruce* in her hull design represented the avant-garde, the forerunner of the famous Dutch motor coaster, or schoot, as it was generally called.

The vessel is shown in the colours of Walford Lines, Ltd. of London, who owned her for the greater part of her career, but she was in fact bought by them when six years old. As the *Aleksander* she was built in a small Dutch yard, that of the Gebr. van Diepen at Waterhuizen. Of 553 tons gross, she had a deadweight tonnage of 740 tons on a load draught of only 9 ft 11½ in. Her length overall was 170·5 ft (157·5 ft b.p.), breadth 27·1 ft and depth of hold 11·4 ft. Her hull was topped by a 24-ft-long forecastle and a 52-ft poop, while ahead of the latter she had a 49-ft-long, raised quarter deck. Machinery-wise she was quite conventional, being propelled by triple-expansion machinery made by a firm at Breslau.

As an Esthonian ship, registered at Reval (now Tallinn), she spent her early years on the North Sea/Baltic trades. This continued until 1926, when her owners, Act. Ges. fur Holzbearbestung A. M. Luther, sold her to Walford Lines, who owned a considerable fleet of *Jolly* coasters. These were so numerous that their names, one for each letter of the alphabet, extended from *Jolly Angela* to *Jolly Pierre*. Like the rest of these, the *Jolly Bruce* was thereafter engaged in the U.K. coastal and near-Continental trades. A change of name, but not of ownership, came about 1932 when, in conjunction with a Dutch firm, Walfords' opened a regular service between London and Dordrecht. The British contributions were the *Jolly Bruce* and the *Jolly Angela*, which were renamed *Theems* and *Rijn* respectively. War inevitably brought its great occasions and twice the *Theems* was able to carry a human load across the Channel to Britain, once with refugees and once with troops—efforts for which her Master was later decorated. The vessel was sold out of the Walford fleet in 1951 to become the *Marvia*. Converted to oil-burning by her new owners, the Medimar Navigation Co. (Hugo Pace & Sons Ltd.) of Valletta, Malta, she continued trading until December 1954 when, while loading at Marseilles, she caught fire and capsized. Although raised, she was declared a constructive total loss and broken up.

79   s.s. TOPAZ, 1920, Great Britain

The *Topaz* was representative of the most numerous of all coaster designs built in Britain during the first quarter of this century. The layout was simple, with a raised forecastle, a short bridge deck aft of the well and then a long quarter deck which extended half the length of the hull. For this size range with two hatches, certain mast variations were possible, the most popular (after that shown) being the provision of an extra mast and derrick just forward of the funnel. The *Topaz* had a small mizzen right aft, its function being to carry a steadying sail. Originally this was normal practice, but in later years this was generally dispensed with. Instead, it became customary for the bridge top—hitherto open as on *Topaz*—to be made more habitable by the addition of a wheel-house. The stern shape also provided some scope for individuality, the bulwarks there being either vertical or else sloping, as on the much larger *Chartered* (plate 28).

On ships like the *Topaz* the accommodation for seamen, firemen and the 2nd mate was forward and that for the steward and two engineers aft. Amidships, under the bridge deck, would be the Captain's and chief mate's cabins, the saloon and a pantry. Sometimes there would be a bulkhead beneath the bridge, so forming two holds, but the *Topaz* had none. Aft of her long single hold was the crossbunker space, which had a capacity of about 70 tons. The *Topaz* is shown as she spent nearly all her career, in the livery of William Robertson of Glasgow. A subtle Company recognition feature, which applied to all his many 'Gem' coasters, was a short white bar which was painted just beneath the bridge, a tradition which still holds good today. Originally she was known as the *Collooney* and she was the sixth of a series of eight coasters of virtually identical pattern which came from the yard of J. Lewis & Sons, Ltd. of Aberdeen. Although this design was accepted as part of the Government's wartime standard ship programme, it was based on the steamer *Dragoon*, which was built by Lewis in 1917. The *Collooney*, which was completed in January 1920, was first owned at Goole by Wilmott & Buttle. Their only vessel, she was sold to Robertson in 1922.

Her tonnages, gross and deadweight, were 577 and 770 and her load draught 13 ft 2 in. She measured 164·8 ft b.p. × 27 ft × 11 ft depth of hold. The depth moulded was 13 ft 3 in., her forecastle 23 ft long, bridge deck 11 ft and quarter deck 94 ft. At Lloyd's she was classed '100A1'. Her main machinery, supplied by her builders, was of the usual triple-expansion type, with cylinders of 14, 24 and 39 in. diameter and 27 in. stroke. Steam at 180 p.s.i. was supplied by one single-ended boiler. In 1925 Wm. Robertson bought another of the same series, the *River Dee* (ex-*War Exe*), which he renamed *Opal*. She foundered near the Longships in 1931, but the *Topaz* continued working around the British coast until 1956, when she was scrapped at Port Glasgow.

80 s.s. GANNET, 1921, Great Britain

The *Gannet* was one of a group with a profile which was quite unique and found only in the fleet of the General Steam Navigation Co. This old-established firm possessed a large fleet, most of which were employed on regular services between London and ports in Germany, Holland, Belgium, France and Portugal. Of the rest, a few larger ones traded to the Mediterranean and various small ones operated coastwise. Besides all these, the Company owned a number of very popular excursion ships.

The G.S.N. ships, or 'Navvies' as they were familiarly known, were mostly of modest size and the 250-ft *Gannet* and her sisters were among the largest of them, excepting only the few Mediterranean traders. For many years the Company's cargo vessels had mostly been very conventional and unremarkable as to layout. However, in 1909, a ship of an entirely new, engines-aft layout joined the fleet. This was the 240-ft *Laverock*, which was joined a year later by her sister *Corncrake*. Their success led to the construction of further vessels, the series culminating in 1920–21 with the introduction of the five sisters *Lapwing, Petrel, Auk, Teal* and *Gannet*.

Most obvious of their distinguishing features were the very tall funnel and midship mast, also the placing of the latter by the bridgehouse. This mast carried the only derrick, reliance instead being placed on cranes, of which six were fitted, two for each hatch. Since before the turn of the century the paint scheme for the Company's cargo ships had been a black hull with white ribbon, brown upperworks and masts, royal blue lifeboats and an all-black funnel. The break-away came in the mid-'thirties when the Company's newest and largest Mediterranean ships appeared; these were the first to be painted as shown. From 1947 the practice became general and the ships were re-painted as opportunity or overhaul allowed.

Of the *Gannet* and her sisters, she and three others were built and engined by Bow, McLachlan & Co. Ltd., of Paisley, while the *Petrel* came from the Ailsa yard at Troon. The *Lapwing*, lead-ship of the whole group, was completed in September 1920. The final one was the *Gannet*, which was launched on 3 September 1921, and completed that December. Her main dimensions were: length b.p. 250 ft, breadth mld 37 ft and depth mld 16 ft 6 in. The load draught, 16 ft 1 in., corresponded to a deadweight of 1,800 tons. The gross tonnage, originally 1,443, was later reduced to 1,336. In 1923 she was given some refrigerated space, amounting to 13,000 cu. ft. She had a single screw and steam triple-expansion machinery of 1,700 i.h.p., and with cylinders of 22, 35 and 57 in. diameter and 39 in. stroke. Two S.E. boilers supplied steam at 180 p.s.i. and remained coal-fired, although some of the other ships were later converted to oil. The service speed was about 12 knots.

As a new ship the *Gannet* was used on various of the Company's routes, including those to Fecamp, Antwerp and Hamburg, but latterly it was most often Hamburg. In the course of the Second World War, three of her sisters were sunk. The *Gannet* survived, although in September 1940 she was bombed and damaged by enemy aircraft, while off the Scottish Coast near Rattray Head. The *Teal* had meanwhile been sold—in 1939—to a French firm, and renamed *Penestin*. Thus, by the end of the war, the *Gannet* was the last of her type in the G.S.N. fleet. She returned to the Hamburg trade in 1946 and she remained on it until early 1953, when she was switched to the London–Amsterdam run. Late that year she was withdrawn and in December 1953 she arrived at T. W. Ward's yard at Grays, near Tilbury, where she was scrapped.

81 s.s. MALINES, 1922, Great Britain

Although the *Malines* is best remembered as a London & North Eastern Rly. ship, she was in fact the very last one to be built for the Great Eastern Rly. and was owned by them for less than a year. A twin-screw, geared turbine steamer of 2,969 tons gross, she was one of a group of three designed for the Harwich–Antwerp service, or the 'British Mail Route to Belgium' as it was then advertised. In terms of design, she and her sisters *Antwerp* (1919) and *Bruges* (1920) represented a very great advance on the previous G.E.R. ships such as the *Brussels* of 1902. One vessel had indeed been ordered in between these. Laid down as the *Stockholm*, she had been taken over by the Government while still on the stocks and launched instead in 1917 as H.M.S. *Pegasus*, one of Britain's first seaplane carriers.

Her sisterships both came from Clydebank, but the *Malines* was built by Sir W. G. Armstrong, Whitworth & Co. Ltd. of Newcastle. She measured 337 ft overall (321·7 ft b.p.) × 43 ft breadth mld × 26·5 ft mld to shelter deck. Her deadweight capacity was just over 700 tons. For propulsion she had twin screws and four Brown-Curtis S.R.-geared turbines of 12,500 s.h.p. These took steam at 200 p.s.i. from five boilers of return-tube type, which worked under forced draught. These could burn either coal or oil, the respective bunker capacities being 190 tons and nearly 100 tons. The cruiser stern was common to all three ships in this class, but was otherwise new to the G.E.R. fleet. So too, was the very long (128-ft) forecastle which reached to and linked with the boat deck which, in turn, extended for another 110 ft. Beneath the shelter deck she had two other continuous decks. For cargo there were four holds and five hatches, these being served by five derricks and steam winches, which were of a type silent in operation. All eight lifeboats were handled by Welin davits.

The *Malines* is generally shown as of 1921 construction. It would seem however that this refers to the date of registration, not, as is usual, to completion. She was launched into the Tyne, at High Walker, on 6 January, 1921, but it was not until 9 March, 1922, that she ran final trials. On these she attained a mean of 21½ knots, one half knot in excess of the guaranteed speed. On 21 March she entered service. Hers was normally a night crossing, so the emphasis was on sleeping accommodation which provided for 263 first-class and (aft) 110 second-class passengers. The time taken for the Harwich–Antwerp crossing (approx. 135 miles) was between 9 and 10 hours, of which only about 5 hours were spent in open water.

Ownership by the Great Eastern Rly. ended on the last day of 1922 and from New Year's Day, 1923, the *Malines* and the rest of the G.E.R. fleet became part of the London & North Eastern Rly.–Harwich Section. Her long service on the Antwerp route ended with the war. She and her two sisters were involved in the evacuation from Dunkirk, in the course of which the *Bruges* was sunk. Later the *Malines* was used in the Mediterranean, but in July 1942 she was torpedoed near Port Said. When salved, the ship came under the ownership of the Ministry of War Transport. Thereafter, managed by the General Steam Navigation Co., she operated from Harwich, but as a government troopship. Her career ended on 24 April, 1948, when she returned to the Tyne—scene of her birth—to be broken up at Dunston. Although the third vessel in this class, the *Antwerp*, was returned to the L.N.E.R., she never made another commercial voyage, and was used instead for the B.A.O.R. Harwich–Hook of Holland service until she was scrapped in 1951.

82   s.s. BERNICIA, 1923, Great Britain

For many years the Tyne Steamship Co. Ltd. of Newcastle and the Tees Union Shipping Co. Ltd. maintained their separate passenger services to and from London. In 1903, partly to meet outside competition, the two merged to form the Tyne-Tees Shipping Co. Ltd. Losses during the First World War were heavy, but soon afterwards, under the new and energetic chairmanship of Sir Arthur Sutherland, the Company embarked on a major expansion policy. To attract more custom to their main passenger service, the fare between Newcastle and London was reduced to £2 10s. 0d. (£2·50), which included berth and food. A year later, in 1923, the Company introduced its finest ships ever, the *Bernicia* and the *Hadrian*. They came from different Tyneside yards, the former being built by Hawthorn Leslie & Co. Ltd., Hebburn and the latter by Swan Hunter & Wigham Richardson Ltd., Wallsend.

Basically very alike, but not exact sisters, their most important difference lay in their engine rooms, where the *Bernicia* had triple- and the *Hadrian* quadruple-expansion machinery. The *Bernicia* had a gross tonnage of 1,839 and her cargo capacity was 1,700 tons, the corresponding draught being 17 ft. Her overall length was 295 ft (282·3 ft b.p.), breadth mld 40 ft and depth mld 17·5 ft. She had a single screw and triple-expansion engines of 3,000 i.h.p., with cylinders of 26, 43½ and 73 in. diameter and 48 in. stroke. Steam at 200 p.s.i. was supplied by three S.E. boilers which used forced draught. These consumed about 43 tons of coal per day, the amount carried being just short of 160 tons. The hull had three decks and three holds, while the deck equipment included six cranes, plus a 15-ton derrick on the foremast and one of 5 tons on the mainmast.

Amidships, under the bridge deck, she had cabins for 136 first-class passengers. For them there was a dining saloon above, which faced forward and just aft of this, a smoking room and bar. Right aft, by the stern, she had accommodation for 100 second-class passengers, some of their dormitories being permanent, others removable. It seems quite probable that the *Bernicia*'s accommodation was later modified, although the figures sometimes given seem quite unrealistically large.

Construction was rapid. Although they were only ordered at the beginning of 1923, the *Bernicia* was launched on 1 May and the *Hadrian* 14 days later. Both were delivered in May 1923 and they then started a very successful period on the Newcastle–London run. Their service speed was 15 knots, but they had ample power in reserve and made the Tyne Pier–Gravesend passage in about 20 hours, the total time, berth to berth, being about 24½ hours. At the height of the summer season up to 1,200 passengers a week travelled to and from London, many of them being football fans. A later boost to popularity was an arrangement by which passengers could eat and sleep on board during their stay in port. But within a few years this trade was virtually killed by the long distance motor coach and in 1932 both the *Bernicia* and *Hadrian* were laid up and their places were taken by smaller ships.

In September 1934 the *Bernicia* was sold to the Hellenic Coast Lines Co. Ltd., Piraeus, for a price of about £30,000. As the *Ionia* she became the newest, if not quite the largest, of a fleet numbering about 30 steamers. In 1939 this fleet was divided. The majority, consisting of coastal ships, remained with the old firm while the *Ionia* and the few others which were engaged on longer Mediterranean routes were transferred to the newly created Hellenic Mediterranean Coastal Lines. She was one of the very few Greek passenger ships working out there which somehow escaped the bombs of German aircraft. However, in December 1944, while on Greek Government service and returning from Thessaloniki to Piraeus, she was wrecked near Skiathos. Her near-sister *Hadrian* lasted much longer. Sold to the Khedivial Mail Line in 1934, she became first the *Fouadieh* and then, in 1956, the *Isis*. After many years of service to and from adjacent Arab countries she was broken up in Egypt in 1968.

83   s.s. AVOCETA, 1923, Great Britain

Just as Bibby passenger liners become well known for their four-masted profile, so too did the three-masted Yeoward Line ships. Yeoward Bros. of Liverpool, had started business as fruit importers and merchants in 1894 and became pioneers in the Canary Islands fruit trade. They bought their first ship in 1900, this being the fifteen-year-old *Avoceta* of 1,219 tons gross. As business developed they bought two more of similar size and type from the same source, the Cork S.S. Co. Ltd. All three had been built by the same Dundee firm, that of W. B. Thompson & Co. Ltd., and had had the same three-masted profile which was to become the hallmark of the Yeoward fleet.

After these three purchases Yeowards' decided to build, not buy, and for their first new ship they turned to the same shipyard, which by then had become the Caledon Shipbuilding & Engineering Co. Ltd. Over the years all new Yeoward ships came from Caledon. It is always fascinating to observe the development of a theme; despite the steady progression towards larger and more ambitious ships there was remarkable constancy in the fore and aft positioning of funnel and masts in relation to length of hull. As seen in profile it was the upward changes which were most apparent, the steady trend towards greater height of hull and taller, more elaborate superstructures.

The Yeoward fleet was never a large one. In all, between 1900 and 1955 when they sold their last ship (the 3,712-ton *Alca* of 1927) they owned 13 steamers and also, for a two-year period, a small, inter-island, auxiliary ketch. Of these, 11 steamers were three-masted, the exceptions being two bought in 1915 and 1916 to replace war losses. The service soon developed into a weekly one, the usual itinerary being Liverpool–Lisbon–Casablanca–Madeira and the Canary Islands. At its peak the fleet comprised six ships, but in later years four proved to be sufficient to maintain the service. In 1922–23 the Yeoward Line took delivery of the sisterships *Alondra* and *Avoceta*. The first was completed in the Spring of 1922, while the *Avoceta*, launched on 21 September, was completed about January 1923. The seventh and penultimate ship in the Caledon/Yeoward sequence, she was of 3,442 tons gross and about 3,700 tons d.w. Her length overall was 330 ft (319 ft b.p.), breadth mld 44 ft and depth mld 28 ft 9 in. The load draught was 20 ft 9 in. A single-screw, 13-knot ship, she had triple-expansion machinery of 2,500 i.h.p. with cylinders of 25, 42 and 68 in. diameter and 42 in. stroke. The three single-ended boilers were coal-fired and worked under forced draught at 180 p.s.i. She had three holds and four hatches and was designed to carry general cargo outward and return with fruit. For the benefit of the latter she had two tiers of 'tween decks, these indeed extending the full length of the hull.

The *Avoceta* carried up to 150 passengers, all first-class and in outside cabins, their accommodation being spread over the upper, shelter and promenade decks. In her early days she operated alongside the *Andorinha* (built 1911), the *Ardeola* (1912), the *Aguila* (1917) and her twin, the *Alondra*, of 1922. The advent of the *Alca* in 1927 raised the fleet to six and it stayed at this figure for some years until the sale of the *Andorinha* and *Alondra* in 1930 and 1938 respectively. Only one Yeoward ship, the *Alca*, survived the Second World War. The *Avoceta* was the second to be lost, being torpedoed and sunk by a submarine on 25 September, 1941, when in position 47·57N, 24·05W. Homeward-bound at the time, she sank rapidly and out of her full complement of passengers only about 20 were saved.

84   s.s. INVERLAGO, 1925, Great Britain

The Maracaibo tanker, or 'mosquito tanker' as it was often called, was a specialist type born in the 'twenties to meet a particular need of the time. Although Venezuela and Maracaibo were extremely rich in oil, the entrance to the Maracaibo Lagoon was so shallow as to prevent the passage of large tankers, while mountainous terrain made the cost of a pipeline prohibitive. However, 140 miles distant and some 30 miles off the Venezuelan coast lay the Dutch island of Aruba and this, at San Nicolas, provided a convenient site for a new oil refinery and a deep-water loading berth for large tankers.

The first development came when, after the end of the First World War, a number of redundant warships came on the market. Several small, shallow-draught monitors were bought and converted to carry oil and these, in service, proved far superior to the tugs and barges used previously.

This led to the construction in series of several fleets of specially designed shallow draught tankers. Of these the first comprised the *Inverlago* and her three sisters. They were manned by local crews, but had white officers; their movements, normally in large convoys, had to be related to a high-water arrival at the Maracaibo bars. The sea passage from Aruba and the crossing of these bars was followed by a further 50 miles up the lake to the loading point. The day was spent loading or waiting to load. Then followed a carefully timed departure, a further night at sea and a day spent discharging at Aruba.

The *Inverlago*, of 2,373 tons gross, was the first of a quartet built 1925 by Harland & Wolff, Ltd., Belfast, for the Lago Shipping Co. Ltd., a subsidiary of the Lago Petroleum Corporation. These four ships were given *Inver-* names, the others being the *Invercaibo*, *Inverrosa* and *Inverruba*. They were followed in 1926–28 by a further dozen or so for the same company, these differing only in that they were given local names such as *San Nicolas*, etc. As a result of dredging operations subsequent vessels were of progressively larger size.

The main features of these ships were twin screws, steam machinery and the considerable beam made necessary by the light draught. All had a trunk deck reaching from poop to forecastle. The *Inverlago* had a load draught of only 11 ft 7 in., yet her deadweight tonnage was 2,350. Her overall length was 315 ft (305·7 ft b.p.), breadth 50 ft and depth mld 15 ft. A. & J. Inglis Ltd. of Glasgow supplied her two sets of triple-expansion machinery. These took steam from two oil-fired boilers and, at 1,100 i.h.p., gave a speed of 10½ knots. The bunker capacity was 78 tons and the daily consumption about 14 tons. Her pumproom was forward and the cargo spaces divided by two longitudinal bulkheads into a series of centre and wing tanks. The tank above—nearly half the width of the ship—was used for oil expansion.

For the first ten years or so the Lago fleet was managed by Andrew Weir & Co., then by the Anglo-American Oil Co. Ltd. In 1949 the *Inverlago* was sold, her purchasers being the newly formed Trinidad Shipping Co. Ltd. of Port of Spain who, in the following year, acquired the other three ships. In 1960, although ownership remained unchanged, she was put under the management of Challenger Ltd. of Hamilton, Bermuda. This continued until 1965, when she was sold to breakers.

85   s.s. NERISSA, 1926, Great Britain

A passenger and cargo steamer of 5,583 tons gross, the *Nerissa* was the final ship to be built for the old-established Red Cross Line service between New York, Halifax, and St. John's, Newfoundland. Her registered owners were the New York, Newfoundland Steamship Co. Ltd., the managers of which were C. T. Bowring & Co. Ltd., of Liverpool. The latter had opened this service in 1884, the first ship used being their then brand new *Miranda*. Winter conditions could be arduous and to face up to the icefloes the *Nerissa* was given a specially strengthened hull with an icebreaker type stem, which from a point near the waterline, sloped back sharply to the keel.

Her length b.p. was 349·5 ft, breadth mld 54 ft and depth mld 33 ft. The net tonnage was 3,116 and the *Nerissa* could carry 3,110 tons d.w. on a draught of 20 ft 8 in. She was built by Wm. Hamilton & Co. Ltd., Port Glasgow, and her machinery by David Rowan & Co. Ltd. of Glasgow. This was of 4-cylinder, triple-expansion type, with cylinders of 27, 45 and 54 (two) in. diameter and 45 in. stroke. Her boilers, four in number, were oil-fired and had a working pressure of 200 p.s.i. The hull had two continuous decks with a third one in the holds. Their cargo capacity was 197,430 cu. ft, this including 7,290 cu. ft of insulated space. Her passenger capacity was given as 163 first-class and 66 second-, and the cabins and public rooms for the former were described as 'bordering on the luxurious'.

In all she was an exceptionally well-equipped ship, yet she was built in a remarkably short time. Her owners needed her for the opening of the 1926 season and when they stressed this on 3 November, 1925—the day when the contract was signed—many thought that Hamilton's would never achieve the deadline. However, the keel was laid within a week and the ship launched on 31 March. She ran preliminary trials on 27 May and during further runs in loaded condition she did over 15½ knots. On 5 June she was away on her maiden voyage to New York.

The Red Cross Line relied largely on the American tourist traffic and this became increasingly affected by the trade depression. By 1927 it was decided that the service must be closed down and at the end of 1928 the Red Cross Line with its three ships, *Nerissa*, *Rosalind* and *Silvia* were sold to the Furness Withy Group. They then became part of the Bermuda & West Indies Steamship Co. Ltd., with their funnels repainted in Furness Withy style, black with two red bands, one narrow and one wide. The *Nerissa* continued on the New York–Halifax–St. Johns (N.F.) run at least until 1931. She was then switched to warmer routes, still based on New York but running to Bermuda, also to the West Indies as far south as Trinidad and Demerara. But she met her end in other waters, for it was in position 55·57N, 10·08W (to the N.W. of Ireland) when, on 30 April, 1941, she was torpedoed and sent to the bottom by a German submarine.

86 m.v. ULSTER MONARCH, 1929, Great Britain

On the Belfast–Liverpool passenger service steam had reigned for 110 years before giving way to diesel. The *Ulster Monarch* of 1929 was not only the first motorship built for that route but also the world's first cross-channel ship to be so propelled. Her owners were the Belfast Steamship Co. Ltd. which, since 1919 had formed part of the Liverpool-based Coast Lines group. The previous generation of ships employed comprised the steamers *Graphic* and *Heroic* (built 1906, approx. 1,900 tons gross) and the 2,254-ton *Patriotic* of 1912.

Like them the *Ulster Monarch* and her two sisters were built and engined by Harland & Wolff, Ltd., Belfast. Their design proved so successful that a further ten of the same general pattern were built between 1930 and 1957. Thus variants of the *Ulster Monarch* became standard on all the main non-railway operated U.K.–Irish services. These were the Liverpool–Dublin (2 ships, plus 2 post-war replacements), Fishguard–Cork (1, plus 1 replacement) and Glasgow–Belfast (2). The remaining two vessels, built 1952 and 1957 for the parent Coast Lines' fleet, were moved around as required.

The Liverpool–Belfast service (often advertised as the Ulster Imperial Line) was a night one and called for an average of 16½–17 knots. Time tables generally undergo slight alteration over the years, but in the late 'thirties the pattern was a 22·15 hrs departure from Liverpool and a 07.30 hrs arrival at Belfast. In reverse a 21.00 hrs departure from Belfast, with an 07.30 hrs arrival at Liverpool. Saturday sailings were two hours later. The *Ulster Monarch* and her sisters could carry 700 tons of cargo and this was handled during the day at their respective berths Donegall Quay, Belfast, and Prince's Dock, Liverpool. Public rooms were therefore only used for about three hours each night, while the dining saloon saw an extra hour or so of activity in the morning. Open promenade space was hardly a selling point. The first-class layout was novel, for the public rooms were grouped in a vertical block in the after part of the superstructure. The entrance hall was just aft of amidships on B deck (one below forecastle level). Just aft was the dining saloon, while a large staircase led up to the other rooms. The cabins were all forward of this point. Although small, they were very well planned. Service, as personally experienced, had a warm, personal touch which made one regret the occasional enforced air flight.

As built the *Ulster Monarch* catered for 418 first-class and 86 third-class passengers, but latterly the figures were 391 and 58. The ship had a gross tonnage of 3,735 (finally 3,851). Her overall length was 358 ft 9 in. (346 ft b.p.), breadth mld 46 ft, depth mld 19 ft and load draught about 14 ft 10 in. Twin screws were driven by two 10-cylinder B. & W.-type diesels of 4-stroke, S.A., trunk-piston, airless-injection type. They had cylinders of 360 mm diameter and a piston stroke of 980 mm At 1,600 r.p.m. they developed 7,500 b.h.p., equivalent to about 18 knots.

The *Ulster Monarch* was launched by Harland & Wolff on 24 January, 1929. The *Ulster Queen* followed on 28 March, while on 25 April there was a double event, the launch of the *Ulster Prince* being coupled with a brief introductory trip by the *Ulster Monarch* which took guests down Belfast Lough. At that time her builders were bedevilled by a protracted joiners' strike and the ship could not enter service until 11 June. Such delay however, was nothing compared to that inflicted on the others, which were not finished until 1930.

The three operated as planned until the war, during which the *Ulster Prince* was lost at Nauplia in 1941. Nor did the *Ulster Queen* return. First used by the Admiralty as a Landing Ship Infantry and then altered out of all recognition into a Fighter Direction Ship, she was scrapped in Belgium in 1949. The *Ulster Monarch* which did survive, had a most arduous and varied wartime career and appeared to have a charmed life. She carried troops to France and as a Combined Operations Ship participated in the Norwegian invasion, the Dunkirk evacuation and the occupation of Iceland. After some trooping she was fitted with landing craft and was in the vanguard of the North African landings. Later she circumnavigated Africa and took part in the Italian campaign. She was bombed and set on fire off Tripoli; on other occasions she was hit by a torpedo and had a bomb pass through her, but both failed to explode.

She returned to commercial service in the Autumn of 1946 and operated with the 4,303-ton *Ulster Prince (II)* which, as the *Leinster*, had been built in 1938 for the Liverpool–Dublin run. Both were withdrawn early in October 1966. Later that year the *Ulster Monarch* was sold to Van Heyghen Freres to be scrapped at Ghent, where she arrived on 8 December. Her post-war running mate, like so many others of this series, eventually went to Greece for further use in the Mediterranean.

The *Ulster Monarch* is portrayed in her original colours, but later she was given a black hull with white ribbon and had a very narrow blue band added to her funnels. Her profile also underwent some modification in 1962 when, among other things, her mainmast (slightly shortened) was re-stepped about 24 ft further forward. Since 1967 the Belfast–Liverpool service has been maintained by the 4,270-ton *Ulster Prince (III)* and *Ulster Queen (II)*. Of these the former was built at Belfast, the latter by Cammell Laird.

87 s.s. BATAVIER II, 1920, Holland

The policy of giving ships in a particular fleet a common name followed merely by a distinguishing number is one of doubtful merit. While a unified image, like that of a bus fleet, may be achieved, it is undeniable that, to the outside world at least, the ships involved suffer a loss of individuality. This was so with the ships of the Batavier Line which, for well over a century, maintained a regular passenger service between Rotterdam and London. These were named *Batavier I* to *Batavier VI*, some numbers being repeated over the years. Most of those built this century, including the *Batavier II* (illustrated), conformed to one basic design, the notable exception being the final passenger ship which was built in 1939 and became a war loss. Only after years of group working did the *Batavier II* appear to acquire a positive identity of her own, this when with her consorts lost in war, she alone was left to reopen and maintain the Company's passenger service. This took its name from the 640-ton paddle steamer which made the first Rotterdam–London crossing in April 1830, a ship which subsequently featured in Thackeray's *Vanity Fair*. Initially the service was operated by the N. V. Nederlandsche Stoomb. Maats., but in the 'nineties it was taken over by Wm. H. Muller & Company.

At Rotterdam the *Batavier* ships had their berth close to the City, while at the British end the train journey from the passenger terminal took only about an hour. This was appreciably less than on the alternative route via Harwich (Parkestone Quay) and Flushing, which involved a longer journey London–Harwich and an extra, admittedly short, one between Flushing and Rotterdam. The *Batavier* fares were remarkably low. In publicity literature dated *circa* 1910 the saloon- and second-class single fares were £1 and 13 shillings respectively, including the train journey, which was then Tilbury–London. The ships left Rotterdam at 16.30 hrs daily, Sundays excepted, and arrived at Tilbury about 07.00 hrs. A brochure issued *c.* 1930 shows the corresponding fares as £2 16s. od. (£2·80) and £1 14s. od. (£1·70), the train journey being Gravesend–London. At that period the ships left Rotterdam and Gravesend about 19.00 hrs, arriving at about 08.00 hrs or soon after. Above Gravesend/Tilbury the *Batavier*s proceeded up the Thames to Custom House Quay, just above the Tower of London, where all cargo was handled.

In her general design the second *Batavier II* was very similar to an earlier one built (by Gourlay, of Dundee) in 1902. The *Batavier II* of 1920 and her sister *Batavier V* which followed a year later (and was sunk in 1941) were both built and engined by the Wilton Engineering and Slipway Co., of Rotterdam. The former, of 1,573 tons gross and 965 tons d.w., had a load draught of 16 ft. Her hull, which had two continuous decks, measured 260 ft b.p. × 35 ft × 15·5 ft depth of hold. Two boilers (later converted to oil) and single-screw, triple-expansion machinery of 2,250 i.h.p. gave a speed of 15 knots. For cargo she had two holds and four hatches which were served by six deck cranes and one derrick and steam winch. As built she carried about 72 first-class and 53 second-class passengers. In 1924 sailings were stepped up once more to six per week in each direction and this continued until the war. Over the ensuing years the *Batavier II* served the Allied cause first as a depot ship, then as a hospital ship. Seven years elapsed before the vessel, by now the last of her group, reopened the Rotterdam–Tilbury service. Her passenger capacity had been cut to about 40 or so, first-class only and she normally sailed weekly in each direction, from Rotterdam on Wednesdays and London on Saturdays.

Over the years her promenade deck, originally open, had been given progressively more glass protection. At first it was right forward where, under the bridge, a sheltered observation area was created. Next the glazing was extended half-way and then, finally, the full length of the superstructure. On her post-war return to service the *Batavier II* had no mainmast but later, to carry the second steaming light, a new one, shorter than the foremast, was stepped, this time much closer to the funnel. In 1958 the passenger service was discontinued and not long afterwards the *Batavier II* was withdrawn.

88   s.s. KNIGHT OF MALTA, 1929, Malta

The *Knight of Malta* was without doubt the most important ship of her type ever built for Maltese owners. Fast and with a finely modelled hull, she had much in common with some of the older French passenger ships used on the Marseilles–Corsican run. Far better looking, however, with her very well balanced, classic style of profile, it is difficult to resist the idea that someone concerned with her initial design had in mind memories of those famous P. & O. fliers, the 1,800-ton *Isis* and *Osiris*. Up to the First World War these operated on an express Mediterranean service carrying the Overland Mail between Brindisi and Port Said, where they linked with their owners' ocean mail ships. This idea becomes the more tenable when one recalls the fact that during the early 'twenties the *Isis*, by then named *Gibel Sarsar*, was owned by Blands' of Gibraltar and used on their fast services to Tangier and Casablanca.

To turn from theory to fact, the *Knight of Malta* was of more modest speed, 15 knots, and was built and engined by Swan, Hunter and Wigham Richardson of Newcastle, to the order of the Casser Company Ltd. of Valetta, Malta. She was specially designed to operate on the mail and passenger service between Malta and Syracuse (on the nearest S.E. corner of Sicily) and also to other Mediterranean ports. Her overall length was approximately 270 ft (260·5 ft b.p.), breadth mld 37 ft and depth mld 19 ft. The gross tonnage was 1,553 and she could carry over 2,000 tons d.w. on a draught of only 15 ft $7\frac{1}{2}$ in. She had a single-screw and triple-expansion machinery with cylinders of 21, 34 and 56 in. diameter and 39 in. stroke. Steam was provided by three single-ended, multi-tubular boilers with a working pressure of 180 p.s.i. She had two decks and holds, the latter being served by two 3-ton derricks and steam winches. Water ballast was carried in the double bottom, but even so the ship had a reputation for rolling. Amidships on the bridge and upper decks, there was accommodation for 63 first-class passengers in one- and two-berth cabins. Their public rooms included an entrance hall/music room, smoking room and dining saloon, while there was a sheltered observation area at the forward end of the promenade deck. Aft there were four-berth cabins and some public rooms for about 30 second-class passengers, while forward there were quarters for 16 emigrants.

The *Knight of Malta* was launched from her builders' Neptune Yard at Walker-on-Tyne on 2 October, 1929, and in December she carried out successful trials, logging over $15\frac{1}{2}$ knots. In her early days she had white, black-topped funnels, but these were later repainted red, as illustrated, to avoid confusion with the Tirrenia Line ships, which also operated in that area. Her houseflag, details of which came too late for portrayal in colour, consisted of a red burgee with a white disc in the centre, which contained a castellated tower under three six-pointed stars. With the war the *Knight of Malta* was taken over by the Ministry of War Transport and managed on their behalf by Harris & Dixon, Ltd., London. After being used in turn as Armed Boarding Vessel and Naval Store Carrier she was sunk by enemy action in March, 1941.

89 m.v. BRABANT, 1926, Norway

The foundations of the present firm of Fred. Olsen & Co. of Oslo were laid in the middle of the nineteenth century by three brothers Fredrik Christian, Petter and Andreas Olsen, of Hvidsten. By 1886, when Petter Olsen's son Fredrik took over the management of his father's two ships, the family had owned nearly 40 vessels. Fred. Olsen's aim was the establishment of a network of regular lines first across the North Sea and then further afield. His first steamship, the *Bayard*, was ordered in 1896 and in 1914 he became the first Norwegian to own an ocean-going motorship, the *Brazil*, of 3,374 tons gross. She was the 74th vessel to feature in the family's fleet list.

The *Brabant* of 1926 (ship no. 127) was notable in being the first Fred. Olsen passenger ship to be diesel-driven. She was expressly designed for the Oslo–Antwerp passenger/cargo service hitherto maintained by two 1,750-ton, four-masted steamers, the *Biarritz* and *Paris*. The first passenger-carrying motorship to be designed for regular North Sea service was the Danish *Jylland* of 1925. Outwardly conventional with a nearly full-sized funnel, she could have been mistaken for a steamer, but not so the *Brabant*. Conforming to Fred. Olsen practice (and indeed to that of most other Scandinavian motor-ship owners), she had no funnel in the true sense. She was three-masted and her twin screws were driven by a pair of diesels, the slim exhausts from which were led up the sides of the mainmast. Just aft of this mast there was a very small 'stove pipe' type funnel, but this was for the galley. Some years later the midship mast and the exhausts were removed and the ship given a normal-sized funnel. However, she is shown as built since, for a passenger ship of her size and type, her profile was virtually unique. As to her cruiser stern, this was a feature which, within the fleet, had hitherto only been applied to one other ship, the previous *Brabant*, the first so named. A fruiter of 3,220 tons gross, she had been built in 1920 and was, incidentally, the Company's first turbine ship. Prior to the advent of the new *Brabant* her name was changed to *Burgos*.

The *Brabant* (*II*), of 2,335 tons gross, was built and engined by Akers Mek. Verksted A/S., Oslo. She measured 282 ft in length o.a. (270·5 ft b.p.) by 40 ft breadth mld by 29·3 ft depth of hold. Her hull was of three-island type, the two wells being protected by almost full-height bulwarks. She had two continuous decks, two holds and three hatches; for cargo-handling there were six electric winches and six derricks. Her deadweight tonnage was 2,400 tons. For propulsion the *Brabant* was given two 6-cylinder, 4-stroke S.A. trunk-piston type engines of B. & W. design. These developed 2,300 b.h.p. and gave a maximum of 15 knots or $13\frac{1}{2}$ in service. Her passenger accommodation, for about 70 first-class and 30 third-class, was of an exceptionally high standard. The first-class cabins, one- and two-berth, were on the bridge, main and 'tween decks. The dining saloon was at the forward end of the bridge deck, with the smoking room above. The third-class accommodation was aft, on and under the poop deck.

The ship was delivered in March 1926 and obviously proved herself to be well suited for the Antwerp run, for in 1937 she was joined by a new and somewhat larger motorship, the 3,285-ton *Bretagne*. She, however, was given a better and more conventional profile with a full-sized funnel and two masts. Late in 1954 the *Brabant* was sold for about £135,000 to the newly formed Sudan Navigation Co. Ltd. of Port Sudan, and renamed *Suakin*. She spent a long period with them and, apart from the occasional longer voyage, traded in the Red Sea, between Port Sudan, Jeddah and Suez. Her running mate during this period was the 1,927-ton *Sudani* which, as the *I.K. Ward* of 1929, had been one of the world's most advanced diesel-driven fruitships. About 1971 both were sold to a local firm, Hussein Mohamed Fayez & Sons. The *Sudani* was renamed *Sikri* and scrapped a year later; but the *Suakin* (ex-*Brabant*) still operates at the time of writing as the *Radwa*.

90   m.v. BELRAY, 1926, Norway

One of the most important new types to appear during the 'twenties was the specialist ship designed to carry extra large or heavy loads. Not long after the war, Armstrong Whitworths' had to deliver 200 heavy locomotives and tenders to the Belgian State Railways. To transport these in the usual manner would have involved several months delay, because of dismantling, re-erection, testing, etc. Hearing of this Captain Christen Smith, an officer of the Norwegian Navy and an expert in heavy lifts, saw his opportunity.

Two existing cargo steamers, the *Belgot* and the *Belfri*, were converted to incorporate his ideas as to the arrangement of suitable lifting gear and the stowage and securing of such heavy items. By the use of these ships, the Belgians were able to put their locomotives into service within 24 hours of discharge, the saving in time and cost more than compensating for the extra freight charges. Soon afterwards Captain Smith was entrusted with the carriage of a large number of locomotives to India. After a visit to Bombay to inspect discharging facilities there, plans were prepared for a series of ships able not only to carry railway rolling stock but also such awkward loads as barges, lightships, etc. A further requirement was the incorporation of extra heavy lifting gear for use when port facilities were inadequate.

The outcome was the design for a motorship of about 3,400 tons d.w. Special characteristics were (1) wide clear holds with the minimum number of bulkheads permissible, (2) large hatches, with specially strengthened covers able to support very heavy loads on top, (3) deep hatch coamings, to compensate for any loss of strength due to the large size of the hatches, (4) a long, single deck, with machinery aft and the narrowest of bridge structures near amidships, (5) extra strong stump masts with steel stays, to support the heavy derricks, (6) heavy winches to operate these derricks and (7) great inherent stability to prevent excessive list during loading/unloading operations.

The first specially designed vessel to join the 'Belship' fleet, as it was known, was the *Beldis* of 1924. She was built and engined by Armstrong Whitworth & Co. Ltd., Newcastle who, two years later, delivered two of a slightly improved design to Captain Smith. These were the sisters *Belnor* and *Belray*. Outwardly very similar to the *Beldis*, they were however about 15 ft longer and 1 ft wider. Taking the *Belray*, her length overall was 328 ft 9 in., length b.p. 318 ft 2½ in., breadth mld 46 ft and depth mld 23 ft 3 in. Her gross tonnage was 2,888 and deadweight tonnage approx. 4,280, the latter corresponding to a draught of about 19 ft. Her single deck was surmounted by a poop, bridge deck and forecastle which measured 83 ft, 23 ft and 26 ft respectively.

Like the other two, she was propelled by a single Armstrong-Sulzer, 6-cylinder diesel which developed 1,350 b.h.p. at 110 r.p.m. and gave a speed of about 10 knots. She had two holds, and of the derricks to work them (all mounted on strong swivel bases) one could lift 100/120 tons and another 45/50 tons. Blocks and pulleys were of high tensile steel while, to aid weight distribution, a large lifting beam was generally used.

The *Belray* was launched into the River Tyne on 15 February, 1926 and was completed in May. She saw long service as one of the Oslo-registered, Christen Smith fleet and in 1946 was re-engined, her new diesel being a virtual repeat, save for the fact that it was built by Sulzers' themselves at Winterthur. In 1960 the *Belray* was sold, put under the Lebanese flag and renamed *Artigas*. As such she remained with the Compania Naviera Soraya (Pateras Bros. Ltd., Piraeus) until the Spring of 1970, when she was sold to West German breakers. Of the other two, the *Belnor* was sold in 1956 for further, if brief, service as the Danish *Lise*. However, the *Beldis*, the first of the trio and sold in 1936, continued on until 1971 when, as the Panamanian *Marietta* (her ninth name), she too was scrapped.

91   m.v. SMOLNI, 1929, Russia

The *Smolni* was one of several refrigerated and passenger-carrying motorships which were built in the U.S.S.R. during the years 1928–30. They were by far the most ambitious group to have been built there since the Revolution, so their introduction into service aroused considerable interest. The first two, the *Alexei Rikov* and *Ian Rudzutak*, both of 3,870 tons gross, were completed in the summer and autumn of 1928 and were then described as the first of a class of six for the Leningrad–London service. All these were built by the Severney Shipbuilding Yard, 'A. Jdhanov', of Leningrad, but the next four ships were of a slightly improved design. Very similar as to size, they differed outwardly from the first pair by having a cruiser—not counter—stern and a quarter deck aft, this being several feet lower than the full-height poop of the others.

These four later vessels were the *Felix Dzerjinsky* (completed September 1929), *Smolni* (October 1929), *Cooperatzia* (December 1929) and *Sibir* (January 1930). All were single-screw motorships with a speed of 12–12½ knots. Their propelling machinery, made by the Russian Diesel Engine Works, consisted of a 6-cylinder, 2-stroke, S.A. unit of 1,900 i.h.p. with a running speed of 95 r.p.m. The *Smolni* (illustrated) had a gross tonnage of 3,767 and an overall length of 341·3 ft, her breadth and depth of hold being 48 ft, and 25·6 ft. Her load draught was 18 ft 8½ in. and cargo capacity approximately 2,300 tons. She had two continuous decks, with an extra one in the two forward of her four holds. Above this there was a 41-ft-long forecastle, a 100-ft bridge deck and a 37-ft quarter deck aft. For cargo-handling she had electric winches and 9 derricks, one of the latter being capable of 12-ton lifts. The first two vessels were stated to have accommodation for 28 first-class, 24 second- and 240 third-class passengers. For the later four the figure quoted was 24 first-class, but this may have been an over-simplification.

For a number of years the six were employed on the Leningrad–London service, making a call at Hamburg en route, but in 1937 the *Alexei Rikov* and the *Ian Rudzutak* were renamed *Andrei Jdhanov* and *Marija Ulyanova* respectively. No reports of these two, nor of the *Felix Dzerjinsky* and *Sibir* appeared after 1945, which suggests that they may have been war losses. Some time after the war the *Smolni* had her port of registry changed from Leningrad to Vladivostok and for some years afterwards she was shown as trading between Shanghai and Yokohama. In 1953 she was re-engined, being given a Swedish-built, 8-cylinder, 2-stroke, S.A. unit of unspecified type. Despite the absence of subsequent reports, her name still features in the current issue of Lloyd's Register. The remaining unit *Cooperatzia*, likewise re-engined in 1958, has been registered in turn at Leningrad, Murmansk and Odessa and is now (1972) operating between Odessa, Varna, Beirut and Alexandria.

92 m.v. SUECIA, 1912, Sweden

In Sweden there had been various small local craft powered by diesels, but the *Suecia* was that nation's first ocean-going motorship. She was owned by the Rederi A/B Nordstjernan, of Stockholm which had been founded by Mr. (later Consul General) Axel Johnson in 1890. His career as a merchant at Stockholm had commenced many years earlier, about 1873, entry into shipowning following in 1885. Prior to the creation of the Nordstjernan fleet, most of Sweden's imports and exports were carried by foreign tonnage and this Mr. Johnson set out to rectify. The Company's first regular line— opened in 1904—was to the East Coast of South America and it was for this that the *Suecia* was designed.

When, on the death of his father, Mr. Axelson Johnson took over the control of the Company, it was regarded locally as being the model of efficiency. Early doubts as to his ability to maintain such a standard were heightened when, about two years later, he ordered two ships to be powered by the then newly invented B. & W. diesel engines. Burmeister & Wain, of Copenhagen, built both the hulls and machinery of these two, which were duly named *Suecia* and *Pedro Christophersen*. Such was Mr. Johnson's faith in this new invention that he decided to order four further ships as soon as the trials of the first two proved satisfactory. It was the classic story of the wiseacres confounded, for both the first two and those which followed proved outstandingly successful.

The *Suecia* was a twin-screw ship of 3,730 tons gross and carried a deadweight of 6,510 tons on a draught of 23 ft 2 in. Her main dimensions were length b.p. 359·4 ft, breadth 51·6 ft and depth of hold 22·2 ft. As to her machinery, this comprised two 8-cylinder, 4-stroke S.A. B. & W. diesels which together developed 2,000 i.h.p. at 140 r.p.m. On trials at 167 r.p.m. she logged 12 knots, but her service speed was about 10¾ knots. Her layout—which was to be widely copied—was then novel, for she had a flush deck with her superstructure placed aft of amidships, four of her five hatches being forward of this. Each of these hatches measured 25 ft × 16 ft and was served by two derricks and two electric winches, the latter representing another courageous decision. Below, she had four holds (No. 2 hold had two hatches) and in them there were two tiers of 'tween decks.

The *Suecia* was delivered in December 1912 and in August 1913 she was joined by the *Pedro Christophersen*. Of the second group, which were similar as to design, the *Kronprins Gustaf Adolf*, *Kronprinsessan Margaretha* and *Pacific* followed in 1914 and the *San Francisco* in 1915. Although the *Suecia*'s career was essentially linked with the Baltic–River Plate trade, war brought inevitable changes. Thus, on her final voyage, the ship was bound from Sydney to Liverpool when, on 16 August, 1942, she was sunk in mid-Atlantic, in position 55·43 N, 25·58 W, with the loss of 9 lives. Of the six ships in this class, four were still with the Johnson Line in 1949, but during the next year or two, several were sold to Germany for further trading. One of them, the *Pacific*, was re-engined in 1963 and, ten years later, is still in service, her current name being *Nedderland*.

93 s.s. BRITANNIA, 1929, Sweden

It is doubtful if any North Sea passenger ships have ever proved quite so successful as the 4,216-ton *Britannia* and her sister *Suecia*. They were delivered to the Rederiaktie-bolaget Svenska Lloyd of Gothenburg in the summer of 1929 and, except for the war years, they were employed on the Company's Gothenburg—London service right up to the autumn of 1966. Even that was not the end of their story, for they then started another successful career in the Mediterranean.

The Swedish Lloyd interest in the London service dates back to 1916, when the

Company bought the Thule Steamship Co. Ltd. of Gothenburg. Among their passenger ships was *Thule* (built 1892, 1,974 tons gross) and the *Saga* (built 1909, 2,809 tons) which alternated with her on this run. A few years later the former was replaced by a purchased vessel which was renamed *Patricia*. Built in 1901, she had a gross tonnage of 3,291. She and the *Saga* maintained the London service until 1929, when they were replaced by the *Britannia* and *Suecia*. It was in June 1928 that the order for the two was placed with Swan, Hunter & Wigham Richardson, Ltd.—who years earlier had built the *Saga*.

The *Britannia* and *Suecia* differed only in their style of decor, this in each case being in keeping with the ship's name. Their main dimensions were length o.a. 376·3 ft, length b.p. 360 ft, breadth mld 50 ft and depth mld to shelter deck 32 ft. The load draught was 20 ft 4 in. and the deadweight approximately 2,230 tons. They had two continuous decks with an extra one in all save the first of the five holds. These had a bale capacity of 142,000 cu. ft, of which 6,300 cu. ft was refrigerated. The ships had 14 derricks and 7 double-barrelled steam winches. Each had a single screw driven by three S.R.-geared Parsons' turbines. The ahead power was 5,700 s.h.p. and 65 per cent of this was available when going astern. The four S.E. boilers used forced draught and had a working pressure of 220 p.s.i. Originally they were coal-fired, but in 1937 they were converted to oil. The service speed was about $17\frac{1}{2}$ knots, but on at least one occasion the *Britannia* exceeded 19 knots. The passenger accommodation extended over three decks and, as built, the *Britannia* and her sister could carry about 220 first-class and 45 second-class passengers. All first-class public rooms were on the bridge deck, excepting the dining saloon which was one deck below, at the beginning of the superstructure. Apart from one four-room suite, the first-class cabins were almost all two-berth, while those for the third-class were either for two or four persons. As with most ships, the accommodation was later remodelled, the final figures being around 127 first-class, and 124 tourist-, plus 92 in dormitories.

The *Suecia* was built on the same slipway as the famous *Mauretania* and was launched at Wallsend on 24 January, 1929. The *Britannia*, built nearby at Walker, was launched on 27 February and both entered service in June. Traffic on the London service increased and this led to the purchase, in 1935, of another ship, the Greek *Patris II* (Plate 43) which was put in service as the *Patricia (II)*. For part of 1937 she and the *Britannia* had to work without the *Suecia*. In March that year, that ship, then at Gothenburg for refit, was being moved to another berth when a tow rope broke just as the tanker *Kollbjorg* was being launched. Sunk by the latter, some time elapsed before the *Suecia* was salved, refitted and able to return to her old run.

War interrupted the service and it was not until 1945 that the *Britannia* and *Suecia* were recommissioned, the *Britannia* being used temporarily first on the London–Antwerp run and then between Hull and Cuxhaven. In due course they returned to their old route, using the Millwall Dock as their London terminal, passengers (except for those on round trips) being handled at Tilbury Landing Stage. Hopes of increased traffic had led to the construction of a new 6,458-ton *Saga* which entered service in 1946. Five years later she was joined by another new vessel, the 7,764-ton *Patricia (III)*, but owing to a steady build-up of air competition both these newcomers had to be withdrawn. So the *Britannia* and *Suecia* were left to carry on alone. Both were lively ships and to reduce their propensities for rolling they were given much wider (one metre) bilge keels. The slight drop in speed which resulted was offset by reducing the aperture between the propeller and rudder. Over the years the two had many modifications made to their profile. As built—and illustrated—they had a 67-ft-long forecastle, but this was subsequently extended to join the bridge deck. For two summer seasons in the early post-war period they were painted white, reverting to black for the winter.

Late in 1966 the *Britannia* and *Suecia* were withdrawn from the London run, their place being taken by the new 7,927-ton *Saga (III)*. The two sisters were then sold to the Hellenic Mediterranean Lines, of Piraeus, the *Britannia* being renamed *Cynthia* and her sister the *Isthmia*. After refit they entered their new service looking as smart and elegant as ever, their hulls being painted light grey over blue boot-topping, the superstructure and masts white and the funnels buff with blue band and, clear of this, a black top.

94   m.v. SVEALAND, 1925, Sweden

Throughout her life the *Svealand* was accepted as one of the outstanding ships of the Swedish merchant fleet. Even when seen against comparable vessels built a quarter of a century later, it was the shaping of detail, such as the stem and counter stern, rather than general layout which betrayed her age. When built, she and her sister, the *Amerika-land*, were the world's largest ocean-going cargo ships. In America there were some which approached her in size, but in Europe none.

The two were owned by the Tirfing Steamship Co. (Angf. A/B Tirfing) of Gothenburg, senior firm in the Brostrom Group of companies. They were designed and built to fulfil the terms of a contract signed in 1922 which called for the construction of two ships to carry ore from Chile through the Panama Canal to the Bethlehem Steel Co.'s plant at Sparrow's Point, Baltimore. The original contract had been signed in January 1914 but, owing to the impossibility of building, a postponement was agreed on. In the autumn of 1922 the two ships were ordered from the Deutsche Werft of Hamburg, their bid of £225,000 per ship being by far the lowest. One of the finest products of a German shipyard, the *Amerikaland* was sunk during the war by a German submarine, but the *Svealand* continued on to give many further years of service.

The two ships had a load displacement of 30,000 tons and a deadweight capacity of 20,600 on a draught of 32 ft 3 in. The gross tonnage of the *Svealand* was 15,357, yet because of special design features the net measurement was only 3,316. The overall length was 571·3 ft, breadth mld 72 ft and depth mld 44 ft. Each of the three holds had a capacity of just over 120,000 cu. ft and together they extended for 367 ft. Despite their heavy dense cargo the ships had an easy motion, for the holds, boxlike in section, were only about 24 ft deep and 31 ft wide. On the return passage the very considerable space between them and the hull sides and bottom was used for water ballast. Including a deep tank forward and the fore and after peaks, the total ballast capacity was 23,500 tons. Features which contributed to the great structural strength required were deep hatch coamings and longitudinal framing, although aft the normal transverse type was used. The ships had no conventional cargo-handling gear, only the posts and winches needed to raise and lower the hinged, corrugated steel hatch covers. These were the full width of the holds, weighed 8 tons apiece and were clamped down on thick rubber gaskets. Twin screws were driven by two, 8-cylinder, 4-stroke S.A. B. & W. diesels which were built under licence by the A.E.G. They had cylinders of 29·13 in. diameter, 47·24 in. piston stroke and developed 4,800 s.h.p. at 110 r.p.m. The loaded speed was 11·4 knots.

The *Svealand* was delivered on 9 April, 1925, and the *Amerikaland* on 29 June and they promptly entered their designed service between Cruz Grande and Baltimore. It was a hard, exacting schedule and the average time spent at sea each year was 320–330 days. At Cruz Grande the 22,000 ton cargo was normally loaded in two hours, although the record was 48 minutes.

Discharging at the other end required about 24 hours. To get under the loading spouts at Cruz Grande the ships were moored alongside a pier where generally there was a considerable swell running. To cope with this, and the steady increase in draught as the cargo came aboard, special mooring winches were needed, these automatically paying out and taking in as the ship moved. Routine engine maintenance was carried out at sea, one of the two engines being shut down for 8 hours per trip. Painting was also carried out while under way.

The two ships maintained their shuttle service from 1925 to 1942 when the *Amerika-land* was torpedoed (in February, off the U.S. Atlantic coast) and the other, released from her charter for the duration of the war, was taken over by the U.S. War Shipping Administration. The *Svealand* returned to the Chile–Baltimore ore trade in 1946 where, by the end of 1947, she had carried more than 3·5 million tons of ore, on 160 round voyages covering 1·5 million miles. In 1949 she came home to Sweden and was used on the Narvik ore trade until 1951, when she was sent to Gotaverken. By them she was thoroughly reconditioned (as shown), and given improved accommodation and new main and auxiliary machinery. Her new 2-stroke S.A., 6-cylinder diesels, of Gotaverken type, had an output of 9,000 b.h.p. and raised her loaded speed to about 12½ knots. This was her second major refit. During the first one—in 1932—her deadweight tonnage had been increased from 20,600 to 22,780, but this was now slightly reduced—to 22,630. Subsequently the *Svealand* was employed on both the Narvik trade and on a world-wide basis.

In May 1969 she arrived at Hamburg, reportedly sold to Eckhardt & Co. G.m.b.H. for scrap. Later she was resold to become the Panamanian *Svea* and under the ownership of the Astra Atlantico Armadora S.A. she left Casablanca on 12 October, bound for Communist China where she was broken up.

95 m.v. MISSOURIAN, 1922 (as a cargo ship), U.S.A.

One of the most remarkable features of American merchant shipping has been the almost universal shunning of diesel engines, at least for ocean-going tonnage. Inevitably there have been the occasional exceptions, and two early motorships of note were the cargo liners *Missourian* and *Californian* of 1922. After years of standard types and governmental ownership it was still something of a novelty for ships of such size to be built for a private firm. The pair were designed for the inter-coastal service of the American-Hawaiian Steamship Co. of San Francisco and New York and their advent raised that Company's fleet to 21. Despite their modest horsepower they ranked among America's highest-powered motorships.

The two were built by the Merchant Shipbuilding Corporation, of Chester, Pa., and their machinery by Cramp's of Philadelphia. The gross tonnage in each case was 7,899, the displacement 16,500 tons and the deadweight 11,450 tons, the corresponding draught being 28 ft 7 in. The length overall was 461 ft 8 in. (445 ft 1 in. b.p.), breadth extreme 59 ft 10 in. and depth mld 39 ft. The hulls were of shelter deck type with two continuous decks and a third one forward of the machinery space. The five holds were served by seven hatches and 21 electric winches. Of the derricks one was capable of 30-ton lifts. The ships had twin screws and these were driven by two 6-cylinder, 4-stroke S.A., B. & W.-type diesels of 4,500 i.h.p. which gave a speed of about 12 knots.

The *Missourian* was launched on 14 December, 1921, and delivered in June 1922, a month after her sister. Their owners were associated with the then newly formed United American Lines, whose ships—among them the *Mount Clinton* (q.v.)—were operating on the North Atlantic. To take advantage of the opportunities there, the *Missourian* and *Californian* and others of the American–Hawaiian fleet were likewise transferred to that trade. So, for a short while, both the *Missourian* and her sister operated on a regular service between North Pacific ports, New York and Liverpool, Glasgow, Dunkirk, London and Hamburg. Subsequently the pair saw many years of service on their designed Pacific–Atlantic trade. In this the ports served included Seattle, Portland (Ore), San Francisco and Los Angeles on the one coast and New York and Boston on the other.

A major transaction which took place in 1940–41 was the sale of over 90 American cargo ships to the British Ministry of War Transport. Among them were several of the American–Hawaiian vessels, including the *Missourian* and *Californian*, which, by a small margin, were the least elderly of all those involved. When the transfer of the two sister-ships took place in the summer of 1940 they were put under the management of Runciman (London) Ltd. The *Missourian* was renamed *Empire Swan*, while the *Californian* became first the *Empire Kite* and then (that same year) the *Empire Seal*. Her career under that name was brief, for in February 1942, while on the Western side of the Atlantic, she was sunk by a U-boat.

That same year the *Empire Swan* (ex-*Missourian*) changed her nationality again, this through a second inter-governmental deal in which a number of British *Empire* ships were transferred to the Belgian Government (then in London) in compensation for war losses. The vessels were all given names commencing with *Belgian*, the one-time *Missourian* becoming the *Belgian Freighter*. Management by the Agence Maritime Internationale (Compagnie Maritime Belge (Lloyd Royal) S.A.) was later followed by actual ownership and in 1946 the C.M.B. decided that their several new acquisitions should, instead, be given *Capitaine* names, the *Belgian Freighter* so becoming the *Capitaine Potié*. As such she traded for two years, first to the Congo, then to South America. The latter represented the final phase of her career as a cargo ship, in the course of which she had sailed under four different names.

96   m.v. MISSOURIAN, 1922 (as a passenger ship), U.S.A.

Apart from the fact that the ship now had a light grey hull, her appearance was virtually the same as it had been at the time of her completion in 1922. So far she had undergone no major structural alterations, but now the pattern was to change. About May 1948 she was sold by the Compagnie Maritime Belge to an Italian concern, the Compagnia Genovese d'Armamento, who had her reconstructed inside and out to carry 800 third-class passengers.

Renamed *Genova*, she was put on a new service between Genoa and the River Plate, many of those she carried being labourers bound for Tierra del Fuego. In 1954 she was withdrawn from this trade and sent to Monfalcone for a much more elaborate reconstruction which lasted until the early part of 1955. Her original engines were replaced by two 5-cylinder, 2-stroke, S.A., C.R.D.A.—Sulzer diesels of 7,200 b.h.p. which raised her speed to $14\frac{1}{2}$ knots. She had previously been given a quite considerable amount of superstructure and internal accommodation (also a funnel), but her accommodation was now greatly enlarged and improved, a somewhat novel feature being the grouping of several enclosed verandas on the topmost deck amidships. Most of the other public rooms were arranged in the base of the superstructure. Forward there was a spacious lounge and two smaller rooms. Next to them was the main foyer, the after part of which gave access to the hospital area, which was provided with an operating theatre. Right aft there was a great dining saloon which seated 480. Above this, on the promenade deck, there was a not over-large swimming pool. Below, on A and B decks, she was fitted with 154 cabins (mainly eight-berth) which could take 1,024 passengers.

In the Spring of 1955 she emerged as the *Flaminia*, as shown, a fully air-conditioned, one-class (tourist) ship of 8,776 tons gross with a reduced draught of 26 ft 8 in. Her owners, the Cia. Genovese d'Armamento put her on what was advertised as the Cogedar Line service to Australia. On this she joined another tourist-class ship, the newly converted *Aurelia* (built 1939, 10,480 tons gross). But while the latter had her European terminal at Bremerhaven, the *Flaminia*'s voyages started from Italy. Like the *Aurelia*, she carried emigrants outwards. After making calls at various Mediterranean ports and also Aden, the *Flaminia* proceeded direct to Australia, but homewards her route was less rigid, often being via the Far East. In 1959 and 1960 she also made some extended voyages, turning around at Bremerhaven.

In the winter of 1961–62 the *Flaminia* was withdrawn from this trade and started running between Marseilles and Haifa, on charter to the Zim Line. While so doing she was sold to another Genoese firm, the Covena S.p.A. That phase was short lived, for about October 1964 she again changed hands, this time to a Saudi Arabian concern, M.A. Bakhashab (Saudi Lines) of Jeddah. As the *King Abdelaziz* her new role was the carriage of Mohammedan pilgrims to and from Jeddah, the port for Mecca. Her first season was not yet over when, on 30 April, 1965, she stranded on the Algaham Reef about five miles West of Jeddah, her 500 pilgrims having to be transferred to another vessel. Refloated a few days later, she was sent to Italy for repairs; in late September she was ready to leave La Spezia for her home port and further service. She was 48 years old when, early in 1970, she was sold to Taiwan breakers and her final voyage ended on 23 March with her arrival at Kaohsiung. By that time the one-time *Missourian* had been owned by five different nations and operated on at least eight different trades.

Abbreviations

aux.	auxiliary-powered (sailing vessel)
b.h.p.	brake horse power
b.p.	between perpendiculars (length)
d.e.	double-ended (boilers)
d.w.	deadweight (tonnage)
i.h.p.	indicated horse power
m.v.	motor vessel
mld.	moulded (breadth or depth, measured over frames, but inside plating)
o.a.	overall (length)
p.s.i.	pounds per square inch
S.E.	single-ended (boilers)
s.h.p.	shaft horse power

Synonomous terms: Derrick posts, King-posts, Sampson posts.

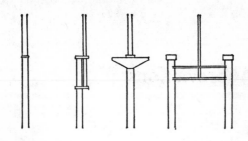

Masts and kingposts
Left to right: Old-style po[l] mast; the same, with fidded top[?] mast; with crosstree and tele scopic topmast; twin kingpost[s] used to carry topmast.

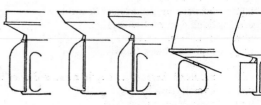

Bows
Left, reading down:
(1) Clipper stem.
(2) Slightly raked with cutaway forefoot (mostly on large passenger ships). Rake exaggerated for clarity.
(3) Maierform.
(4) Normal vertical.

Sterns
Above, left to right: Three varia tions of counter type; styl[e] favoured for cross-channel ship[s] and generally known as Denn[y] type; early cruiser type.

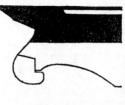

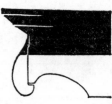

Rudder contrasts
Above: The *Aquitania*'s balanced rudder which was completely immersed. *Below:* Rudder of the *Imperator*.

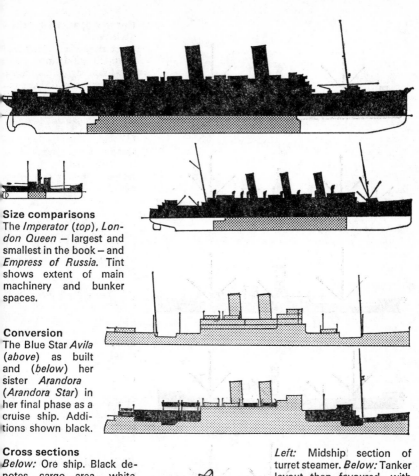

Size comparisons
The *Imperator* (*top*), *London Queen* – largest and smallest in the book – and *Empress of Russia*. Tint shows extent of main machinery and bunker spaces.

Conversion
The Blue Star *Avila* (*above*) as built and (*below*) her sister *Arandora* (*Arandora Star*) in her final phase as a cruise ship. Additions shown black.

Cross sections
Below: Ore ship. Black denotes cargo area, white, spaces for water ballast.

Left: Midship section of turret steamer. *Below:* Tanker layout then favoured, with centreline bulkhead. White spaces denote summer tanks.

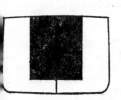

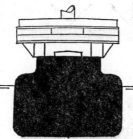

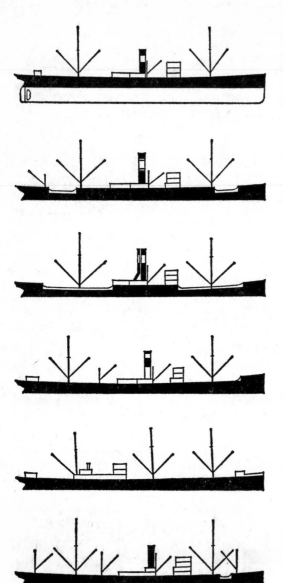

Cargo ships – the basic styles

Most deep-sea tramps buil 1910–29 conformed to a five-hatch layout, the super structure being divided into two blocks. If there was a sixth hatch this was generally aft of the superstructure.

(1) With completely flush weather deck. A minority had bulwarks forward, these ex tending half-way to the fore mast; sometimes also amid ships.

(2) Long bridge deck type with two half-length wells Far less common was a single short well aft, as on *Howick Hall*.

(3) Three-island type. Prob ably the most popular of all Example shown has an auxili ary funnel for donkey boiler Smaller vessels had no mid ship hatch.

(4) Similar to (1), but with short topgallant forecastle The vessel shown has an extra hatch and pair of king posts forward of the main mast.

(5) Typical early motorship style, with composite super structure aft of amidships The exhausts were often carried up one of the masts.

(6) Typical German layout with very short well forward large bridge and casing a base of funnel. All boats b the funnel.

Typical coaster/small ship layouts

In these a half-height quarter deck was normal. Nos 1 and 2 were especially popular. Nos 3 and 4 show alternative mast positions. No. 5 was a prototype for subsequent motor coasters.

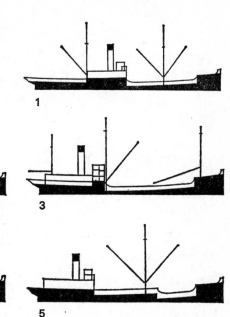

1

2

3

4

5

Tanker comparisons

Above: Normal type, length 420–460 ft, with three islands. *Below:* One of the then giants, maximum length about 540 ft. These, if not flush-decked, had a short raised forecastle.

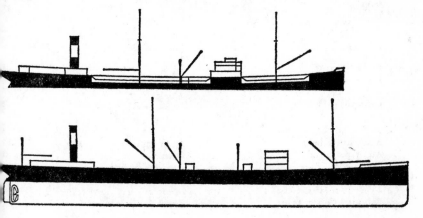

List of ships illustrated, grouped according to nationality

Australia
Indarra, 1912

Belgium
Stad Antwerpen, 1913

Canada
Empress of Russia, 1913
Lady Rodney, 1929
Princess Marguerite, 1925

Denmark
Selandia, 1912

Finland
Carelia, 1921

France
Commandant de Rose, 1918
Eridan, 1929
France, 1911
Providence, 1914

Germany
Barbara, 1926
Imperator, 1913
Isar, 1929
Orinoco, 1928

Great Britain
Aba, 1918, rebuilt 1921
Aquitania, 1914
Automedon, 1922
Avila, 1927
Avoceta, 1923
Balmoral Castle, 1910

Beaverford, 1928
Belgic, 1917
Benrinnes, 1914
Bernicia, 1923
British Marshal, 1912
Capable, 1918, converted 1924
Chartered, 1921
Corchester, 1927 (see Chartered)
Cretecable, 1919 (see Molliette)
Darino, 1917
Doric, 1923
Erinpura, 1911
Gannet, 1921
Highland Chieftain, 1929
Howick Hall, 1910
Huntsman, 1921
Inverlago, 1925
Jervis Bay, 1922
Jolly Bruce, 1920
Kedah, 1927
Laconia, 1911
Lady Cloé, 1916
London Queen, 1910
Macclesfield, 1914
Malines, 1922
Margretian, 1923
Melrose Abbey, 1929 (see Maccles-field)
Minnewaska, 1923
Molliette, 1919
Nerissa, 1926
Normannia, 1911
Olympic, 1911
Pacific Reliance, 1927
Parracombe, 1928
Rotorua, 1911
Royal Scot, 1910

San Jeronimo, 1914
Shantung, 1915
Southern Empress, 1914, rebuilt c.
　1928
Topaz, 1920
Ulster Monarch, 1929
Uskhaven, 1923 (see Margretian)
Vauban, 1912
War Mingan, 1918
War Viper, 1918
Yorkshire, 1920

Greece
　Patris II, 1926
　Vasilefs Constantinos, 1914

Holland
　Baloeran, 1929
　Batavier II, 1920
　Karimoen, 1911
　Klipfontein, 1922
　Spaarndam, 1922

Italy
　San Guglielmo, 1911

Japan
　Arabia Maru, 1918
　Suwa Maru, 1912

Malta
　Knight of Malta, 1929

Norway
　Belray, 1926
　Brabant, 1926
　Brant County, 1915
　Canis, 1888, rebuilt c. 1918 (see Cap-
　　able)
　Sardinia, 1920
　Stavangerfjord, 1918

Portugal
　Cunene, 1911

Russia
　Smolni, 1929

Spain
　Infanta Beatriz, 1928
　Infanta Isabel, 1912
　Reina Victoria-Eugenia, 1913

Sweden
　Atland, 1910
　Britannia, 1929
　Suecia, 1912
　Svealand, 1925

U.S.A.
　American Merchant, 1920
　Matsonia, 1913
　Missourian, 1922
　Missourian, 1922, as rebuilt
　Mount Clinton, 1921
　President Harding, 1921
　President van Buren, 1920
　Tivives, 1911

List of ships illustrated, grouped according to type and trade

Lady Rodney
Nerissa
Tivives

North Sea, Passenger and Cargo
Batavier II
Brabant
Britannia
Macclesfield
Melrose Abbey
Smolni

U.K. *Coastal Passenger and Cargo*
Bernicia
Lady Cloé
London Queen
Royal Scot

Railway and Cross Channel
Malines
Normannia
Stad Antwerpen
Ulster Monarch

Emigrant/Pilgrim
Arabia Maru
Flaminia
Jervis Bay
Karimoen
Mount Clinton
San Guglielmo
Spaarndam
Vasilefs Constantinos

Special Features

Aba	world's first passenger motor liner
Baloeran	stepped-in superstructure
Belgic	austerity completion
Brabant	no-funnel passenger m.v.
Matsonia	early engines-aft passenger liner
Rotorua	five masts
Yorkshire	last 4-masted passenger steamship built for Britain

CARGO

Cargo Liners
American Merchant
Arabia Maru
Automedon
Beaverford
Benrinnes
Brant County
Cunene
Darino
Howick Hall
Huntsman
Isar
Karimoen
Klipfontein
Margretian
Missourian
Pacific Reliance
Sardinia

Selandia
Suecia

Tramps
Atland
Carelia
Commandant de Rose
Parracombe
War Mingan
War Viper
Uskhaven

Coastal/Home Trade, cargo
Gannet
Jolly Bruce
London Queen
Molliette
Topaz

(And see above, 'Passenger', 'U.K. Coastal Passenger and Cargo' and 'North Sea, Passenger and Cargo')

Fruit Carriers
Avoceta
Darino
Sardinia
Tivives

Colliers
Chartered
Corchester

Oil Tankers
British Marshal
Inverlago
San Jeronimo
Southern Empress (whale oil)

Specialist, Heavy Lift/Heavy Cargo
Belray
Svealand

Pioneers
Barbara
Margretian
Selandia
Svealand

Wartime Standard Types
American Merchant
Commandant de Rose
President Harding
President van Buren
War Mingan
War Viper

Wartime Expediency

Belgic	completed without superstructure
Canis	converted from sail
Capable	converted from sail
Commandant de Rose	wooden hull and sail and steam
Cretecable	concrete
Molliette	concrete and sail
War Mingan	wood hull

Special Features

Huntsman	4 masts
Isar	,, , Maierform bow.
Benrinnes	clipper stem
Parracombe	semi-clipper stem
Howick Hall	2 funnels, etc.
Brant County	,, ,,
Cunene	layout
Gannet	,,
Margretian	,,
Carelia	mast arrangement
Beaverford	,,
Karimoen	,,

Index of Ship Names

Figures in bold type refer to plate numbers. Other references are to page numbers.